The EVERYTHING. Christianity Book

Dear Reader:

Baptized a Catholic, raised in Anglican schools in Canada, and having attended Methodist, Lutheran, Presbyterian, and Episcopal services as an adult, I may have one of the most eclectic Christian backgrounds of anyone I know. I guess I'm just a good example of religious diversity and tolerance in North America today. In fact, my mother jokingly listed me as a Druid in an elementary school roster once and giggled herself all the way to the mailbox. My parents were all about diversity, not to mention humor!

My father, an historian and scholar, may have been my greatest teacher of all things Christianity—after all, he seriously considered becoming a Jesuit in his youth! However, instead of choosing a life in the church, he surrounded himself with Jesuits in some of the finest learning institutions in the country and was certainly one of the best teachers I ever had. It would have been amazing to have had his input while writing *The Everything® Christianity Book*, but I'm sure he was watching me from his well-deserved seat in heaven. He was the inspiration behind my research.

One thing my father always loved was the ritual of Christian services, the more traditional the better—the incense, a good Latin mass, perhaps a Gregorian chant or two . . . he loved it all. I've noticed through my own Christian experiences that the major differences from service to service are their degrees of formality and ritual. For example, you will not find any incense waved through the pews of a Lutheran service, nor will you see images of Jesus on the cross in a Presbyterian Church. The one thing you will find they all have in common, however, is devotion to Jesus Christ.

Despite all the differences, the years of persecution, burnings, hangings, corruption, and general chaos, Christians in most parts of the world eventually came back to the very thing that united them in the first place—the man and his message.

The EVERYTHING® Series

Editorial

Publishing Director	Gary M. Krebs
Managing Editor	Kate McBride
Copy Chief	Laura MacLaughlin
Acquisitions Editor	Bethany Brown
Development Editor	Patrycja Pasek-Gradziuk
Production Editor	Jamie Wielgus

Production

Production Director	Susan Beale
Production Manager	Michelle Roy Kelly
Series Designers	Daria Perreault
	Colleen Cunningham
Cover Design	Paul Beatrice
	Frank Rivera
Layout and Graphics	Colleen Cunningham
	Rachael Eiben
	Michelle Roy Kelly
	Daria Perreault
	Erin Ring
Series Cover Artist	Barry Littmann
Technical Reviewer	Janice Hildreth

Visit the entire Everything® Series at everything.com

THE
EVERYTHING®
CHRISTIANITY
BOOK

A complete and easy-to-follow guide to Protestant
origins, beliefs, practices, and traditions

Michael F. Russell, M.Div., and Amy Wall

Adams Media
Avon, Massachusetts

An Everything® Series Book.
Everything® and everything.com® are registered trademarks of F+W Publications, Inc.

Published by Adams Media, an F+W Publications Company
57 Littlefield Street, Avon, MA 02322 U.S.A.
www.adamsmedia.com

ISBN: 1-59337-029-6
Printed in the United States of America.

J I H G F E D C B A

Library of Congress Cataloging-in-Publication Data
Russell, Michael F.
The everything Christianity book / Michael F. Russell and Amy Wall.
p.   cm.
(Everything series book)
Includes bibliographical references.
ISBN 1-59337-029-6
1. Christianity. I. Wall, Amy. II. Title. III. Series: Everything series

BR121.3.R87 2004
270–dc22

2003021794

This publication is designed to provide accurate and authoritative information with regard to the subject matter covered. It is sold with the understanding that the publisher is not engaged in rendering legal, accounting, or other professional advice. If legal advice or other expert assistance is required, the services of a competent professional person should be sought.

—From a *Declaration of Principles* jointly adopted by a Committee of the American Bar Association and a Committee of Publishers and Associations

Many of the designations used by manufacturers and sellers to distinguish their products are claimed as trademarks. Where those designations appear in this book and Adams Media was aware of a trademark claim, the designations have been printed with initial capital letters.

This book is available at quantity discounts for bulk purchases.
For information, call 1-800-872-5627.

Contents

Protestant Globalization / 139

Calvinism / 151

Presbyterianism / 163

Reformation in England / 175

The Church of England / 189

Counter (Catholic) Reformation / 201

Acknowledgments

I'd like to thank everyone at Adams Media for their advice and guidance; Jacky Sach of Bookends for her continued support; and Pastor Mike Russell for his invaluable knowledge and assistance throughout this project. I'd also like to thank my parents for the Easter baskets, the Christmas readings from the *King James Bible*, and the shiny black patent leather Sunday school shoes (or "Mary Janes")—but mostly I'd like to thank them for encouraging me to learn everything I can about the world around me with an open mind.

Top Ten Protestant Reformers
and Reform Movements

1. **John Wyclif (1328–1384):** Led English Bible translation movement.
2. **John Hus (1369–1415):** Critic of Roman Catholic Church practices.
3. **Martin Luther (1483–1546):** Founder of Lutheranism; credited with starting the Protestant movement.
4. **John Knox (1505–1572):** Founder of Presbyterianism.
5. **John Calvin (1509–1564):** Founder of Calvinist movement.
6. **Ulrich Zwingli (1484–1531):** Founder of the Anabaptist movement.
7. **Henry VIII (1491–1547):** Established the Church of England.
8. **William Tyndale (1494–1536):** Translated Bible into English.
9. **John Wesley (1703–1791):** Founder of the Methodist movement.
10. **Charles Wesley (1707–1788):** Cofounder of Methodism with brother John Wesley.

Introduction

▶ IT IS REALLY QUITE REMARKABLE that a country so diverse with multiethnicities and cultures is capable of maintaining a structure that includes religious tolerance. Americans live in a society of Christians, Hindus, Buddhists, Muslims, those of Jewish faith, and many more religions, yet we manage to live in harmony, for the most part. Of course, there are problems that arise—no society is perfect—but overall, in a world where religious warfare is status quo, the United States remains true to the original intention of the colonists. After all, it is the air of religious freedom that inspired the American leaders to write the Declaration of Independence, to which we still adhere.

As you delve into the world of Christianity and the Protestant Reformation in this book, you will not only see why this is true, but you'll also learn the chronology of events that brought us to this point. It all began with a man named Jesus and a handful of his followers. While most European countries still lean toward one particular faith, the ideal of religious tolerance has taken hold in most portions of Western society. For example, the Church of England still dominates England, but you will also find Methodists, Lutherans, and Presbyterians—just like you do in the United States.

The Protestants and Catholics still struggle with one another in some regions of the world, but great strides have been made to find peaceful solutions. Of course, it will take work, time, and a change of mind-set, but nothing is impossible, as you will learn from the struggles the Christians have faced over the last 2,000 years.

If you look around the world in which you live, you will see Christian influence everywhere. There are churches and cathedrals on almost every street corner, Western governments have established national holidays around the Christian rituals, and we live by a calendar that measures time by "before" and "after" the life of Christ. Some might argue that these are the markers of a noninclusive society—and they are most likely correct—but the more we understand about each other and our various faiths, the more chance we have of keeping the peace.

Chapter 1
Early Christianity

In the sixteenth century, the Christian church went through a religious revolution, or Reformation, from Catholicism to what we now refer to as Protestantism. It was a gradual change with origins often credited to a man named Martin Luther. But in order to understand its effect on the Christian world today, we need to go all the way back to the beginning of Christianity itself.

In the Beginning

The birth of Christianity goes back to the time when Jesus traveled the Middle East region of the world teaching the word of God. Although Jesus has been referred to as "Jesus of Nazareth," the town of Nazareth was in the green, mountainous region of Galilee, so he was also called a "Galilean." It is actually in the region of Galilee that Jesus chose to begin his ministry.

Jesus Christ

According to the Bible, Jesus was born to Mary (daughter of Anne and Joachim), who was chosen by God to bear His son. The Bible states that Angel Gabriel appeared to Mary and announced: "You will be with child and give birth to a son, and you are to give him the name Jesus" (Luke 1:31, NIV). In a state of grace, Mary accepted God's will.

Mary was engaged to an older man, the carpenter Joseph. At that time, bearing a child outside of wedlock was considered disgraceful. Joseph considered leaving Mary, but an angel appeared to him to explain that he would be head of a household in which Mary would bear the son of God. And so Joseph too accepted his role.

FACT

Roman Catholics believe in the doctrine of "Immaculate Conception," which recognizes that Mary was sinless (or without sin) when she conceived Jesus. Other Christians simply believe that Jesus' birth was a miracle.

The Roman Empire

Jesus was born during the time of the Roman Empire (about 400 B.C. – A.D. 476), under the rule of the Roman emperors. At least 200 years before he was born, and for at least 200 years after his death, what we know today as Europe, the Middle East, and parts of northern Africa were ruled by the Romans. As the Roman armies swept across the region, they toppled existing cultures and governments by violent means, installing their own societal and governmental influences in their wake. So whatever belief systems existed in many of these areas were buried with their civilizations.

However, this time period was also surprisingly a time of relative peace—a time referred to as "Pax Romana." The Romans developed cities by establishing water and sewage systems, public baths, and theatres. However, despite the growth and development of the time, there was still a great deal of religious unrest resulting in an outpouring of spiritual prophets. Many considered Jesus to be one of them, but he was not simply a prophet. He was the Son of God, and his influence took hold and became one of the biggest religions of all time.

Christian Influence

Today, it's hard to imagine what the Western World would be like without the dominating influences of Christianity: We see it in our schools, in our jobs, and even in our politics.

Our calendar year is based on the birth of Jesus; we live in the twenty-first century (which really means twenty-one centuries after the birth of Christ); and to help us put history in comprehensible perspective, we refer to events or dates as being A.D. (anno Domini or "in the year of our Lord") and B.C. (or "before Christ").

So if it all started with Jesus, why do we have so many different factions of Christianity today? What does it all mean? Catholic? Protestant? Evangelical? Born Again? How did so many different beliefs come from the humble beginnings of one man and a group of his followers? The only way to make sense of any of it is take a step back into history.

Although many refer to Jesus as "Jesus Christ," Christ wasn't his last name, but a title. In Hebrew, "The Christ," means "The Messiah" and serves as the root of the word Christianity. In his time, Jesus would have been referred to as Jesus of Nazareth— the area in which he was raised.

Religion Before Jesus

Human beings have always relied on some sort of belief system to help them understand the world mysteries. It's hard to believe that the earth is here merely by luck and that we are born, live, and die for no good reason at all. Religion, myth, and legend have always been comforts to help people find answers to questions that would otherwise be unanswered.

While Eastern culture developed many different "universal" belief systems several centuries older than Jesus, Western Civilization did not have a universal religion. Before Jesus, Judaism was the predominant religion in Palestine, which was part of the Roman Empire.

Judaism was also around long before the Romans conquered the region, but Roman leaders did not see the Jewish people as a threat—they chose to keep to themselves and helped maintain law and order within their societies. Besides, if they continued to pay their taxes to the Caesar, the Emperor of Rome, the Romans had no reason to feel they would cause any kind of trouble for the Empire.

The Pagans

The roots of paganism are the fertility cycle of nature and the existence of gods that were reborn every spring. The Greeks, for example, had an entire belief system built on a society of gods that represented different aspects of their culture.

QUESTION?

What is a pagan?
By dictionary definition, a pagan is a label given to someone who is not Jewish, Muslim, or Christian. However, "paganism" is really a host of various different belief systems based on native societal and cultural rituals and traditions.

Many of the pagan beliefs held to the basic principles that applied to the message of Jesus: the rejection of immorality (sin) and resurrection (rebirth), for example. As word spread of Jesus' miracles—for example, his ability to feed thousands of hungry people with only five loaves of bread and two fish—so did the intrigue surrounding him. Because he changed lives, people continued to gather around him and listen to his teachings.

Judaism in the Midst of Change

The people of the Jewish faith, who represented about half the population of Palestine (about 1 million) felt threatened by the pagan factions that sprang up all over the region. The Jewish people held onto the voice of their past prophets, predicting that one day God would deliver them from pagan influences by sending a Messiah, who would bring an end to corruption and establish the kingdom of God throughout the world. The evil ones would be condemned and the righteous would spend eternity in paradise. With further influence of foreign lords and pagan practice, it was time for the Messiah to arrive.

Politics and Jewish Factions

It's important to understand the society in which Jesus lived in order to realize the magnitude of what he started and his followers continued. At that time, Jewish society was divided into several different political and religious factions, and the one thing these groups had in common was their dislike of the Romans.

Here is a list of the various Jewish power factions:

- **The Pharisees:** A group of staunchly restrictive Jewish leaders.
- **The Sadducees:** A conservative political group that represented the aristocracy of the Jewish society.
- **The Zealots:** A group that believed in armed conflict against the Romans.
- **The Essenes:** A group that was neither politically active nor violent, but that took to the wilderness to study religious writings.

Jesus and His Apostles

Jesus was Jewish—he was raised in the Jewish tradition under Jewish law. Together with a group of his disciples (students), Jesus traveled the region of Palestine to spread the word of God. At a time when people suffered spiritual suppression and craved religious leadership and guidance, Jesus offered them hope of salvation and renewed faith. The message he projected was one that the people desperately needed to hear.

FACT

The word "apostle" comes from the Greek word "apostello," which means "to dispatch." Another Greek word, "apostolos," means "one who is dispatched" or entrusted with a mission— a sort of ancient-day ambassador.

The Message

Jesus' message had come from Jewish roots, but it was also new, because he preached "a new and living way" (Hebrews 10:20, NIV). He taught the people the word of God, which would lead them to salvation, and that God wanted them to live their lives in goodness, love, and simplicity—which is more important than living life according to laws made by powerful politicians.

The Followers

To help him spread his message, Jesus chose twelve friends to be his closest disciples (also called "apostles" or "followers"). However, he also had many other disciples who set off ahead of Jesus on his travels to help prepare his way.

Here is a list of Jesus' twelve apostles:

1. **Simon**: From Bethsaida; Jesus gave him the name of Peter (Greek) or Cephas (Aramaic), both of which mean "rock"; he is often considered the leader of the twelve.
2. **Andrew**: From Bethsaida; Simon Peter's brother; he and John were the first disciples Jesus called.

3. **James** (son of Zebedee): John's brother; he was killed in A.D. 44 by Herod Agrippa I and is considered the first apostle to die as a martyr.

4. **John** (son of Zebedee): James' brother; one of the closest friends of Jesus; the author of the Gospel of John.

5. **Philip**: From Bethsaida, as Peter and Andrew.

6. **Matthew**: The tax collector; also known as Levi; the author of the Gospel of Matthew.

7. **Thomas**: He has the nickname "Doubting Thomas" because he wanted to actually see and touch Jesus' scarred body after his resurrection; Didymus is the Greek version of his name.

8. **Bartholomew**: From Cana; one of the disciples to whom Jesus appeared at the Sea of Tiberias after his resurrection.

9. **James** (son of Alphaeus): He is also known as James the Younger, or James the Less; the author of John's epistle.

10. **Thaddeus**: Also known as "Judas, the brother of James."

11. **Simon**: Also known as the Zealot; evangelized Persia and Ethiopia.

12. **Judas Iscariot**: The only disciple not from Galilee; the one who betrayed Jesus and then committed suicide after Jesus was condemned to die.

The Miracles

Christians believe that one of the reasons the message of Jesus was so powerful, spread so quickly, and had such a lasting and profound impact has to do with word of mouth and the witnessing of miracles. In his day, many people believed Jesus was the Messiah—the Savior who came to save the Jews as predicted in the Old Testament. Later Christians found even more answers to the miracles he performed by the belief in the Trinity, the idea that the Godhead is a three-in-one entity: the Father, the Son, and the Holy Spirit.

But what did Jesus do that made people think he was a divine being? The miracles are almost too many to count, and some of them have become so much a part of our culture that they are instilled in our language. For example, where did we get the expression: "to walk on water," which has become a metaphor meaning that a person is some kind of exceptional human being?

Well, Jesus is believed to have truly walked on water, and this is how the story goes: Jesus was separated from his apostles when he went to a mountain to pray. When he finished praying, Jesus headed for the sea where he saw the apostles in a boat. He began to walk to them across the water. The apostles thought he was a ghost at first, but Jesus calmed them down and told them to not be afraid. The apostles had faith in his words, and Jesus joined them in their boat.

The bigger message in this story is that walking on water was Jesus' way of helping the apostles keep their faith in him. Although it is impossible for a human being to walk on water, by performing the seemingly impossible, Jesus demonstrated that placing your faith in God means anything is possible. If the apostles let him into the boat, it was because they had faith that it was really Jesus and not a ghost that was walking toward them.

In another story, Jesus is believed to have fed 5,000 hungry people with just five loaves of bread and two fish, and, afterward, there were enough leftovers to fill twelve baskets. Here, Jesus once again showed that with faith in God, anything is possible. The food is actually a symbol of spiritual enrichment. Receiving Jesus' spiritual message and accepting knowledge are all food for the soul.

The Parables

The Bible is a teaching tool. It explains to Christians how the world began and answers questions about life's greatest mysteries. How does it do this? Quite simply: through the telling of stories, which enables a spiritual truth to be more easily understood. Here's an example from the Gospel of Matthew 13:31–32 (RVNS):

"He put before them another parable: 'The kingdom of heaven is like a mustard seed that someone took and sowed in his field; it is the smallest of all the seeds, but when it has grown it is the greatest of shrubs and becomes a tree, so that the birds of the air come and make nests in its branches.'"

What is Jesus saying? What is this mustard seed to which he refers? How is God's kingdom like a mustard seed? Well, you can interpret it however you want, but most theologians believe Jesus' message is that faith begins as the smallest seed in the hearts of human beings. When the seed is sown and nurtured, it grows into something bigger, stronger, and more beautiful. To sow the seed is to accept the word of God, which in turn will transform the person from within in the same way that the seed is transformed into a plant or a tree.

This is just one example of how Jesus spread his message. There are parables like this one throughout the New Testament of the Bible—stories told by Jesus and repeated in the scripture that still hold great meaning for Christians today.

Politics and Religion

Jesus' message touched the hearts of the masses, and stories of his healing powers spread through the region like a brush fire. Although the presence of the Messiah brought hope to the people, it also brought fear to the ruling Jewish factions. Jesus had become too powerful—too influential—and as result threatened the status quo. Additionally, he seemed to undermine the Jewish faith by violating Sabbath laws and denouncing the validity of other governmental laws. This obviously made the Pharisees and the Sadducees very nervous, especially since undermining the Jewish laws was considered a direct threat, not only to the religion itself, but also to the political bodies that set and enforced them. As a result, the Sadducees and Pharisees formed an alliance against Jesus, and they called for his arrest, trial, and execution.

The Betrayal and the Trial

Ironically, the Sadducees and Pharisees found the way to Jesus through one of his apostles, Judas Iscariot. There are many stories as to why Judas betrayed Jesus, but most distill it down to one fact: He was greedy. According to the Bible, Judas was paid "thirty pieces of silver" to turn in his friend to the authorities in what would become one of the most legendary betrayals of all time.

FACT

Many Roman leaders let the Jewish people take care of their own, which is why Pontius Pilate was in the picture to begin with. The Romans gave Pilate control over the fate of Jesus and, fearful of the pressure from Rome, Pilate turned Jesus over to the soldiers for crucifixion.

Jesus was arrested quietly for fear of riots and was put on trial as a traitor to Rome. It was Pontius Pilate, a Roman governor, who tried him. When the word had spread that Jesus had been arrested, Pilate was afraid of the masses that gathered outside the palace fortress. Pontius Pilate did not believe Jesus had done anything wrong, but in an effort to appease Caesar, he ordered him flogged and then put to death by crucifixion.

The Last Supper

The night before his arrest, Jesus shared a meal with the twelve apostles—an event that has come to be known as "The Last Supper." At this meal, Jesus told his followers to drink the wine and eat the bread (some Christians interpret these as actually being or representing his blood and his flesh): "Do this for the remembrance of me," he said. This event is known today as "the new covenant" and is one of the things that set one Christian branch apart from another after the Reformation. The tradition of taking "communion" became one of the first sacraments of the Catholic Church, and the ritual of taking the bread and wine at the altar would come to be known under many names, including the "Holy Eucharist."

QUESTION?

Did Jesus mean the wine and bread should be actually transformed into his blood and flesh?
The answer depends on to which branch of Christianity one ascribes. The ritual known as "transubstantiation" is still enacted in Christian churches today, but the actual meaning of the holy rite would become an issue during the period of the Reformation.

Jesus Is Crucified

Jesus was crucified on the cross on a hill outside of Jerusalem. Over his head, the Romans inscribed the letters "INRI" (Latin translation: "Iesus Nazarenus Rex Iudaeorum") meaning "Jesus of Nazareth, King of the Jews." Since Jesus was still seen as the leader of a Judaic sect, the inscription on the cross was to serve as a warning to the Jewish people and any potential future "trouble-makers."

In the days that followed Jesus' death, hopelessness seemed to prevail among his followers, with the lingering question: How could Jesus be the Messiah? He was gone and the people still lived under the same Jewish leaders in the same Roman Empire.

Resurrection and the Pentecost

Hope was renewed as rumors started to spread that Jesus had risen from the dead. His tomb was empty and several people reported that they had seen him, which was enough proof to the followers that Jesus was divine and that he truly had been sent by God to redeem his people.

ESSENTIAL

Mary Magdalene, a friend and follower of Jesus, was the first to see him after he had been resurrected. It is a tale told in all the Bible gospels, and here is one version from the Gospel according to John, Chapter 20: " . . . she turned around and saw Jesus standing there, but she did not know that it was Jesus. Jesus said to her, 'Woman, why are you weeping? Whom are you looking for?' . . ." (John 20:14–15, NRSV).

Mass Conversion

As the apostles celebrated the Jewish Feast of Weeks (known as Shavuot in Hebrew and Pentecost in Greek), the Holy Spirit came down upon them and the apostle Peter announced the resurrection of Jesus to a huge crowd, claiming it was prophesied in the Old Testament. Having received a message from Jesus, the apostles told the people to go and be baptized in the name of the Holy Spirit. So in about A.D. 33, over three thousand people were baptized—an event that is considered the start of the Christian Church and celebrated by some Christians during Pentecost.

Following in Jesus' Footsteps

After Jesus' death, the apostles continued to spread the word of Christ—the Messiah—calling him their Lord and their Savior. Jesus had been sent to the people to spread God's word of love and redemption, and was then sacrificed to save the souls of all people. Those who would believe in him, accept his message, and be baptized in Christ would be redeemed and their souls would spend eternity in paradise. Ⓔ

Chapter 2

The Early Years of the Catholic Church

As you've learned so far, Christianity began as a branch of Judaism that spread quite rapidly to pagans and Gentiles in highly tumultuous times. When Jesus was crucified, he left behind a host of followers, who continued his work by traveling vast regions and spreading the news of his life and resurrection.

The Spread of Christianity

It would be impossible to talk about the growth of Christianity without mentioning the apostle Paul, who was not one of the original apostles. In fact, Paul was an outspoken opponent of Jesus' teachings at first, both during Jesus' life and after his death. It is then a surprise that Paul became a vigilant missionary after he was strangely blinded on the road to Damascus. According to the Bible, the Holy Spirit visited Paul and returned his sight, which then led Paul, as a new convert, to spread the message of Jesus and establish Christianity throughout the world—at least the parts he could reach in a lifetime.

Paul's Mission

Paul became the perfect ambassador for Christianity and was able to bridge the gap among Jews, Romans, and Greeks. He had been raised strictly in Judaism; he spoke fluent Greek; and he was a Roman citizen. He was also educated in Greek literature and thought and could, therefore, express the doctrines and teachings of Jesus to the Gentiles. As a Roman citizen, he had certain freedoms that allowed him to travel and continue the work that Jesus began. Paul managed to bring his message to areas of the world that Jesus never reached, such as Turkey (then known as Asia Minor) and Greece.

According to the scriptures, in particular the Book of Acts in the New Testament, Paul made three major trips during his life:

1. Palestine and Antioch (Syria)
2. Thessalonica (ancient Macedonia)
3. Philippi and then on to Corinth and Turkey (Asia Minor)

However, it wasn't long before authorities caught on to Paul and his continuing Christian teaching. Upon his return to Jerusalem, after he opened a church in Ephesus (a city in the country we now call Turkey), Jewish authorities arrested Paul, fearing an uprising of Jesus' followers and the possible undermining of Judaism. Paul appealed his case to Rome, where he spent the rest of his life awaiting trial. In A.D. 64,

Emperor Nero decided to eradicate the Christians from Rome, and Paul was never seen or heard from again.

New Christian Ground

After the fall of Jerusalem to the Romans (about A.D. 70), the seat of the Christian faith was forced to find new ground. By that time, Christianity had gathered thousands of followers and was powerful enough that finding a new home did not take very long. The second home of the Christian faith became, not surprisingly, Antioch in Syria, where Paul had spent a good amount of time preaching. It seemed the most likely place for the new church home, but it didn't stop there.

FACT

On his travels, Paul managed to convert many Gentiles to the teachings of Jesus Christ and during his third trip, he wrote his famous letter to the Thessalonians, which later became a book in the New Testament.

Paul Leaves His Mark

Christianity found its way to India and northern Africa, as Paul made his way to Italy and Spain. By the end of the fourth century—400 years after the birth of Jesus, there were about 500,000 people living in Antioch and half the population was Christian. By the middle of the third century, there were 30,000 Christians living in Rome.

However, Christianity did not spread as quickly to the West as it did to the East. France (or Gaul as it was known then) only had one known church, based in Lyon, by the middle of the first century, and there were only a few churches in Spain, despite Paul's work.

The New Testament

When Paul got word of newly formed churches that were struggling with certain Christian issues, he wrote many letters to explain the various teachings of Jesus Christ. In an effort to spread the word of God, the

Christian leaders often struggled with putting the ideas into effect in a way that everyone could understand. Paul's letters—combined with the writings of apostles Peter, James, John, and Jude, as well as the books written by Mark, Matthew, Luke, and John (the Gospels)—formed the foundation of the new Christian Bible.

The word "Bible" actually means "book." It is a French word that originates from the Latin world "biblia" and the Greek word "biblios."

Letters and Unity

There were at least thirteen letters, which were highly valued and passed around for about 150 years after they were written. Paul's letters, along with the four Gospels and other writings, served as highlights to the Old Testament, and were eventually compiled into the New Testament. Christian leaders passed the letters from region to region, using them as preaching tools in an attempt to form a church with universal beliefs and laws—the beginning of Christian unity. The writings of the apostles were passed around so much after the death of Christ that it wasn't until the end of the first century that the books and letters of the New Testament were completed.

QUESTION?

What did they use for writing material in these times?
The most commonly used "paper" was papyrus, which came from the papyrus plant, an expensive product that only the rich could afford—but then again, only the rich could read and write, anyway. The papyrus plant grew in regions of Syria and Egypt and was shipped throughout the Middle East via the Syrian port of Byblos.

Some believe that it would not have been possible to finish the writings because the early Christian followers were awaiting Christ's second coming, which is prophesied in the Old Testament. As time went by, however, and Christians realized that the second coming might not be imminent, they completed the writings of the New Testament.

Combined Written Works

The word "gospel" in Greek means "good news," and the good news of Jesus Christ was depicted by Matthew, Mark, Luke, and John in their various accounts of the life and work of the Messiah. Each story takes a different perspective. Mark wrote of the persecution of Christ; Matthew explained that Jesus was the Messiah and was here to fulfill Jewish prophecies as indicated in the Old Testament. The gospel according to Luke expressed the good news that Jesus, the Savior, does not discriminate against any group of people—especially race and class; and John's gospel explained the divinity of Jesus—perhaps the hardest concept for people to grasp.

FACT

The first time the term "Catholic" was used in relation to Christianity was by Ignatius, Bishop of Antioch. The bishop said, "Wherever Jesus Christ is, there is the Catholic Church." He used the word "catholic" with its original connotation in mind, meaning "universal." The term caught on, and by the end of the second century, the Christian Church was referred to as the Catholic Church.

In the ever-increasing desire to establish Christian unity, several different meetings were held and the scripture changed several times over the centuries. By A.D. 100, there was no definitive scripture—church leaders studied from the various writings of the apostles; by A.D. 200, there were more writings added, and the New Testament began to take shape. Finally by the fifth century, meetings of Christian bishops were held in Carthage and the New Testament was fixed for the West. The result of the Carthage meetings was the agreement that twenty-seven books were to be proclaimed the Christian "Scripture."

Canonization of the Scriptures

In an effort toward unity, church leaders worked furiously to define Christianity in terms of scripture, but it was not an easy road. With Gnosticism and other schools of thought springing up on the church's doorstep, the fate of Christianity was in the hands of its argumentative leaders. How did Christian leaders determine which writings would make up the new scriptures (i.e., the New Testament)? They could not fully rely on the books of the Old Testament if the Messiah had already come and gone, so they needed a scripture. There were many church councils held over the early centuries of Christianity to try to put the issue to rest, but the books and writing that were accepted changed repeatedly over a 400-year span.

> After Jesus' death, the Christians had relied on about twenty writings: the Four Gospels, the Book of Acts, Paul's thirteen letters, First Letter from Peter, First Letter from John, and John's Revelation.

By the late fifth century, twenty-seven books were finally accepted as part of the New Testament, including: Paul's letters; the four Gospels: Matthew, Mark, Luke, and John; the Book of Acts; and Revelation.

The Major Canonization Councils were:

1. **The Council of Laodicea (about A.D. 363):** All books of the New Testament were accepted, except the Book of Revelation.
2. **The Council of Carthage (A.D. 397):** This council was chaired by Augustine, an early church leader and theologian. All twenty-seven books were accepted at the council.
3. **The Council of Hippo (A.D. 490):** This council validated the decision of the Council of Carthage.

The decision-making process was not easy. There were arguments that took over a century to work out. The debate over the texts fell into two categories: the homolegoumena—those in favor of the texts—and antilegoumena—those against them.

The Foundation of Christian Thought

The formation of the New Testament may have been the final step in the division of Christianity from Judaism. After all, the New Testament is based on the belief that the Messiah had come and that He was Jesus of Nazareth. Those who didn't believe that the Messiah had arrived were bound to the Old Testament. The Christians, therefore, faced two choices: to remain a sect of Judaism or to define Christianity as a separate religion. By combining the writings of the founders of the religion, they were able to define themselves, and as a result separated from Judaism.

Christians Versus Pagans

In the early days of Christianity, there was a certain purity in the acts of Christ's followers. In the absence of Jesus himself, Christians took over his good works of helping the sick and feeding the poor. Because they practiced a new religion, their ways were seen as odd, and they were forced to disassociate from mainstream pagan society in order to practice their beliefs. As a result, even as word of their good deeds spread, so did fear. The pagans considered Christians to be atheists and, therefore, a direct threat to pagan worship.

FACT

Christians negated the importance of pagan worship by virtue of their own belief in monotheism (the belief in one god). The pagans' worship was based on polytheism (the belief in many gods/goddesses).

The unconverted pagan worshippers felt that Christianity was an enemy. Not only did such a sentiment breed fear, but it also caused a great deal of social animosity between the two groups. A Christian, for example, could not attend a pagan feast—and an unaccepted invitation was considered rude. The Christians wanted to set their own standards of living in accordance with their own beliefs, which meant they had to ignore certain social and economic ways of life that had previously been the norm. This was just the beginning of the widespread hatred of Christians to come.

Persecution

The Romans set out on a fierce mission to eradicate Christianity, since it was a threat to their pagan belief system. Christianity was growing and was a direct threat to Rome and its emperor. The Christians did not recognize the emperor as a deity and didn't acknowledge more than one god—meaning they were not obeying the laws of the Roman Empire.

The Holy Trinity is the Christian belief that God is three-in-one (three "persons" in one): The Father, The Son, and the Holy Spirit. The Trinity can be understood in this way: "The Father" indicates the personal relationships Christians can have with God; "The Son" represents the human (flesh and blood) aspect of God through His Son, Jesus Christ; and the "Holy Spirit" represents the divine aspects of the deity.

Rome in Flames

In A.D. 64, Rome burned to the ground, and some speculated that Emperor Nero had set the fire himself. In an effort to divert the allegations from himself, Nero used the growing fear of the Christians. He blamed the Christians for setting the fire to destroy the Roman way of life, and this marked the beginning of Christian persecution. Christians were arrested, tortured, and murdered in hideous ways.

It is believed that Peter and Paul were both executed during this time of Christian persecution. It is said that Peter was crucified, but he demanded to hang on the cross upside-down because he was not worthy of dying by the same means as Jesus. Since Paul was a Roman, he is believed to have been beheaded rather than crucified. This may have been the worst era of Christian persecution. There were times later in history when the Christians were left alone, but the threat of another onslaught of persecution was continuously present.

The Early Heretics

The writings that eventually culminated in the New Testament were critical to Christian unity. As the Christians struggled to put together the foundation of Christian thought and avoid the sword of persecution, there were plenty of false documents floating around Christian societies. The mission of the Gospel writers was to formulate one Christian message— that Jesus came to the people "in the flesh" but was a divine being—a holy spirit. In so doing, the apostles condemned all false news that tried to impose Jewish and/or Roman legal requirements.

Fighting False Gospels

The four Gospels of the New Testament were written to define the terms of Christianity and to dispel any false depictions of Christ. John may have had the toughest job in his Gospel, because he had to convince believers who upheld two different schools of thought.

FACT

A Jewish-Christian sect, the Ebionites, was amongst those who believed that Jesus was a mere man and was made the Messiah by his acts, while Docetism became the philosophy that Jesus appeared in the image of man but was not flesh. In a way, these two groups were the earliest Christian heretics. The root of the word "docetism" comes from the Greek verb: "to seem."

There were those who thought of Jesus as having come to earth as God, in the image of man, but not actually as a human being with flesh and blood. Part of the Christian thought was the miracle that not only was Christ a flesh-and-blood man, he was also a holy spirit. As an explanation, John wrote of the crucifixion. Even in the Catholic Church today, the depiction of Christ's bloody wounds and the pain he endured while he died on the cross are critical to outline this point of view.

There were others who believed that Jesus was just a man and that by virtue of his work on earth, he became the Messiah. John had to dispel this notion as well.

The Gnostics

Of all the break-away Christian factions in the early years, Gnosticism may have had the biggest effect on the development of church scriptures. The Gnostics believed that Jesus was divine and not made of flesh. In fact, the Gnostics believed that Jesus, as a divine being, could not be made of anything as base as matter. Matter was evil to a Gnostic and therefore could have nothing to do with God.

QUESTION?

If the Gnostics didn't believe in matter, then how could they explain their own existence?
The Gnostics explained this by saying that somehow the purity of the human soul, as created by God, became mixed up with matter, and it was the purity that had to be redeemed.

The Orthodox or Apostolic church leaders had a tough time fighting the Gnostics and their "false" gospels. The Gnostics claimed to have secret documents left with their teachers by Jesus to protect the information from the materially blinded Jewish leaders of his time. It's hard to prove something false if it is said to be a secret.

The Gnostics managed to stay around the perimeters of Christianity in the second century because they believed several of the basic Christian doctrines. Specifically, they believed:

1. That Jesus Christ was the Messiah, just not made of matter
2. In the idea of one supreme deity
3. In the idea of salvation

Creationism and Evil

Gnostics differed from Orthodox Christians in that they felt their beliefs needed to be redeemed from the base and vile level to which the Christians had reduced them. They took their belief system to extremes with their conviction that the world was divided into dueling forces: good and evil. So, if the world is made of matter and God created it, then the Orthodox God that created it must be evil, too.

The Gnostic God was also set apart from the Christian God of creationism. The Gnostics believed that the divine spirit of God, in the form of Jesus, came to earth to redeem the souls from the evil nature of the material. When Jesus died, the deity left his flesh-like form and ascended back to heaven. Therefore, the body that died on the cross was not a deity, but mere matter.

This is where the Orthodox Christians drew the line and had to set themselves apart from such heresy. They had to set the rules of Christianity so that their teachings and their scriptures were not lost in all the fringe groups that were beginning to pop up.

Despite the hard work of Christian leaders to defy the influence of Gnostics and other heretics, some Gnostic philosophy did manage to dribble its way to later generations of Christianity. The idea that flesh is evil and the soul is all-important is an issue with some of the more radical Christian factions of today: to deny the flesh is to enhance the soul.

The Apostolic Creed

The Orthodox Christians followed the belief that Jesus was made of flesh and sent by God as a divine spirit to save the souls of His creations. Any other branch of Christianity undermined the fight for unity, and this is where the Apostolic Creed came into the Christian services. It was a reminder of what the Orthodox Christians believed—a way of setting the foundation of Christian thought in concrete.

This is the early Apostolic Creed:

I believe in God the Father Almighty;
And in Jesus Christ, his only Son, our Lord;
Who was born of the Holy Spirit and of the Virgin Mary;
Crucified under Pontius Pilate and buried;

The third day He rose again from the dead,
He ascended into Heaven,
Sitteth at the right hand of the Father,
Whence He shall come to judge the living and the dead.
And in the Holy Ghost
The Holy Church,
The forgiveness of sins
The resurrection of the body.

In this statement, the Orthodox Christians eradicated all threatening Gnostic belief by stating that Jesus was made of flesh as are we all. The Apostolic Creed later added the belief in God Almighty "maker of heaven and earth"—and with that, the Orthodox Christians refuted yet another Gnostic belief: The earth is matter made by God and we are here to enjoy His creation. The problems, however, were not solved, just quelled for the time being. There would be more creeds to come in the future.

The Body and Soul Issue

Perhaps, to the Orthodox Christians, the most threatening stance of the Gnostics was their refusal to believe in "The Event," which is the belief that the Son of God was born of the Virgin Mary, crucified, buried, and resurrected. This is the foundation of the Christian faith. The Gnostics disbelief in "The Event" was another reason that stating the Apostle's Creed needed to be put into practice. The Orthodox Christians had to refute the Gnostic belief that human beings were made of good souls and evil bodies and, therefore, must be redeemed. Rather, the Orthodox Christians viewed the body as a gift given by God, and the reason for redemption was the selfish choices human beings make—they follow their own way versus the way of God. As a result, Jesus was sent to help save human beings from themselves. Ⓔ

Chapter 3

Christians and Rome

How is it that the Christian faith, which started out with one man and a few followers (and one that many thought was just a tiny sect of Judaism), managed to sweep a huge region of the world and eventually the entire world? Well, it wasn't an easy road—there were many bumps along the way—yet the growth of Christianity remained constant.

Roman Catholics

After everything you've read so far, putting the words "Roman" and "Catholic" together seems like an oxymoron. Nevertheless, Christianity did manage to take hold in Rome, but only after Christian leaders and believers underwent some very trying times.

When the Romans took over countries, they brought peace and stability to many nations previously ruled by tyrannical dictators. This era of "Pax Romana" (Roman Peace) lasted about 200 years, and most people of the Roman Empire were actually grateful for their newfound liberties and modernization. They built temples to worship the goddess Roma, the deity that they felt was the reason for this peace. This worship was gradually transformed to a human symbol—and what better symbol than the emperor of Rome himself? Temples previously built in honor of a pagan goddess were now built to honor Caesar.

Caesar Worship

At first, the Roman emperors were not thrilled by the idea of being worshipped. The Emperor Claudius I (who ruled from A.D. 41–54), for example, thought that such worship would be insulting to his fellow Romans. Eventually, however, the idea began to make sense. The Roman Empire was huge, stretching from the Euphrates River in the Middle East all the way west to the Irish Sea. The concern of the empire was how to unify such a vast region of cultures and languages. It made sense to take care of the problem by enforcing a common religion—and why not worship emperors? After all, that was the one thing all the regions under the rule of Caesar had in common. Soon temples recognizing the emperor as a living god were constructed all over the empire.

The first temple to honor the emperor of Rome (Caesar Augustus) as a deity was built in the city of Pergamum (western Asia Minor) in about 29 B.C.

The Brewing Conflict

It seemed like a good idea for unification of the empire, but it meant any other kind of worship was unacceptable. If religion was the one thing the Romans saw as a unifier, then anything else would lead to possible chaos. By the third century, Caesar worship was mandatory and universal—with the exception of the Jewish people.

The Jewish people were not required to pay homage to Caesar as a deity because Rome knew that they would fight to death before worshipping anyone other than their one God. In an effort to keep the peace, Rome left them alone. Those of Jewish faith paid their taxes and maintained a lawful society, so why stir things up? Judaism showed no interest in expanding— you were either Jewish or you weren't. As long as the Christians were seen as a sect of Judaism, they too were left alone by Rome. However, when the Jewish people denied any association with the Christians, the Romans changed their tune, and the persecution of the Christians began.

The Christian Lord Versus the Roman Lord

Once a year, all good citizens of Rome were expected to go to a temple, burn a piece of incense, and say, "Caesar is Lord." A certificate was then issued after the ceremony. If you didn't acknowledge Caesar as Lord, you were automatically branded a traitor to Rome. Well, no good Christian would ever acknowledge Caesar as Lord. The Christian Lord was Jesus Christ, not the emperor of Rome. So what were the Christians to do in this situation? Declare themselves traitors to Rome, or betray their faith? As long as they stood their ground and maintained loyalty to their God, they were considered enemies of Rome. Now that the Romans had found the key to unification, they were not about to let the Christians threaten their stability.

At this point in time, there were some gross misunderstandings regarding who the Christians were and what they believed. Rome considered any Christian who did not declare Caesar as Lord to be an atheist. Christians were also thought to be cannibals because of the Eucharist (the Lord's Supper). In this sacrament, non-Christians accused the Christians of eating real flesh and drinking real blood.

The Christians, in turn, saw Rome as a threat to their own existence. They weren't going to let the Roman Empire interfere with their faith. To Christians, their faith was more important than life itself.

Christian Persecution

The worst period of Christian persecution occurred in A.D. 250, during the reign of Emperor Decius. He saw the Christians as enemies and blamed them for any problems that existed in the empire. As a result, he forced all Roman citizens to sacrifice to the traditional Roman gods, to declare Caesar as Lord, and to get their certificates to prove that they had done so. Many Christians complied to save their lives, while others managed to obtain certificates either through forgery or bribery, and still thousands of other perished in order to stay true to Jesus Christ. However, anyone who did not comply, or feign compliance, was tortured until he denied Christ or died.

The Romans believed that the way to abolish Christianity was to burn the scriptures. They thought that once the written word was gone, the Christians would flounder. What they didn't take into consideration, however, was that Christianity was founded and grew without the written word, so destroying the scriptures could not possibly squelch the faith nor halt its growth. The persecution of the Christians continued until Decius was killed in a battle in A.D. 251.

The Christians who did not succumb to the torture but died as a result were declared "martyrs" (which actually means "witness"). If a Christian survived the torture but stayed true to his faith by not declaring Caesar as his deity, he was called a "confessor." Those who gave in to the torture and denied Christ were considered the "fallen ones."

Christian Martyrs

Dying for your love of and belief in Christ was the greatest thing a Christian could do. The admiration of these believers by fellow Christians was tremendous, and to commemorate their sacrifice, the church leaders kept ledgers of their names and the days on which they died. They also held celebrations in their memories at their tombs. Martyrs and confessors were the first Christian "saints."

Redemption

Christians were amazed by the ability of the martyrs and confessors to withstand torture, and considered it a gift from God. They believed that these special few had been ordained by the Holy Spirit, and since they had been touched by God in this way, they were able to absolve people of their sins.

But there was a problem: What do you do with the fallen ones? Some argued that the martyrs and confessors could absolve them by virtue of their own merits.

Penance

Confronted with these new questions, Christian leaders devised a system of degrees of guilt (or sin). They believed it was possible for the fallen ones to plead that, while their bodies had given way to the torture, their souls had not—that they remained true to the Holy Spirit. So it was decided that if a fallen one came before the church in a sackcloth and with ashes on his head as an act of humility and penance, the bishop could forgive him and restore him in good standing to the church.

Not everyone agreed with this idea, however. Some Christians did not believe in showing any kind of leniency toward the sinners or that any church leader could forgive the unforgivable—that such sin could only be forgiven at the gates of heaven.

FACT

Bishop Cyprian, a church leader of the time, did not agree with the blanket redemption idea. The fallen ones had committed one of the unforgivable sins of "apostasy" (or "denial of faith") and must be rejected by the church. However, he did favor some tolerance for the fallen one (or sinner) after penance and the passage of time.

The Turning Point

One of the most outspoken and powerful Christians at that time was a scholar named Novatian. He felt that the church had a say in the redemption of unforgivable sins only at the time of death. However, Cornelius, a church leader who was later ordained bishop of Rome, espoused that as ordained ministers of God, the bishops could forgive the most grievous sins in the name of God. While Cornelius' argument won majority approval, groups of Novatianists built their own congregations to uphold the more hardline school of thought.

The church eventually excommunicated (deprived of membership) Novatian in A.D. 251, which was considered to be yet another split in early Catholicism—a split between the old and the new church. It was also a huge turning point for the church on a couple different counts: The bishop now had power over the spirit as ordained by God, and the Christian Church now held to two sacraments: baptism and penance.

In the first two centuries, early Christians believed that baptism cleansed a person of all sins in the eyes of God. However, there were a few unforgivable sins that, although forgiven by God by virtue of baptism, would not be forgiven by the church. The three most unforgivable sins were murder, sexual immorality (adultery), and the denial of faith (apostasy).

The Emperor Diocletian

The death of Decius provided Christians some time to regroup and reunify, but it wasn't long before the next emperor, Diocletian, followed in Decius' footsteps. It remains a mystery as to why Diocletian chose to persecute Christians when he had pretty much ignored them for the first eighteen years of his reign. Also, his wife and daughter were Christians, and Christians held high-ranking positions in his court. Christianity continued to grow during his rule until one day the emperor snapped and launched the most vicious attack against Christians in their history.

Diocletian and Politics

Many historians consider Diocletian to have been one of the greatest of all the Roman emperors, mainly for the way he managed and organized the empire during his reign. Although he was born into slavery, he became a great military leader, and as a result, was elected emperor of Rome in A.D. 284.

Having seen the chaos of the battlefield and the constant threat of assassination against the Caesars and their families, Diocletian was concerned about the state of the empire and felt it was unmanageable due to its enormous size and expanse across the region. Diocletian then divided the empire into four imperial seats of power—and not one of them was in Rome. He placed his own court in Asia Minor, where he could keep an eye on potential foreign invaders from the East. He proclaimed the other leaders as the "Augusti" and gave himself the title of "Caesar," thus lessening the threat of assassination. It is this strategic maneuvering that gave Diocletian the historical seat of being one of the empire's greatest political leaders.

According to the scriptures, Jesus said: "Blessed are those who are persecuted for righteousness' sake, for theirs is the kingdom of heaven. Blessed are you when people revile you and persecute you and utter all kinds of evil against you falsely on my account."
—MATTHEW 5:10–11, NRSV

The Last Persecution

About A.D. 303, Diocletian went on a rampage against the Christians. The first step was to rid his army of all Christians, which was soon followed by the destruction of all church buildings, including many that had been built under his reign. He also abolished Christian worship, destroyed the scriptures, and tortured and executed many Church leaders. Although Diocletian abdicated in A.D. 305, his successor, Augustus Galerius, continued the reign of terror, wanting to eradicate Christianity from the Roman Empire altogether. What followed was one of the most bloody eras in the history of Christianity.

World Intervention

However, the brutality of Galerius did not sit well with regions outside of Rome. Constantius Chlorus, one of the Diocletian-appointed Augusti, demanded the end of the terror, and pagans from various regions rejected the persecution as well.

The pressure to end the eradication of Christians was so great that on his deathbed Galerius issued an "edict of toleration," which ended the last of such prolonged acts of violence against the Christians.

Constantine the Great

If it wasn't for Emperor Constantine, it's hard to know whether Christianity would have had much of a future at all. After the Diocletian and Galerius reigns of terror against Christians ended, a power struggle ensued that changed the course of history. In A.D. 312, Constantine led an army to Rome after he supposedly had a dream in which he saw a cross and heard the words, "In this sign conquer." Constantine saw his victory as a sign of the power of Christ and his conversion to Christianity began.

FACT

Constantine was baptized shortly before he died in A.D. 337. After his baptism, he rejected the emperor's purple imperial robes and chose to wear only his white baptismal robes. Constantine was a firm believer that baptism would wash away all sins, and, as a result, waited until the last minute to be baptized.

Here are some of the actions taken by Constantine that catapulted Christianity into the spotlight and set its course for the future:

- Abolished crucifixion
- Stopped public battles of gladiators as a means of punishment
- Gave Christian ministers exemptions from some taxes
- Made every Sunday a public holiday
- Built church buildings
- Raised his children as Christians

The rule of Constantine was a far cry from the life Christians had led under the previous two emperors.

Constantine's City

Since 1930, Constantinople has been known as Istanbul (Turkey). Before it was Istanbul, the city was called Byzantium, which was changed to Constantinople (Constantine's City) under the reign of Emperor Constantine.

Constantine chose the city Byzantium to be the new capital of the Roman Empire because of its supreme location on the Bosporus waterway between the Black Sea and the Mediterranean Sea. He recognized it as a potential gold mine for international trade and realized the waterway was narrow enough to keep an eye on foreign invaders.

The Danger of Riches

Although Constantine stopped the persecution and put Christianity into the limelight, his foresight was so great that it also drew the attention of the greedy. With the newly found wealth of the church under Constantine, along came those willing to feign Christian beliefs for the love of money and political gain. Some say that before Constantine's time, the church was comprised predominantly of true believers, but after Constantine, it was anybody's guess as to who truly believed and who was just in it for wealth and glory. Some would even argue that the legitimization of Christianity by Constantine actually caused people to become too complacent in their faith and in their involvement with the church. (E)

Chapter 4

Early Christian Leaders

After the apostle Paul began spreading Jesus' message, Christian churches started to appear throughout the empire, but still needed leadership. As a result, early church leaders turned to Paul for answers to some of the questions that would bombard the Church for centuries to come. Through his letters, Paul attempted not only to unify each individual church, but the entire Christian community.

Church Leaders

In the early years of Christianity, the bishops (or popes) played just a small role in Christian life, but their influence was undeniable. As you read earlier, it was the bishops who originally called for church unity, prompting Paul to write the letters (e.g., Romans, 1 and 2 Corinthians, Galatians, Ephesians, Philippians, and Colossians) found in the New Testament of the Bible. The church did find a sort of unity in ancient times with the letters, Gospels, and books inspired by the apostles; however, it would be some time before it reached an agreement on what it actually believed in. There were many struggles ahead for the unification of the Christian church, especially in terms of spiritual teachings.

Prophets and Teachers

The apostles were the first Christian leaders—after all, they were the ones who personally knew Jesus and listened to his teachings (except for Paul, of course). Next in line, in terms of Christian authority, were the prophets and the teachers, who wandered the earth teaching the words of the Messiah. But the church required resident teachers to forge a unity within the community, regions, and eventually the world. The power of the bishops was a slow-growing process, but one that seemed very natural for such a rapidly growing religion.

FACT

The apostle Paul did not meet Jesus until after the resurrection, at which time he experienced a visit by the Holy Spirit on the road to Damascus and converted to Christianity. Today, Paul is known as the greatest missionary of the early church.

Paul's Letters

Paul knew that it would be important to establish church leadership, especially in ministering to the spiritual needs of the people on a day-to-day basis. He was only one man, and the other apostles could never spread themselves that thin, so leaders had to be established.

Some of Paul's letters (also referred to as "epistles") were written to help a church at Corinth (located in modern-day Greece) find direction in its leadership and traditions of worship. Although he may not have intended them for universal application in the Christian community, they were later accepted into the canon. As a result, Paul's letters served to unify church leaders who were geographically scattered but looking for direction.

There were about 200 followers of Christ living in Corinth during the time Paul was writing his letters to the church. The Corinthian Christians were a tight-knit community and lived and worshipped in large households. Paul visited Corinth in about A.D. 50.

Elders and Deacons

While the apostles remained the traveling spiritual leaders of the age, the church welcomed a new brand of leadership that oversaw the instruction and day-to-day practices. These leaders were divided into two groups called "elders" and "deacons." The job of the elders was to maintain law and order, oversee public worship, and teach new Christian converts, while the "deacons" served as their assistants.

Eventually, there was a shift in leadership, so that just one bishop presided over each church congregation and was assisted by a group of elders and deacons. This would soon become the standard hierarchy of church leadership and remains so to this day.

Controversial Points of View

Over the centuries, several arguments cropped up that threatened the unity of the Christian church. Christ's teachings were still a relatively new way of thinking and given the limitlessness of their geographical reach, it is understandable that other groups came forward espousing new ideas. However, these ideas did not sit well with the established Christian communities. With each new growing movement, the bishops felt that the control and unity they had worked so hard to maintain could easily slip through their fingers.

Councils

The controversies that arose over different church teachings forced the leaders to further solidify Christian doctrine by holding councils—a sort of ancient-day convention of church leaders. In the council meetings, church leaders tried to adopt a universal standard for controversial subjects that they felt could threaten the original intention of Christianity. The goal was to reach one conclusion on each controversy that would withstand the ages and reaches of Christian teaching. Over the years, there were hundreds of subjects with which the church would struggle. The councils often helped church leaders find compromises on topics ranging from the nature of Christ to the offering of the Eucharist. But it would take centuries and many council meetings to formulate the Christian doctrine.

QUESTION?

What exactly is a "heretic"?
A heretic is someone with a point of view dissenting from the traditionally accepted views of the church. In the early Christian church, a heretic was anyone who opposed the view of the unified church governed by the bishops.

The Challenge

In the centuries after Christ died, there was much debate over the central ideology of the church. Perhaps one of the most provocative events that took place in the early fourth century was when Pope Alexander of Alexandria called a council of elders (or "presbyters") to discuss the Holy Trinity. As Alexander lectured about the idea of the Father, Son, and Holy Ghost, a man named Arius from Libya stood up and challenged Alexander. He claimed that if God begat the Son, then there was a time where the Son did not exist; thereby, openly stating that if Jesus was born of God, he was lesser than God, acting only as a mediator between God and humankind. Arius also maintained that if Christ was not always the Son, then God was not always the Father.

For church leaders, Arius' statement was highly provocative because it challenged the firm Christian belief in the Holy Trinity. The church espoused that Christ is God, and God is three-in-one: Father, Son, and Holy Spirit. He existed as the Triune (three-in-one) God at the time when Christ was of the flesh; he was the Trinity before that; and he will always be.

The two controversial ideas for the early Christian church were:

1. The Trinity (Who is God?)
2. Christology (Who is Jesus Christ?)

The Trinity

This may have been one of the most complex ideas to grasp in Christian doctrine, which is why so many church leaders opted out by calling it a mystery. Just as it is hard to help a child understand the concept of the Trinity today, it was equally difficult to explain it to a fledgling community of Christians.

Here is the breakdown of the Trinity (or the Triune God):

1. God the Father
2. God the Son
3. God the Holy Ghost (or Spirit)

Questions of the Era

The Trinity means that God consists of three persons making up one entity. What does that mean? Isn't God . . . just God? And aren't humans just flesh and blood? Well, what was Christ then? Son of God? Or God himself? Was he a divinely inspired prophet created by God? Or a man, like any other, made of flesh with perhaps the soul of God?

The pagans believed in several different gods, while those of Jewish and Muslim faith found the idea of God being "three-in-one" offensive and disrespectful. Even within the Christian community, there was argument over the concepts of the Trinity and of Jesus' divinity. This was one major disagreement that had to be resolved if there was to be any kind of lasting unity in the future.

It is hard to give a secular description of the Trinity. It can't be explained by history or logic. Those of Christian faith, pastors, and their congregations alike struggle to put "the mystery" into words. That's because it is just that—a mystery—a rather complicated one at that. But to Christians, understanding and accepting the mystery is a matter of pure faith.

Three-in-One

When Christians refer to God as a "person," they don't actually mean a human being of flesh and blood. The literal translation of "person" comes from the Greek word "persona" or "mask." What the Christians mean when they say that God is "three persons in one" is that God has three identities (not that he is three different beings).

When God reveals himself, he removes his masks. For example, in the Old Testament when God reveals himself to Moses, he reveals himself as the Father, a divine authoritarian. In other words, the Trinity of Father, Son, and Holy Ghost represents the *fullness* of God. When he reveals himself as a carpenter from Galilee in the form of Jesus the Messiah, God comes as a flesh-and-blood man—the Son. And, finally when he reveals himself at the Pentecost, for example, inspiring thousands to seek Christianity by means of baptism, he comes as an essence—a spirit. These are the three revelations of God that make up the one being that is God.

FACT

The four Gospels of the New Testament of the Bible are called Matthew, Mark, Luke, and John, named after the four apostles. It is believed that the first three Gospels (Matthew, Mark, and Luke) were written by those apostles, and it is generally accepted that John the Beloved—also known as John, son of Zebedee—wrote the Gospel of John.

Question of Faith

For many Christians, the concept of the Trinity is the very essence and the basis of their faith. In some ways, it is also a mystery; most modern-day Christians are content to leave it at that, while those of perhaps a more analytical mind want the idea of the Trinity to be spelled out in plain English. That was certainly true in the early days.

Here are some ancient arguments against the Trinity:

- **Monarchianism (Adoptionism):** Belief that Jesus became the Messiah only at his baptism and was adopted by God (the Father) after his death.
- **Sabellianism (Modalism or Patripassionism):** This school of thought espoused that onc God reveals himself in three ways—as Father the creator, as Son and redeemer, and as Holy Spirit and life-giver—and the difference between this belief and that of the Trinity lies in the "word" rather than the "person."
- **Arianism:** This school of thought proclaimed that Jesus Christ was not God, just created by God.
- **Semi-Arianism**: Belief that Jesus was not God but made of similar essence—a subordinate to God.
- **Macedonianism:** This school of thought denied the Trinity and believed that the Holy Spirit was one being created by the Son (Jesus Christ), and was, therefore, subordinate to both the Father (God) and the Son (Jesus Christ).

Christology

Who exactly was Jesus Christ? This was a question that was broached even in the apostolic era. The Gnostics, with their ideas of good and evil in relation to matter and spirit, were the most outspoken dissenters to orthodox beliefs at that time. The apostolic leaders felt the Gnostics had been successfully dealt with in the past, so why was Christ's identity taken into question again?

Well, over the centuries, theologians had emerged with a lot of questions. They had plenty of time to think and analyze, and with the growth of Christianity, there were those with serious political ambitions who wanted to put their opinions forward as a means of acquiring religious and political power.

FACT

The mingling of God with humanity is referred to as the "incarnation." Jesus is the first God-man. He is a being with two natures: humanity and divinity. The incarnation implies three things: That Jesus Christ is a divine person; that Jesus Christ is of human nature; and that there is a hypostatic union in Jesus Christ (the mingling of the human with the divine nature in the divine person of Jesus Christ).

Figuring It Out

This was a period when a great deal of thought went into the ideas that the life of Christ put forth. Again, all the questions boiled down to the issue of mystery. In this case, the mystery was the incarnation and the question of the Trinity. Did God appear in the form of a man? Was Jesus a man with the soul of God? What actually happened, and who is Jesus Christ, and, for that matter, who is God?

Here are some of the dissenting movements regarding the identity of Christ:

- **Apollinarianism:** This school of thought believed that Christ had no human spirit (His soul was that of God), rather his soul was the Divine Word ("Logos" in Greek), and he was connected to humans by means of physical flesh only.

- **Nestorianism:** This school of thought believed that the Divine Word (Logos) existed inside Jesus, but that his flesh and blood being was not a deity—in fact, Nestorians believed that there were two versions of Jesus: one born of Mary (the human Jesus) and the other made from God (the divine Jesus).
- **Eutychianism:** This school of thought put forth that Jesus was flesh, but his human attributes were completely absorbed by his divine nature. Eutychianists also believed that Jesus was not the redeemer.

Theology and Unity

All of the abovementioned groups were considered the early heretics, but it was these "heresies" that forced the church leaders to fully analyze religious doctrine and to iron out some very complex issues. Even though the church won Arius' argument regarding the Holy Trinity, Arianism maintained a powerful hold with its "heretical" point of view.

When the word of this heresy reached Emperor Constantine, it started a barrage of letters between the bishops and Rome. At first, Constantine had no clue as to why this was a problem and didn't think the priests should be making such a big deal of it. However, he also knew that disunity in the church could be a threat to the power of Rome.

ESSENTIAL

In an effort to end the Arian heresy, Constantine ordered all writings of Arius' to be burned and anyone caught with an Arian book to be put to death. However, Arianism had taken a strong hold in regions of the empire, and it took a while before the movement faded away to levels that were not threatening to Rome.

Constantine's Solution

It's not easy to explain mysteries, but it's easy to lose ground and fall apart under several dissenting points of view. That is exactly what concerned Emperor Constantine, as some of these issues loomed heavy and large over his reign. Concerned that all this theological griping would threaten the stability of his empire, he called a council to meet in Nicea (in Asia Minor) in A.D. 325, where he brought the church leaders together to put an end to this religious quarrelling.

The Council of Nicea

If you're a Christian, you're most likely familiar with the Nicene Creed, which originated from this council held only 325 years after the birth of Christ. The council, called by Constantine himself, was organized to put an end to some of the religious bickering that not only threatened the stability of Christianity but, because of the newfound power of the church in Rome, the stability of an entire empire. The result of the council was the determination that Jesus Christ (the Son) was co-equal with the Father (God)—that they were, essentially, one and the same.

QUESTION?

How was the news of the council organized and communicated?
Constantine sent messengers to all parts of the empire with invitations to the bishops. Each bishop was allowed to bring two presbyters and three slaves. An estimated 1800 people—from church leaders to common men—made their way to Nicea.

The determination was consecrated in the unifying words of the Nicene Creed, which attempted to discredit all other dissenting points of view.

The version that the Council of Nicea came up with was not nearly so lyrical—it was a complex topic, which was put into words in a chaotic and incomprehensible way. The Nicene Creed was altered at the Council of Constantinople in A.D. 381, but it didn't get final approval until A.D. 451 at the Council of Chalcedon.

Here is the modern-day version of the Nicene Creed:

Nicene Creed

We believe in one God,
the Father, the Almighty,
maker of heaven and earth,
of all that is, seen and unseen.
We believe in one Lord, Jesus Christ,
the only Son of God,
eternally begotten of the Father,
God from God, Light from Light,
true God from true God,
begotten, not made,
of one Being with the Father.
Through him all things were made.
For us and for our salvation
he came down from heaven:
by the power of the Holy Spirit
he was born of the Virgin Mary,
and became man.
For our sake he was crucified under Pontius Pilate;
he suffered death and was buried.
On the third day he rose again
in accordance with the Scriptures;
he ascended into heaven
and is seated at the right hand of the Father.
He will come again in glory to judge the living and the dead,
and his kingdom will have no end.
We believe in the Holy Spirit, the Lord, the giver of life,
who proceeds from the Father and the Son.
With the Father and the Son, He is worshiped and glorified.
He has spoken through the Prophets.
We believe in one holy catholic and apostolic Church.
We acknowledge one baptism for the forgiveness of sins.
We look for the resurrection of the dead,
and the life of the world to come.
Amen.

Chapter 5

The Monks

There were several early church leaders who influenced the Catholic Church over the ages—so much so that their words and ideas can still be heard in church teachings today. As the scholars and thinkers of the age, the monks may have had the most powerful influence of all the Christian leaders.

Who Were They?

Right from the early years of Christianity, there were many Christians who wanted to worship in the way they believed Christ meant them to: reflectively, introspectively, with purity of body and mind—and so they did. In most cases, this meant relinquishing their belongings and denouncing their families and past existence for a life of isolation in a place that they felt would bring them spiritually closer to God and the true message of Christ.

Although different monastic orders took their own set of unique vows, generally speaking, a monk vowed:

1. To lead a life of poverty.
2. To lead a life of chastity.
3. To lead a life of obedience to the monastic order and to God.

As a result of such purity and servitude, monks were considered the most holy and idolized persons of medieval society.

Desert Hermits

Monks were also considered desert "hermits"—Christians choosing to live apart from society, dwelling in caves, for the most part, and walking in Christ's footsteps. They were usually highly educated and from wealthy backgrounds. Yes, the early monks were hermits, in the true sense of the word, but they were not crazy. They were Christians who were perhaps influenced by the Gnostics in their belief that only the spirit should be nurtured and all things physical should be denied. One way or another, they preferred an isolated life, hidden away anywhere they could be left alone to devote themselves to their faith. These hermits were purists who knew what they believed and didn't need bishops, emperors, councils, and heretics to tell them how to manifest their faith.

The first of these early-day hermits were actually women, who were known in Latin as "nonnus," or nuns, and later, their communities became known as "convents." They joined the convents for several reasons: to avoid arranged marriages; to answer God's call to worship; or to save their fathers from having to come up with their wedding dowries.

Life in the Monasteries

The hermits eventually realized that life alone might not be the best way to go. They looked to the book of Genesis in the Bible to help them find the road to communal living: "Then the LORD God said, 'It is not good that the man should be alone; I will make him a helper as his partner.'" (Genesis 2:18, NRSV).

Although this reference from scripture points to the creation of Eve as a companion to Adam, these were some of the words that the monks lived by when choosing monastic living. Many of these monks later became saints.

In choosing communal living, the monks also found a means of returning to God's original intentions for humankind before Adam took a bite of the forbidden fruit of the tree of the Knowledge of Good and Evil. Adam and Eve lived in the Garden of Eden—a paradise on earth. This meant living with no death, no pain, no suffering—just peace and harmony. God promised them eternity in this garden as long as they did not eat a bite of the forbidden fruit. But, tempted by Satan in the appearance of a serpent, Eve gave the fruit to Adam, who took a bite, and all hopes for peace on earth came to a sudden halt. They disobeyed God and as a result, they were punished and expelled from the Garden of Eden. God also mandated that all of their offspring, and therefore, all future human beings, would be born into sin and the pains of life that we know in this world. This is what is referred to as "original sin" in the Christian Church. " . . . I commanded you, 'You shall not eat of it,' cursed is the ground because of you; in toil you shall eat of it all the days of your life . . . By the sweat of your face you shall eat bread until you return to the ground, for out of it you were taken; you are dust, and to dust you shall return" (Genesis 3:17,19 NRSV).

" . . . And the LORD God planted a garden in Eden, in the east; and there he put the man whom he had formed. Out of the ground the LORD God made to grow every tree that is pleasant to the sight and good for food, the tree of life also in the midst of the garden, and the tree of the knowledge of good and evil."
—GENESIS 2:8–9, NRSV

What does this have to do with the monks? Well, the monks believed that a return to simple living in their own gardens would bring them back to "Eden"—to the days before "the fall" of Adam and Eve. In a shared community, helping each other, they grew their own crops, tended their own animals, grew their own herbs to make their own medicines, and eventually even came to manufacture wine and cheese in order support their way of life. In essence, monastic life was like crawling back into the womb of creation to start anew and live as Adam and Eve had lived before original sin. This kind of life, they believed, would bring them closer to God and help them lead a more spiritual existence apart from the sinfulness of the world beyond their gardens.

Because many of the monks were inspired by the apostle Paul—and the Gnostic belief in the evils of the physical world—they believed that part of monastic life should also include celibacy. Celibacy meant that one should not marry and therefore, should not have sex.

Church leaders also began to promote the idea that they had power that reached beyond the common folk. They tried to widen that gap by putting themselves on a higher spiritual plane, which included denying themselves the physical aspects of the common layperson: marriage, consummation, and children.

The Saints

It takes a long time to achieve sainthood in the Catholic Church, but the early Christian monks all earned the respect of church leaders through their scholarly contributions to the church, their devotion to their monasteries (and therefore to God), and in some cases for their good deeds to humankind.

Here are some of the Christians, amongst the more notable monks, who eventually achieved sainthood:

- St. Anthony
- St. Jerome
- St. Benedict
- St. Gregory
- St. Augustine

St. Anthony

Saint Anthony (A.D. 251–356) was the first Christian who lived a life of solitude, and many people consider him the father of monasticism. Anthony believed that one's Christian soul is strengthened through physical deprivation, and although this was a common philosophy of the early Christian monks, it was not always practiced at the same level of severity.

As a young man, Anthony sold his land, gave his money to the poor, and went off to live in a desert. A friend brought him some bread and water from time to time so that he could survive. His first claim to fame was his willingness to combat demons—Anthony claimed he had fought demon images: raging images of lions and bears, creeping snakes, and a wolf on the attack. One day, the cave in which he battled the demons opened, and he heard the voice of God saying that, since Anthony had persevered, He (God) would be with him forever.

Anthony's Ministry

Anthony never actually founded a particular monastery, but throughout his 105 years of life people flocked to the cave to catch a glimpse of the famous demon-battling monk. Anthony spent the rest of his life seeking guidance in seclusion, as well as giving spiritual direction to those who sought it through his public ministry. He was believed to have exorcised demons, reconciled enemies, and ministered to the sick.

Many monasteries popped up in Anthony's lifetime and for many years thereafter, which is why he is referred to as the father of the monks.

FACT

Located in Egypt, the Deir Mar Antonios (or St. Anthony's monastery) was founded just after St. Anthony's death in A.D. 356 and still observes the original rituals of the fifth century. It is the oldest active monastery in the world and contains a library of 1,700 handwritten manuscripts. The cave in which St. Anthony is said to have battled his legendary demons is just a short distance away.

St. Jerome

Saint Jerome (A.D. 342–419) was another one of the early Christian hermits. He rejected all things physical to the point of refusing to bathe, believing that baptism was all the cleansing he needed. He was a scholar who admired the pagan stories of lust and rage, as well as other physical passions, which put him in quite a religious and intellectual quandary. Jerome was tormented by his physical urges because he couldn't reconcile them with his Gnostic tradition of denying the physical.

Return to Rome

Jerome was one of the many monks who decided living alone was not the best way, so he returned to Rome, where he befriended two women: Paula and Marcella—also brilliant scholars devoted to the denial of all things physical. While Paula remained a lifelong companion, Marcella was the one to finance Jerome's scholarly goal of translating the Bible from its original Hebrew to Latin.

Before Jerome's translation, the most commonly used scripture was the Septuagint, which, by more advanced standards, was considered a rather rough translation of the Judaic scriptures from Hebrew to Greek. Other translations to Latin had been made from the Septuagint, so Jerome's idea was to start from scratch.

The Vulgate

In his translation of the Bible, Jerome used easily understood words to make the text more readable. Because of its straightforwardness, several Christian scholars called his translation the "Vulgate," meaning "common." Jerome completed the translation before his friend Paula died in A.D. 405. His work became one of the most popular translations of the Bible, and is still used in churches today. Jerome died in A.D. 419.

St. Benedict

Benedict (A.D. 480–550) and his twin sister, Scholastica (who was also made a saint), were born in Italy. Benedict was one of the first monks to start a community of Christians living apart from society. He is legendary for several reasons, including that he smashed one of the remaining pagan altars that sat on a hillside and on the same spot built his first monastery. Nearby, Scholastica founded a convent, and the two continued their Christian work in neighboring communities. However, in A.D. 589, an invading army of "barbarians" burned Benedict's monastery to the ground, and the monks fled to Rome.

FACT

You may see ancient drawings (or modern-day movies) depicting monks with shaven heads. Shaving the crown of the head was practiced mostly between A.D. 400 and A.D. 600 to symbolize when a novice became a monk. The ritual was called the "tonsure" and was abolished by Pope Paul VI in 1972.

The Benedictine Rule

Benedict is perhaps best known for giving "The Rule" to Christianity, a guidebook for Christian community living. It was not considered to be a book of extremes in the same way other monastic living writings were, but taught a rather mellow way of living in true devotion to Christ. The book expressed that the best way to live as a community of Christians was to balance work, Bible reading, and prayer on a daily basis. His rules also consisted of chastity, poverty, obedience, and stability.

The principles of the Benedictine rule were similar to the vows taken by monks. However, by putting it into one manuscript, Benedict was able to outline what he considered the ideal form of monastic living. Benedictine orders of monks exist to this day and still live by "The Rule," with the aim of burying one's will in monastic living and devotion to God.

St. Gregory the Great

Gregory (A.D. 540–604) was a powerful Roman politician who suddenly, in about A.D. 574, became a monk. Gregory earned the love of his fellow Romans when he left his monastery, during a plague that was ravaging Rome, to tend to the sick and the dying.

QUESTION?

Who were the "barbarians"?
The "barbarians" were nomadic tribes who lived on the fringes of the Roman Empire. They were accused of all sorts of savage behavior—and aside from plundering and pillaging, they were particularly ridiculed for their lack of "table" etiquette. The Goth and Vandal tribes, as well as the Huns, were all referred to as barbarians.

Gregory and England

Christianity had arrived in England in about A.D. 300, but hordes of Saxon barbarians had raided the land and destroyed all the churches. When the Roman overseer died, Gregory was appointed to his position, and his priority was to make sure that the barbarians changed their pagan ways to become Christians. As a fan of Benedict's Rule, Gregory, in A.D. 599, delegated forty-one Benedictine monks to England on a mission of conversion. It only took a few months before 10,000 Anglo-Saxons were baptized, and Gregory has since been considered one of Christianity's greatest missionaries.

Gregory and Augustine

Not only was Gregory influenced by Benedict, but he also read a great deal of Augustine's writings. One of the things that struck him, however, was Augustine's dilemma over what happens if someone who has led a good Christian life dies without confession.

Gregory found his answer in his doctrine of "purgatory," a place where the unabsolved souls go and still experience God's presence—a sort of an intermediary stop between heaven and hell. Gregory was also concerned with the music of the church and as a result, the Gregorian chant, a Roman form of "choral" singing, was named after him.

FACT

Purgatory became a Roman Catholic belief found in the Apocrypha (books such as Tobit and Maccabbees, which are considered "noncanonical"—not part of the official scriptures—by today's Protestants).

St. Augustine of Hippo

Given the life he led before he was a monk, it is almost ironic that the writings of St. Augustine (A.D. 354–430) became the most coveted and admired in Christian theology. But, on the other hand, it is perhaps his past that enabled him to have so much understanding of Christianity.

A Changed Life

St. Augustine's path to the monastery was a difficult road full of repentance and prayer. He was a ladies' man and frequently prayed to God to take away this sin from his life. His Christian mother, Monica (now a saint as well), was concerned about her son, especially when he decided to go to Italy. She was convinced that the trip would only add to his wicked lifestyle, but much to her surprise, it had the opposite effect. Augustine heard a speech given by Ambrose of Alexandria, and it changed his life—he decided that he wanted to be a monk.

Inspired by stories of conversions, Augustine decided to retreat to a place where he could devote himself to God without external temptations—he chose the desert. Soon afterward, he was appointed the overseer of Hippo in North Africa (part of the Roman Empire).

The Fall of Rome

St. Augustine was a scholar—considered, perhaps, one of the greatest scholars in Christian history. At fifty-six years old, while still in Hippo, he heard that Rome had been sacked (one of the many times) and decided to help by taking in Roman refugees, feeding them, and finding places for them to live. His next step was to turn inward and analyze what had happened in Rome and what this would mean for the future of Christianity.

The City of God

Inspired by the horror of what happened to the Christian capital, Augustine wrote his epic, *The City of God,* in which he discussed what Christians owed to God and what they owed to the emperor for the next fifteen centuries to come. It was his look into the future—a way of making sense of the chaos that had brought a blight upon the Christian seat of power.

In *The City of God,* Augustine also discussed the roles of the church and the state. The church, Augustine believed, supported the soul of the citizens, and the citizens were the power behind the community—the supports behind the city—while the state existed to maintain law and order. But the state was rooted in the power of sin and, therefore, had to submit to the power of the church.

Augustine's *The City of God* would become a cherished piece of writing and would remain so well into the Middle Ages. It gave people hope for better things to come.

Pelagius, the Heretic

Pelagius is believed to have been British, but no one knows for sure. He made his way to Rome and was later renowned as one of Christianity's most infamous heretics. A highly educated monk and theologian, who spoke Latin and Greek fluently, Pelagius caused some trouble for Augustine, who did not want Pelagianism to manifest itself in Hippo. The basis of Pelagianism, and the ideas that the church found most threatening, were the negation of original sin and the disbelief that people can only achieve salvation through the grace of God.

There are many saints of the same name in the Christian church. So most saints are identified by their place of birth, their place of leadership, or their position in the church.

What Is Pelagianism?

Pelagius claimed that no one is born sinful and that the story of Adam and Eve is merely an allegory to show an example of what it means to sin, but that it does not say anything about the moral condition of humankind. Pelagius also believed that faith alone is enough to achieve salvation—one's salvation does not depend on God's grace. In general, Pelagius argued that leading a good life and achieving salvation has everything to do with self-control.

Augustine's Struggle

Augustine, from his own experience, believed that only the grace of God had saved him from a life of sin. He believed that all people are natural-born sinners and the constant desire for salvation is what keeps people from sinning any further. Augustine's own struggle to achieve the grace of God was, as he said, what kept him a Christian. He believed and taught that all humankind shared Adam's fall and as a result was doomed to damnation—except for the grace of God.

Council of Ephesus

One of the many things to come out of this council, including issues of Christology, was the negation of Pelagianism. This "heresy" had reached to the far corners of the Christian world, and at the Ecumenical Council of Ephesus in A.D 431, Pelagianism was crushed in the East. And with the help of Augustine's manuscripts, it didn't take long before Pelagian's influence faded throughout the Christian world altogether.

Monastic Scribes

One of the great legacies left behind by these educated monks was their books. Book production in the monasteries began in the seventh century and continued well into the thirteenth century. The monastic scribes recorded religious works by translating them into Latin and hand writing them into complete manuscripts. The "illuminated" manuscripts were works of art, with drawings telling the story of the text.

FACT

One of the greatest existing examples of an illuminated manuscript is the Irish *Book of Kells* (a Latin translation of the Gospels). If you can't make a trip to Trinity College in Dublin, Ireland, to see the manuscript with your own eyes, samples from the *Book of Kells* can be seen on the Internet: *www.dubois.ws/people/paul/kells*. It is truly worth the time to look over these magnificent drawings.

Worship Through Transcription

The monks worked (usually in silence) in the "scriptorium" (a room inside the monastery), and they stored the books in massive libraries. It's hard to know if the books were translated from their original, or if the monks chose to translate them into works that would be beneficial to the church. Any way you look at it, the books are artistic masterpieces. The creation of these manuscripts was considered an act of religious worship. The monks spent months working on a single chapter, and their work was not seen as making books but a way to manifest the word of God.

In the thirteenth century, book production was secularized and was done not as an act of worship, but as a means to observe the world. Universities, for the most part, took over transcribing manuscripts, and books were not necessarily found only in the libraries of the monasteries, but on the shelves of scholars to be shared with the outside world.

Chapter 6

The Early Middle Ages

The Middle Ages are often referred to as the "Dark Ages," which may have to do with the fact that Rome fell to barbarian hordes, the Crusades saw the slaughter of thousands, and the world of art and education was not flourishing. But, in all likelihood, the era was considered "dark," in hindsight, because of the exciting period of "enlightenment" that was to follow 1,000 years later.

The Fall of Rome

Even though Rome was never the center of the universe, it *was* considered the center of the Christian world, and the barbarians wanted to gain the power and wealth attributed to the empire. In A.D. 410, the city fell at the hands of Alaric the Goth, and this event marked the beginning of the Middle Ages.

Alaric the Goth

The tribes, or the barbarians (as they were called), wanted to share the benefits of the empire, but Rome was not interested. The Goth tribal leader, Alaric, wanted the emperor in the West to give him farmland, gold, and silver, so the Goths could start their lives within the bounds of the Roman Empire. Rome, however, refused and the Goths attacked. They were successful in shattering the city in a three-day rampage of looting and pillaging.

According to legend, Alaric the Goth faked his own death to save his people from capture by the Romans and Vandals after his attack on Rome. It is said he went "underground," and ruled the later Visigothic kingdoms for several decades until his supposed real death in the year A.D. 470.

A Traumatized Society

At the time, Rome was considered invincible—it was the sacred city, the seat of Christianity—so it's no wonder that the barbarian invasion shook the empire's political system, rattled the security of the church, and most importantly, wounded the proud Roman soul.

While the citizens of the realm stumbled amongst the confusion, trying to make sense of the mess, Augustine of Hippo turned their confusion into hope by writing his book *The City of God.* You read about this earlier, but it's critical to note just how important Augustine's words were to the Christians.

In *The City of God*, Augustine claimed that two cities exist: a City of God and a City of Mankind. He said that although the two cities interact, there will come a day when the City of Mankind will fade away, but the City of God will be left in the hearts of humankind—a faithful Christian spirit will conquer the physical world of power and riches. When Rome collapsed, Augustine's words served as a reminder to his fellow Christians that God would never forsake them.

Barbarian Invasions

The fall of Rome in A.D. 410 was just the beginning of a series of attacks that would continue to challenge the strength of the empire. In A.D. 452, the most infamous of all barbarians, Attila the Hun, paced the borders of the Roman Empire. As Attila and his Huns entered Rome, they suffered no resistance—no army and no emperor—but there was the Roman overseer, Leo, who did his best to control the hordes.

FACT

The Huns were an invading army from Asia that entered the West and quickly crushed the Ostrogoths (eastern German tribe) in the fourth century. Their leader, Attila, is known, even today, as one of the most vicious and aggressive tribal leaders the world has ever known.

Leo, who later became the first pope of the Roman Catholic Church, actually managed to strike a bargain with Attila, and the Huns retreated. However, Leo was not as successful when the Vandals (another "barbarian" tribe) darkened his doorstep in A.D. 455. He did manage to convince them not to kill or rape, but he could not stop them from looting and destroying property.

The tribes who attacked Rome were mostly from the north (Scandinavian region of Europe), and here is a list of some of them:

- **Franks:** A powerful Germanic tribe (French, as we know them today), with their name originating from the word "fierce" or "free" in the Frankish language.

- **Goths (Visigoths and Ostrogoths):** A Germanic tribe that settled on the Danube River and eventually formed an army to ward off the Huns.
- **Vandals:** A Germanic tribe from Jutland (what is now Denmark).
- **Angles and Saxons:** The Angles come from "Angeln," a district of what we now know as Denmark, and the Saxons were a warring tribe that came from a region of Germany.
- **Huns:** A nomadic Mongolian tribe that invaded southern Europe in the fourth century. The Huns were highly successful in their invasions of the western Roman Empire, maintaining their dominance as they fought off the Goths and several other defensive tribes.

The Western Collapse

In A.D. 476, a very tired and ravaged Rome was occupied again by Odovacar, who deposed the last of the Western Roman emperors and, thus, brought down the Western Christian Empire (the Eastern Empire still remained intact in Byzantium, or Constantinople). As a result, church leaders found themselves shouldering the burden of their lost politicians, which had a drastic impact on Christianity over time.

Monastic Inspiration

With all these attacks on Rome, and the witnessing of its demise, many religious scholars returned to monastic living. They felt their ministries and spirituality would be better served away from the chaos of Rome. In the monasteries and convents, one could nurture the spirit (The City of God) and flee from all the killing and mayhem that had become so much a part of the empire (The City of Mankind). After Augustine put his thoughts into words, even more men and women fled to the monasteries and convents, where they could work on their respective cities.

During the Middle Ages, Christianity was also flourishing in the Celtic society of Ireland. Because Ireland was a long way from the regions of the Roman Empire, the Christian Church there developed its own way of doing things. It wasn't until the meeting of Christian leaders at Whitby in A.D. 664 that Celtic and Roman churches became one.

Christian Invaders

In the early days of the Middle Ages, the pagan Franks (Germanic tribes) held the primary Western power—and they were not complete strangers to the empire, since they had battled it out with the Romans for centuries. Rome had also engaged in trade with these tribes, and the Benedictine monks had gone on several successful conversion missions within tribal territory.

Escape from the Huns

When the Huns started their rampage on the West, the Visigoths (western Goths) sought refuge in Rome, which offered them protection. Rome also invited some German tribes to settle on vacated land within the empire, and by the fifth century, most of the Western army was comprised of Germans. The empire also recognized them as potential future defenders of the empire.

FACT

At the end of the fifth century, Clovis, the Frankish battle chief and leader of the nation of Gaul, accepted the Nicene Creed, which began a domino effect of conversions among the citizens. When he was baptized on December 25, A.D. 496, his loyal army of 3,000 reneged their German gods and followed their leader to the baptismal font.

The Plague

The Western Empire was invaded by yet another challenging assailant: the plague. This voracious disease, referred to as "Black Death," was as bad as any barbarian tribe, taking lives by the thousands, including that of Pope Pelagius II. However, out of fever, ruins, and desperation emerged a strong region that we now call Europe—with Christianity playing a huge part in strengthening this society even further.

Pope Gregory the Great

The pope who succeeded Pelagius II was Gregory the Great—the same Gregory who had once been a monk. He arrived in Rome as the new overseer during the time of the plague, but wasn't crazy about the job. He had been a monk and preferred the life of solitude.

Gregory was amongst many who believed that since the state of affairs had gotten so bad, the world might be coming to an end. The invading armies and the plague had ravaged the empire, leaving towns empty with the smell of death in the air. However, despite his dislike of his papal role, he was determined to bring control to this world of chaos. He managed to ward off an invasion by the Lombards (another Germanic tribe) by making peace with its leaders, and after an invasion of central Italy and the destruction of imperial rule, he stepped in to feed the hungry and collect the land taxes that would otherwise have been collected by the local authorities.

ESSENTIAL

Throughout his life, Gregory suffered from continuous ill health, especially from indigestion, attacks of fever, and for the last years of his pontificate, from gout (a form of arthritis). His suffering, both physical and mental, especially manifested itself during the last few years of his life.

Gregory died in A.D. 604, after serving fourteen years as the leader of the Western Christian World. Here are some of the powerful influences that Gregory had on medieval Christianity (and on the future of the Christian church in general):

1. **The power of the Eucharist:** Offered by the priests for the sins of humankind.
2. **Purgatory:** Those who live a life without sin will go to heaven, while those who lead a life of evil will go to hell. Those who have sinned but are not evil will go to a "holding ground," called purgatory.
3. **The sacredness of the Holy Mass:** The Mass can also serve to redeem those who have sinned.
4. **The power of relics:** Gregory encouraged Christians to collect remains of the saints and martyrs, believing that they held great powers.

The Post-Invasion Years

It's hard to imagine that such a solid, sophisticated society like the Western Christian Empire could fall to wreck and ruin so quickly. It took a few different tribal invasions, but eventually, the empire was left with no government, no money, no schools, and no law enforcement. This was the former Western Empire at the start of the Middle Ages—a period that would span the next 1,000 years.

Christian Influence

The fall of Rome did not stop the growth of learning, and it was the Christians who were able to salvage a future from the ruins. The church was the unifying force amongst the various new kingdoms that helped continue the cultural and spiritual evolution started by the empire. Christianity became the source of learning and culture that spurred future generations into the age of enlightenment during the fourteenth century (otherwise known as the "Renaissance," which is French for "rebirth").

The Feudal System

One of the few sources of wealth remaining after the collapse of the Roman Empire was land, which was divided into several principalities, each ruled by a warrior—later to be called a prince. The warrior, or prince, also became the local government of that region. From this new government structure came the feudal system, which had the same kind of social impact as any caste system: the rich stayed rich and powerful, while the poor stayed poor and subservient.

Lords and Vassals

The landowners (or "lords") earned their living from the peasants ("vassals") that farmed the land ("fiefs") of their plantations ("manors"). The lords gave the peasants only what they needed to survive and nothing more. There was no way for a peasant to become a landowner, because there was no way for the peasant to make any money.

However, in the early days of feudalism, with the empire gone, the system did offer a means of survival. People got roofs over their heads, food to eat, and protection from foreign invaders. But once in the system, there was no way out, and for future generations, who may not have remembered the barbarian hordes, the trade-off hardly seemed worth it.

ESSENTIAL

The vassal formally received the fief in the ceremony of homage. He knelt before the overlord and then swore an oath of fealty, promising to be faithful to the overlord and to perform the services due him. The overlord then usually kissed and raised the vassal to his feet. The ceremony was meant to seal the personal relationship between the two.

The System Order

While the vassals were subservient to the lords, the lords were subservient to their king (or prince), and while the land fed the lords and the vassals, it also fed the kingdom. This is one of the ways the landowners earned their money. In a ceremony, known as "the act of homage," the vassal placed his hand on a Bible or other religious item and swore an oath of loyalty and servitude to his lord of the manor. In another ritual, called "investiture," another symbolic item, such as a glove or a lance, was handed to the vassal to signify his jurisdiction over the fief. The contract between lord and vassal was considered sacred, and to break the oath was considered a felony.

While the vassals were expected to provide unpaid military service to the lords, the lords would also hire knights to protect their land. Often several lords living in one kingdom would share their knights to protect all of their manors.

Lay Investiture

Hiring knights for a manor was one thing, but the lords also paid priests to minister to their manors. Given the constant invasions and the lack of government structure, it was in the interest of the clergy to benefit from the protection of the lords. Bishops and abbots also became vassals like any other layperson. The pope didn't object if a church leader sought the landowner, but when the landowner appointed the church leader, that was considered stepping over a line and the church did not tolerate it.

QUESTION?

If the landowners paid the clergy, then who was subservient to whom?
This was a tricky position for the church because it still saw its ultimate loyalty to the Lord of heaven, not to the lord of the manor. The corruption began when the church leaders forgot which lord they were supposed to serve.

The Eastern Empire

Up to this point, you've read very little about the Eastern Christian Empire, primarily because the Western Empire had been a focus of a huge region of the world over a long period of time. But after the destruction of the Western Empire, the East still had a hold on its Christian seat of power. The Eastern Christians (the ones we now refer to as Orthodox Christians) drifted away from Western Christianity very early on in the church's history.

Icon Worship

The belief in Jesus was the main factor unifying Eastern and Western Christianity—and that was not about to change—but one of the biggest areas of contention was the idea of icon worship. The Eastern Christians actually worshipped images of Christ, the cross, and their saints. In fact— and this is true today as well—part of their worship was to kiss the image of the saints upon entering a church. As a result, Eastern Christians were called "icon kissers" or "iconodules."

The Western Christians did not believe in icon worship because it was a throwback to paganism. The pagans worshipped their gods in the form of icons, and the Christians did not want to associate themselves in any way with what they believed to be heathenism.

While the Western Christians maintained religious relics, images, and remains of the saints, they didn't actually worship these items. Worship was resigned to love and devotion of Jesus Christ—not the love of his image.

FACT

The major difference between the Eastern and Western Christian Churches had to do with a few added words to the Nicene Creed. While the original Creed, as established by the Nicene Council, reads that the spirit "proceeds from the Father," the Eastern Church adopted a version created by a church in Spain, which added that the spirit "proceeds from the Father and the Son."

The Muslims

The Muslims, which translates from Arabic as "those who submit" to Allah, believed in a completely different God than the one the Christians worshipped. Their God was (and is) Allah, and their religion became known as Islam, meaning "submission."

Muhammad

Muhammad was the founding father of Islam. He was from Mecca, which, at the time of Muhammad's life in the early seventh century, was a small Arabian trading post. Like the Western Christians, Muhammad reviled icon worship and preached against it throughout the Middle East.

The words of Muhammad, however, did not sit well with the icon vendors who made a living off the propagation of the idolization of objects. As a result, Muhammad was chased out of Mecca in A.D. 622 and wasn't able to return until several years later. When he did return, he gathered an army of followers and called them Muslims.

The Muslims became a powerful force to reckon with as they began rampaging their way through the Middle East, sacking entire regions. Here is a list of some of their conquests in the early Middle Ages.

- They conquered Arabia, Syria, and North Africa after Muhammad's death in A.D. 632.
- They sacked Jerusalem in A.D. 637.
- They conquered Spain and Portugal by A.D. 711.

The Muslims were so successful in their conquests because they allowed the Christians in the conquered regions to maintain some religious freedom. Even though they forced Christians to wear identifying clothing and symbols and forced them to pay higher taxes, they did not stop them from worshipping their own God. In fact, the early Muslims protected any holy writings, including the Christian scriptures.

Despite their distaste for icon worship, the Muslims were not the iconoclasts of the era. "Iconoclast" is the term used for anyone who attacks a religious tradition or belief, or an entire religious belief system. In the case of eastern Europe, there were those who felt it necessary to destroy all the religious relics in an effort to stop icon worship.

In addition, the Muslims were able to convert all those whom the Eastern and Western Christian churches had rejected, including the North Africans, who were formerly a part of the Roman Empire. (E)

Chapter 7

The Late Middle Ages

The second half of the Middle Ages presented some hard times for Christianity. With the fall of Rome, Christians had to reestablish their foothold in a new world. It would be a long haul, but it may well have been worth the wait as the nations of the region now called Europe moved toward a rebirth in a new era.

Charlemagne and Leo III

At the end of the eighth century, Pope Leo III sought the assistance of a king as he found himself in the middle of local warfare. Loyalists of the previous pope, Adrian I, wanted the ouster of Leo. They accused him of all sorts of corruption, including adultery and perjury. Leo's enemies then kidnapped him and hid him in a monastery in Greece. He was rescued, but the unrest did not stop there. Street fighting broke out amongst the people of Rome, and with no emperor in the Western Empire, Leo found he needed some outside assistance. He would certainly not turn to a woman—Empress Irene, who ruled over the Eastern Empire—so he called upon Charles, the King of the Franks, a long-time supporter of the papacy.

King of the Franks

He was called Charles the Great, but you may know him as Charlemagne (a name he was given by later generations). Charlemagne first stepped into the spotlight of Christian history when he traversed the Alps to Rome, where he intended to put an end to the city's troubles.

On December 23, A.D. 799, Leo took an oath on the holy Gospel that he had not committed the crimes of which he was accused, and Charlemagne added his stamp of approval—declaring to the world that Leo was innocent of all charges.

ESSENTIAL

The reason Charlemagne was so readily accepted by the Western Empire goes back to his grandfather, Charles Martel, or Charles "the Hammer." He was renowned for saving the kingdom of the Franks from the invading Muslim armies. Later, the pope declared Charles' son, Pepin the Short, the King of the Franks, which was the beginning of an amicable relationship between the Franks and the Romans.

The next day, on December 24, at a Christmas Mass, Leo crowned Charlemagne emperor. The congregation cheered as Leo knelt before the king. This was the first time in history that a pope had appointed an emperor—a symbolic gesture for the future of the empire and the papacy. Charlemagne had restored the Christian Roman Empire (Holy Roman Empire) and was declared on that day to be a great and peaceful leader—a reputation that he would carry through the Middle Ages to modern times.

Establishing Christendom

By using Augustine's *The City of God* as his reference, Charlemagne was responsible for pulling the Catholics together again. Who knew that one monk's scholarly effort could have such tremendous influence over an entire religion for centuries to come?

As King of the Franks, Charlemagne had three goals in mind:

1. He wanted enough military power to follow in his grandfather's footsteps, with the ability to crush any threatening enemy.
2. He wanted the religious power to guide the souls of his people.
3. He wanted enough intellectual strength to teach people to nurture both mind and soul.

Charlemagne was successful in his vision, and as a result, established a new political order for Europe under the jurisdiction of the Catholic Church. As emperor, Charlemagne had the same vision for Christendom as he did for the Franks of his own kingdom: He wanted to present the world with a unified society of Christians mingling the eternal with the temporal. In other words, Christendom would be a cohesive society that blended the spiritual truth with earthly (or political) matters.

Church and State

Despite the unification of religious and political leadership, the question always remained: Who should control whom? Should the church control the state or should the state control the church? The papacy proclaimed its dominance over the emperor, but the emperor declared himself independent of the pope. Charlemagne managed to escape the argument to some degree because he was seen as a sort of father figure for Christianity *and* for the empire. With his natural ability and involvement in the land of the church, there was never any real dispute about who was in charge. Charlemagne made sure of this, too. He appointed envoys to keep an eye on local governments—and on the pope.

FACT

Charlemagne's envoys were called "missi dominici" (Latin for "the king's envoys"). They traveled in pairs, with one party being a bishop and the other a layperson of noble rank.

The Age of Charlemagne

Charlemagne's efforts to improve society included the decree that every monastery must provide education for boys. This meant that the monks were to teach boys singing, arithmetic, and grammar. Charlemagne himself opened a palace school in Aix-la-Chapelle, in Gaul, where boys were educated in grammar, spelling, rhetoric, and logic. These were the baby steps toward rebirth, and with these steps Charlemagne solidified himself as one of the world's great leaders and a forefather of the Renaissance.

Here are some of the benefits Charlemagne extended to society during his rule:

- He restored law and order to a ravaged society.
- He extended Christianity throughout Europe.
- He started a movement of education and learning, which would continue to grow well into the future.
- He set the standard for an imperial ideal that would last until Napoleon Bonaparte put an end to the Roman Empire in 1806.

Cluniac Reform

The Benedictine monks at the monastery in Cluny (France) were amongst the first to speak out against the merger of the leadership of church and state, particularly related to church leaders as vassals. The Cluniacs started a movement for monastic reform, which gradually became a cry for church reform. They called for the celibacy of the clergy and an end to the buying and selling of church offices, also known as "simony."

One of the main political reasons for banning the clergy from marrying and reproducing offspring was to prevent them from appointing their children to church offices—which is an exclusive practice, and history would show that it would only lead to further corruption within church ranks.

The Cluniac Reform called for the separation of church and state. Reformers wanted to put an end to secular control of the church and wanted the church to fall under complete papal authority. These changes eventually happened and even went one step further by removing the papacy from any secular control, with the creation of the College of Cardinals. Starting in 1059, these new church leaders (the cardinals) elected the pope, and this is still practiced to this day.

Today the pope's primary role is as the spiritual head of the Roman Catholic Church. While the pope is the sovereign leader of Vatican City, he is not a political leader in the sense of western-style government as we know it today. However, the influence he has in the Christian world has profound political implications.

The High Middle Ages

The glory and majesty that the church achieved during the Middle Ages can be seen in the gothic architecture of the twelfth and thirteenth centuries. Notre Dame Cathedral in Paris is but one of these examples. Cathedrals like Notre Dame spread throughout Europe and were built thirty and forty stories high—a symbolic representation of humankind reaching toward the heavens to reach God.

Chivalry

The Christian influence managed to infiltrate the feudal system: Knights and the feudal barons were expected to conduct themselves according to a code of ethics based on Christian virtues. The ideal of treating fellow human beings with decorum and respect, and the ideal of living one's life according to a code of spiritual ethics may have been more romanticism than reality. But, that said, the church did attempt to curb feudal warfare by establishing a code of ethics.

Here are two important ways in which the church attempted to control methods of warfare in the eleventh century—neither method worked, but it showed that the church cared about the battlefield in terms of the Christian ideal:

1. **The Peace of God:** Those who pillaged sacred places or refused to spare noncombatants were denied the sacraments.
2. **The Truce of God:** Established certain times when fighting was not allowed—from sunset on Wednesday to sunrise on Monday and during religious seasons like Lent.

The Crusades

Christians today see the Crusades (Holy Wars) as a blight on their history—and this is understandable, because it was seven centuries of purposeless bloodshed. The mission of the Christian crusaders from the West was to expel the Muslims from the Holy Land. But they failed over and over again. Even though the Muslims had controlled Jerusalem since A.D. 638, and the First Crusade was in 1095, there are several reasons why the Christians went on the attack all those years later.

Pilgrims

To prove their devotion to God and to absolve themselves of their sins, Christians went on pilgrimages to the Holy Land—usually Jerusalem. The Muslims never objected to these pilgrimages, but the Turks (Muslim converts) decided to start charging heavy tariffs on the roads to the Holy Land. From the point of view of the church, to impede a pilgrimage was to jeopardize a Christian's salvation. But the Crusades were not about road tolls—that was just an early sign of trouble ahead.

Events came to a head when a fanatical group of Turks called the "Seljuks" seized Jerusalem, expelled the Muslims, and began to persecute Christian pilgrims. The Seljuks spread into Asia Minor, and, at the Battle of Manzikert in 1071, they captured the Eastern Emperor. With his army scattered and territories seized, the emperor turned to the West for assistance.

Pope Urban II declared the battle cry of the Crusades to be: "Deus Volt," which translates from Latin to English as "God wills it." The word "Crusade" means "taking the cross," in the same way Christ had. On the way into battle, the Crusader left with a cross on his breastplate and, if he returned, he wore the cross on his back.

The First Crusade

In 1095, Pope Urban II responded to Eastern Emperor Alexius I's appeal for assistance by calling the First Crusade (A.D. 1096–1099) to regain the Holy Land. The first Crusaders may have felt that they were redeeming the soil on which Christ had lived. They were idealists, although many faced a conflict between their spiritual beliefs and their sense of religious justice. In fact, Pope Urban promised complete redemption of all sins to all Crusaders—that meant that if they committed the sin of murder, it wouldn't matter, because their souls were automatically safe.

So Much for Chivalry

During the Crusades, all the rules of warfare first established by Augustine and then reestablished under the code of chivalry fell by the wayside—there was to be no mercy shown to noncombatants and prisoners; there was no respect for property; and looting, rape, and slaughter were considered just a side effect of a Holy War.

An Effort in Futility

In 1099, in the very place that Christ had lost his own life, the Crusaders slaughtered both Jews and Muslims—the Crusaders were said to be knee deep in blood on Temple Mount—all in the name of Jesus Christ. Jerusalem fell to the Crusaders and returned to Christian control, but not for a long time. In 1291, the Muslims once again regained control of the city.

Women in Christendom

Women had extremely powerful roles in the history of the world, and civilization simply would not have been possible without them. It would also be very difficult to ignore the roles of some medieval women, and more and more scholars of today have begun to delve into their fascinating lives.

QUESTION?

What happened to the women when their husbands, fathers, brothers, and sons took off for the Crusades?
They were left behind to tend to the manors, caring for the land, overseeing financial matters, and often having to take up arms to defend their homes and children.

Overlooked but Not Forgotten

Women were seen in the church and in society as being subservient to men, but in reality, in many cases, they were anything but. If a woman's husband did not return from the Holy War, or even if he just died of natural causes, the woman's role on the manor was not completely forgotten: She was given at least a third of the property and assets, which was hardly what she deserved, yet better than nothing.

Paul wrote: "Women should be silent in the churches. For they are not permitted to speak, but should be subordinate, as the law also says" (1 Corinthians 14:35, NRSV). There is nothing in the scriptures to point to this as a Christian reality, and many scholars suggest that because Paul was writing to a particular church, this scripture was not meant to be applied universally.

Women at Work

It's interesting that so many people today think that the trend of women in the workplace started with the Women's Liberation movement of the 1970s. But that's a preposterous thought. Women have worked since the beginning of time, and medieval women were no exception.

Women outside the feudal system were shopkeepers, bakers, seamstresses, and spinners (spinning wool into thread). They were artists creating magnificent tapestries and other fine thread-work. They were scholars (often within the confines of a convent—the only place a woman could get an education), writers, thinkers, queens, empresses, and even soldiers. There was nothing a woman couldn't do.

Here is a list of some exceptional medieval women whose power and influence would have a lasting effect on world history.

Helga of Russia

Helga (Olga) of Russia was the first Russian Orthodox saint. She avenged her husband's murder (Prince Igor I of Russia) by means of mass execution. She ruled Russia as regent from A.D. 945–964, and was known for her ruthlessness. Helga was baptized a Christian in Constantinople in about A.D. 957. It was because of Helga that the Russian church remained separate and autonomous from the Byzantine Church.

Matilda of Saxony

Born in A.D. 895 and raised by her grandmother in a convent, Matilda was one of the many women sold off to marriage for political purposes. She married Henry the Fowler of Saxony, who became king of Germany. Matilda used her power and influence to open convents and monasteries, and she was known for her generosity to many charities. She had four children: Otto I, Emperor of Rome; Henry the Quarrelsome, Duke of Bavaria; Saint Bruno, Archbishop of Cologne; and Queen Gerberga of France (married Louis IV of France). Matilda died in A.D. 968.

FACT

St. Joan of Arc is perhaps the most famous female heretic of the Middle Ages. Claiming she heard voices telling her to restore the true king of France to the throne, Joan led troops into battle against the English. She was later captured and sold to the English, declared a heretic, and burned at the stake. Twenty-three years after her death her name was cleared, and on May 16, 1920, Pope Benedict XV declared her a saint.

Adelaide

Saint Adelaide was married to two Italian kings. Her first husband was King Lothair, who died after she was kidnapped by Berengar II (possibly her husband's assassin) in 951. Berengar tried to force Adelaide to marry his son, but Otto I of Saxony rescued her, defeated Berengar, and declared himself king of Italy. He, then, married Adelaide. Later, Otto I was crowned emperor of the Holy Roman Empire and Adelaide became the empress. Adelaide had five children with Otto, and after her husband died, she ruled Italy as regent for five years—her grandson, Otto III, was too young to be king. Adelaide then retired to a convent and died in 999 after founding churches, monasteries, and convents.

Sigrid the Strong-Minded

Sigrid was a very tough woman, as her nickname suggests (she is also referred to as Sigrid the Proud). As a princess of Sweden, she refused to marry the king of Norway (Olaf) because it would force her to become Christian—and she was a devout pagan. Sigrid helped organize a revolt that would eventually lead to the ouster of Olaf. She did, however, marry the king of Sweden and became mother of King Olaf III of Sweden and of a daughter, Holmfrid, who married the king of Denmark (Svend). She divorced the king of Sweden and married Sweyn of Denmark and had two more daughters, one of whom married King Richard II of Normandy. Sigrid died in 1013 after quite an adventurous life.

Blanche of Castille I

Granddaughter of the most famous of all medieval women, Eleanor of Aquitaine, Blanche was married to Louis VIII. She became regent when her son, Louis IX, went off to the Crusades. Blanche quelled rebellions and extended the power of the French dynasty during the king's absence. Her power and influence is believed to have provided the foundation of the France we know today.

Melisende of Jerusalem

Melisende was the daughter of the Frankish king of Jerusalem during the time the Crusaders had taken Jerusalem back from the Turks in 1099. She ruled Jerusalem with her father and then married Fulk V of Anjou (France)—they became joint rulers. Rumors started that she was having an affair with her husband's rival and opponent, Hugh II. Fulk declared war against his wife and her supporters, but she prevailed. Her peace terms included being allowed into the inner circles of the councils of the kingdom. Melisende became a patron of the arts and founded a huge convent.

The Christians blamed Melisende and her troubled empire for losing large amounts of territory back to the Muslims and, as a result, vowed to never let a woman rule Jerusalem again.

Eleanor of Aquitaine

Eleanor is one of the most famous women in history, and definitely the most acknowledged and admired woman of medieval times. Her power and beauty inspired the romanticism of the era—the chivalry; the idealism of the Crusades; as well as the love depicted in songs, art, and poetry. Considered to be a great beauty with an iron will, Eleanor was married to King Louis VII of France at the age of fifteen—a union that joined major portions of Europe.

FACT

You may know the story of King Arthur and the Knights of the Round Table. Whether he existed or not, the story of Arthur, and his ideals of a utopian society, are a good example of the romanticism that came out of the Middle Ages: the kings, queens, ladies, and knights; the jousts and festivals; Merlin, the Druids, and the Christians—it's all in the story of Camelot.

At the age of nineteen, Eleanor offered St. Bernard (the Abbé of Clairvaux) thousands of her vassals for the Second Crusade. But she did not stop there—she took 300 of her ladies and headed off to the Holy Land with the Crusaders, claiming she wanted to "tend to the wounded." Eleanor's marriage to Louis was annulled in 1152, and she retrieved all of her lands that had been part of her marital alliance.

Later Eleanor married Prince Henry of Anjou, who became King Henry II. Henry and Eleanor knew that their union would bring vast regions together, and with that they would rule their own "small" empire. Eleanor and Henry had five children (she had two daughters with Louis), two of whom became kings of England. Preferring to rule Aquitaine with her son Richard, Eleanor led her three sons in a rebellion against their father in 1173. The rebellion failed, and her husband imprisoned her for fifteen years. The pope, then, banned women from attending all future Crusades. Eleanor lived into her eighties and is considered one of the great political powers of medieval Europe.

Chapter 8

Pre-Reformation

The road to enlightenment began with the decline of papal authority and the expansion of education. This struck fear in the hearts of the declining church authority, and a desperate scramble to regain solid footing began. For the scholars, however, it marked a new world of thinking, but it was only the tip of the iceberg.

Church Corruption

Little did Pope Leo III know what would happen when he placed the crown on the head of King Charles. While Charlemagne did have a tremendous amount of influence over government and Western Society as a whole, Leo did not sit back and throw his arms in the air. There was always a disagreement about who should have supremacy over whom. This debate had gone on for centuries and would continue for several more.

But Leo and Charlemagne did manage to come to an agreement separating the powers of the emperor from those of the pope. That agreement, however, lasted as long as Charlemagne was alive. Upon his death in A.D. 814, the agreement was no longer applicable, and it was back to square one.

After the rule of Charlemagne, there was no one next in line with the ability to wield that much power and authority over the empire (nor to achieve the same level of respect). So, naturally, people once again looked to the pope for leadership.

Isidorian Decretals

Despite their illegitimacy, these writings, the *Isidorian Decretals*, were accepted by the people of the empire in A.D. 850, much to the benefit of the papacy. These falsified documents were said to be a collection of writings from the time of the apostles in the first century to the ninth century.

The papers categorically legitimized papal supremacy, giving the pope absolute power over any other leader, including the emperor. According to the documents, the pope alone held specific power over the entire church. The popes did enjoy several centuries of power over the church and the entire Christian world, but it was only a matter of time before absolute authority would turn to corruption, and ultimately decline.

The *Isidorian* (False) *Decretals* are believed to be one of the greatest forgeries in history. The collection hosts sixty letters or decrees of popes, from Clement I to Melchiades; an original essay on the early church and the Council of Nicea, with canons of fifty-four councils; and a collection of papal letters from the fourth to eighth centuries.

Murder and Mayhem

Because of the extravagant accumulation of wealth, the misuse of power, and the complete neglect of Christian value, the corruption of the papacy became obvious to almost everyone in Christendom, and the message of Christ was completely obliterated by the popes after A.D. 850.

Not everyone would sit back and watch, however. Pope John VIII was so corrupt that he was assassinated while in office. In A.D. 955, Emperor Otto the Great forced the equally corrupt Pope John XII to resign. After Otto's death, however, all chaos broke loose again: the popes were fighting the "anti-popes"—those who opposed the existing pope.

The fighting got so bad that Pope Benedict IX threw in his papal robes and sold his office to Pope Gregory VI—only to turn around later and say he wanted it back. Thus began the Great Schism of the Papacy.

Pope Gregory VII (Hildebrand)

In 1073, a man named Hildebrand was elected pope, taking the papal name of Gregory. It was Pope Gregory VII, who reformed the papacy, taking it away from the corruption and turmoil and giving it back legitimacy. He achieved this by banning lay investiture—appointment of a church leader to a church office by a noble or king—which was the root of corruption in Gregory's mind. Gregory wanted to see all of Christendom under papal control, and so he went back to the age-old Christian argument of spiritual supremacy over the temporal—rather than to express this in terms of church supremacy over the state.

Excommunication and Control

Gregory had threatened anyone who practiced lay investiture with excommunication, a threat (and practice) that became popularly used to control people who did not adhere to papal authority or Christian orthodoxy. If a person was excommunicated, it meant that the church denied that individual certain religious and legal rights. An "interdict" was even more powerful because it was an excommunication of an entire nation.

FACT

A ceremony was actually held to pronounce an excommunication: A bishop would read the sentence aloud, a solemn funeral-like bell would be rung, and a candle was extinguished. This was the official cutting-off ritual that would deny a Christian his rites of salvation.

The hope of the papacy was that a threat of excommunication, or an interdict, would force the citizens to place pressure on their leader to obey the supremacy of the pope. Since no king wanted to deal with angry and frightened citizens, he was usually forced to give in to the authority of the pope.

Pope Gregory VII was able to turn the tables for the medieval papacy by wielding his power over the Christian community, and ultimately the "wayward" kings and emperors. Here is what excommunication meant for the unlucky Christian:

- The person could not serve as a judge, juror, attorney, or witness.
- The person could not be a party to a contract (guardians or executors).
- The person was not entitled to a Christian burial—and if the individual was buried in consecrated ground, the body would be disinterred and burned.

While excommunication disabled a person from productivity and certain Christian rites, the interdict was even more threatening to the Christian, since it denied all seven sacraments and public worship—putting one's salvation in serious jeopardy.

Pope Innocent III

Pope Innocent III picked up where Gregory left off, and his time in Rome saw the height of papal strength. In 1215, Innocent III called the fourth Lateran Council, which had a powerful effect on the next generations of Christendom.

ESSENTIAL

In an attempt to end the Muslim threat to the Eastern churches, Pope Innocent III wanted to organize the Fourth Crusade in March 1199. His effort failed, and it wasn't until November of that year when rulers mobilized enough troops to form an army.

During his papacy, Innocent III also settled some doctrinal matters in the church. He claimed that all laymen must make annual confession to a priest; spelled out the doctrine of "transubstantiation" by stating that the bread and the wine are not just symbols of Jesus' flesh and blood, but the real thing; and sanctioned and defined the seven sacraments.

The Seven Sacraments of the Catholic Church were (and are today):

1. **Baptism:** Entry into the church and identification with Christ
2. **Confirmation:** Initial entrance as an adult or full member into the church
3. **Holy Eucharist:** The Lord's Supper (communion)
4. **Penance:** Reconciliation with God and others
5. **Extreme Unction:** Anointing of the sick
6. **Holy Orders:** Entrance to apostolic ministry
7. **Matrimony:** The unity (marriage) of a man and a woman

The Great Schism

While Pope Innocent III made a lasting impact on the Catholic doctrine (which is still evident today), the papal "heyday" rapidly declined from that point on. The bickering and squabbling once again caused a big rift in church leadership, known as "The Great Schism" (A.D. 1378–1423).

Unam Sanctum

After Pope Innocent III died, Pope Boniface VIII took over the papacy in the late thirteenth century, and his "bull," or papal decree, asserting a new church law, was called the *Unam Sanctum* or "One Holy Church."

The *Unam Sanctum* stated that the rulers of all Christian nations—and that meant everyone in the Western World—were subject to him and that anyone seeking salvation must submit to him. But there were certainly some rulers who were not too crazy about that idea.

FACT

Pope Boniface had a crown that contained forty-eight rubies, forty-five emeralds, sixty-six large pearls, and seventy-two sapphires. He was one of the most flamboyant of the popes and was known to declare, "I am Caesar. I am emperor." Little did Boniface know that times were about to change forever for papal sovereignty.

The Disobedient King

King Philip of France was the loudest of the *Unam Sanctum* objectors. When Boniface forbade France from taxing church property, King Philip and King Edward I of England decided to tax the local clergy in an effort to finance their constant battles over territory between their kingdoms. King Philip was not going to let the pope tell him what he was permitted to do in his own nation, and so in an act of retaliation, he ordered that no money leave the French borders without his approval. When Boniface placed an interdict (excommunication of the whole nation) on the country, the French ignored it and remained loyal to their king. King Philip then sent Boniface to prison, thereby ending that dispute.

The Rise of Nationalism

There was a time when Western Civilization held its loyalty strictly to the church, especially during the feudal era, when there was no national unity due to a lack of a centralized government. However, what had once been nonexistent throughout the empire suddenly took the church by surprise—nationalism.

Self-Determination

As principalities grew through royal and noble marital unions and purchases, the population grew and loyalties shifted. With the rise of the middle class (the bourgeoisie) came the rise of self-determination—the people were not sending their money off to the pope any more, but rather they were investing it in their own lives and toward their government's needs.

You can't combat this kind of change. No one anticipated the rise of national pride, not even Rome. With the new and growing loyalty to the government, the pope and the emperor lost a huge amount of power—and money.

The Split

After getting rid of Pope Boniface, King Philip decided he wanted to keep a closer eye on the papacy, so he attempted to get a French pope elected. Again, he was successful, and in 1309, Pope Clement V took the church seat. When Clement took office, he moved the seat of church power from Rome to Avignon, located in the south of France.

The papacy remained in France for the next seventy years, and this period of time came to be known as the "Babylonian Captivity" (a reference to the exile of the ancient Jews in Babylon) of the papacy. The papal palace in Avignon still stands on a cliff overlooking the Mediterranean Sea. In its magnificent setting, it has become a popular tourist spot.

In the collective mind of Europeans, however, Rome was the "Eternal City"—the unifying force of Western Civilization—founded by the apostle Peter (Christianity's first "bishop," or pope). And so, with the move of the papacy seat to France, many felt that the French now controlled the church. When the Hundred Years' War broke out between France and England in 1337, the English saw the pope as being an ally of France, and so he lost credibility and power in England.

Three Popes?

In 1376, Pope Gregory XI restored the papacy to Rome, and after he died, Pope Urban VI was elected. However, the French did not approve of the choice and claimed the election was illegal, so they elected their own pope: Clement VII. Various councils were held to put an end to the chaos, but the only decision made was to have Urban and Clement step down and elect a new pope—which they did at the Council of Pisa. However, despite great effort to make the council legitimate and compulsory, the appointment of Pope Alexander V did not meet with general approval. Therefore, from 1409 to 1417, there were three popes ruling the church.

Pope Martin V

At the Council of Constance in 1417—in an attempt to end the mockery that was being made of the Christian leadership—Emperor Sigismund elected Pope Martin V as the new head of the Christian Church. With this appointment, the Great Schism era came to an end, but severe damage had been done to the legitimacy of the papacy. It wasn't long until a new reform movement began to appear all over Christian nations.

QUESTION?

Was Pope Martin V better than his predecessors?
Martin V was no better than his predecessors—he was just as corrupt, greedy, materialistic, and power hungry. Although he agreed to all the terms of the Council of Constance, Pope Martin V spent most of his years finding ways to reassert papal supremacy and undermine the authority of the councils.

Scholasticism and Rebirth

During the dark years of corrupt popes and church leaders, a more positive movement was underway that would assist in reforming Christianity forever. With the early days of the Renaissance, or rebirth, came the revival of learning, a spirit of adventure and geographical discovery, and the renewal of philosophy. Universities were opening up all over Europe and people began studying, thinking, questioning, and rethinking old ways. Art, literature, music, and science quickly came into the forefront of education.

Education

Like the monastic schools promoted by Charlemagne during the Middle Ages, cathedral schools were also established to promote the understanding of Christianity. These cathedral schools were open to all, and their purpose was to study Christianity within the fixed bounds of church law. A cathedral school education consisted of the seven liberal arts:

1. Grammar
2. Rhetoric
3. Logic
4. Arithmetic

5. Geometry
6. Music
7. Astronomy

The growth of education stemmed from enthusiastic schoolteachers, often monastic scholars eager to spread their wealth of knowledge. This enthusiasm would take many educators away from the restrictive bonds of medieval thinking into a mysterious world of questions just dying to be answered.

FACT

A man named Gerbert of Rheims (later to become Pope Sylvester II) was a brilliant monastic scholar influenced by both Christian bishops and Muslim culture. Gerbert discovered the wonders of the inquisitive thinking of Muslim learning and decided to incorporate them into his own teaching methods.

The Value of the Question

One of the most notable intellectuals of the late Middle Ages was Peter Abelard. He gave his inheritance to his brothers and traversed all of France to learn from the great thinkers. He became a lecturer (professor) in Paris and wrote *Sic et Non* (Latin for "Yes and No"), in which he posed 158 questions with answers from Christian scripture, pagan writings, and church leaders.

Abelard took the ancient Greek method of consistent questioning and applied it to medieval study—something the church leaders did not welcome, but students craved. At the Council of Soissons in 1121, Abelard was condemned for his work on the nature of the Trinity, and was soon living in seclusion in a monastery. Athough his students found him and begged for him to continue teaching, Abbot Bernard de Clairvaux put so much pressure on Abelard that he disappeared to the abbey of Cluny, where he died in 1142.

A New Age of Enlightenment

Once the interest in questioning began, there was no way to stop it, no matter how hard church leaders like Bernard de Clairvaux tried. Schools opened all over the country—not in the ivy-covered stone buildings we are familiar with today, but in homes, sheds, church cloisters, town squares, and rented rooms.

The schools formed a teaching method that incorporated Abelard's format of posing questions and answers. This was the beginning of "Scholasticism," which became known as the method of arriving at difficult conclusions through questions and debate. By arranging information and questioning the details, students would arrive at conclusions by means of logical reasoning.

ESSENTIAL

Less than 100 years after Abelard's death, schools opened all over Europe in Paris, Oxford, Cambridge, and Bologna (among many others). The Europeans called their schools "universitas," which is a Latin word used during the Middle Ages to describe any corporate group.

However, in order to keep the Bernards of Clairvaux at bay, the conclusions had to correspond with Christian doctrine. Christian authorities couldn't argue with that as long as the outcome came out in their favor. Nevertheless, the method by which these scholars achieved their answers was the magic that would lead to new conclusions—ones that would not sit so well with the church.

Influx of New Thinking

By the end of the thirteenth century, the philosophical writings of the ancient Greeks, and other nations outside the empire, were flooding over the borders of Europe—many of which undermined church authority. Many of these writings did not come out in the church's favor. For example, Aristotle's philosophy on the nature of the universe questioned the Christian scriptures; the writings of Muslim philosopher Averroes and Jewish philosopher Maimonides were also giving the church a major headache.

FACT

St. Thomas Aquinas, a Dominican monk and scholar, was called in to examine the texts of Maimonides and Averroes. While he refuted some, he reconciled others with Christian thinking. The result of his work was the *Summa Theologica* ("Summation of Theological Knowledge"), in which he distinguishes philosophy from theology.

Educated Women

Although it was not easy for women to receive an education outside of a convent in the Middle Ages, there were a handful who managed to find their way to the books. Scholars today have spent a great deal of time and research searching for the works of medieval women writers, artists, and musicians.

Anna Comnena

Anna Comnena (1083–1146), for example, is said to be the world's first female historian. She lived in the eleventh century and was the daughter of Alexius I, Emperor of Constantinople, and Empress Irene.

Using diplomatic correspondence, reports from the military to her father, and the imperial archives, Anna Comnena is responsible for chronicling the life and times of Alexius. Her writings include the social, political, and economic life in Byzantium, as well as the Crusades and the relationship between the Eastern and Western Empires. As a child, she received a superb education in the Greek classics, geography, mythology, philosophy, and, of course, history.

Anna married the so-called rightful heir to the throne (otherwise called "the pretender"), Nicephorus Bryennius (also an historian), and at the encouragement of her mother, participated in a rebellion to place her husband on her father's throne. She failed, however, and along with her mother, was sent to a French monastery. It was at this time that Anna wrote her series of fifteen books, *Alexias*, chronicling the life of her father.

Anna Comnena's life was extraordinary; she knew she was privileged to have been given an education and the freedom to write when it was nearly unthinkable to do so.

Heloise

Heloise (1101–1164) has been romanticized over the years for her dramatic "love" story with Peter Abelard. What many don't know, however, is that by the age of sixteen, Heloise spoke Latin, Hebrew, and Greek, and was proficient in ancient philosophy and rhetoric. In fact, as a teenager she was already a recognized scholar in twelfth-century France.

Based on her reputation, Peter Abelard, the greatest French philosopher of his time, became her private tutor. Abelard allegedly seduced Heloise, got her pregnant, and married her against her will. Shortly thereafter the two of them denied the marriage—Peter was afraid the marriage would harm his clerical career and Heloise just didn't want to be married. Her uncle, who was her legal guardian, became so angry with her (and some say abusive) that Peter took her to a monastery, where she became a nun. According to the story, this angered the uncle even further and he had Peter castrated.

Heloise stayed in the convent, and she and Peter spent the rest of their lives writing letters to each other. These letters tell the story of their deep philosophical ideals and have become invaluable documentation of scholarly thought of the times.

Chapter 9

The Renaissance

Despite the growing appetite for learning and the quest for answers, the pre-Reformation intellects would have a long and treacherous road ahead. With the papacy in continuing decline, many Christians wanted to go back to basics: back to the message of Christ, the apostles, and the scriptures. These Christians were the first Protestants—and they didn't even know it.

The First Signs of Change

As the appetite for education continued to grow, the Western World was about to embark on a remarkable journey toward renewal. People were on the brink of a revelation that there is more to life, and Christianity, than what they had come to know so far. But no growth is possible without hardship, as some of the forerunners of the Reformation would learn. To understand what the new Christian movement was about, we have to back-track to its beginning.

While the scholars of the era questioned every aspect of the church, including the sacraments and the legitimacy of church leadership, there were several general key issues the pre-reformers began to address:

- **The Wrath of God:** The church had gradually developed into this method of thinking to the point where the focus of Catholics was no long on faith, but on fear.
- **The Bible:** The pre-reformers pointed out that it is the Bible and the teachings of Christ and his apostles that have ultimate Christian authority, and not the popes.
- **Individual spirituality:** The pre-reformers also pointed out that the relationship a person has with God is personal, and it is not necessary to have a mediator in that relationship.
- **Apostolic poverty:** Many scholars of the time advocated a return to apostolic poverty and to live in the example of Christ—with humbleness and humility.

Poverty

It seems only likely that the back-to-basics movement would include a return to apostolic poverty. With no guidance and no example coming from Rome, or its local priests, people turned away from power politics and the glitter of papal crowns to the original message of Christ. Inspired by Christ and the apostles, a movement began to spread through the Western Empire and inspire men, such as Arnold of Brescia, to observe an austere life.

Protest from Within

In the first part of the twelfth century, Arnold, an abbot of a church in Brescia (located in northern Italy), began to preach about clerical corruption—blaming it on the popes for trying to seize global power. As a clergy member himself, this was an attack from within the church, which held a great deal of credibility amongst Christians. Arnold called for the Catholic Church to return all property to the state and to live a life of poverty, as there is no salvation in wealth. The abbot was highly persuasive and managed to steer the people of northern Italy toward his way of thinking.

FACT

As a young boy, Arnold entered a convent of canons in Brescia, where he was ordained a priest and appointed provost of his community. He reached this high office through the austerity of his life, his detachment from earthly things, his love of religious discipline, the clearness of his intellect, and an originality and charm of expression that he brought to the service.

The Pope Fights Back

The church was not pleased with Arnold's preaching, and in 1139, Pope Innocent II exiled him from Italy. However, Arnold was not silenced forever. He traveled to Paris, where he studied with another "rabble-rouser" and renowned scholar, Peter Abelard.

Later, he came back to Rome, where he joined a movement to overthrow the pope. When the pope was away, Arnold did manage to form, and lead, a secular government in Rome for ten years, with the backing of the Romans. However, Pope Hadrian IV put Rome under an interdict, and Emperor Frederick Barbossa captured Arnold. In 1155, the emperor ordered Arnold to be burned at the stake. His ashes were thrown into the Tiber River.

QUESTION?

What happened to the Eastern Empire?
In 1071, the Turks sacked the Eastern Empire, captured the emperor, and sent his army running. The Byzantine Empire was lost, which was one of the factors that led to the Crusades. Emperor Alexius I pleaded with Pope Urban II to help him recover lost lands.

Peter Waldo

Arnold's words did not fall on deaf ears. Peter Waldo (1140–1218), a wealthy merchant from Lyon, France, was one of the pre-reformers who heard Arnold loud and clear. But it is believed that his inspiration to act came from an entirely different and unlikely source: a song.

A Song of Inspiration

Waldo heard a troubadour (traveling musician) singing a song about monastic living using an allegory about a man who returned home from the Crusades only to turn away from the riches of his youth to a life imitating that of Christ. He lived in the streets of his hometown in complete poverty and self-denial. He was unrecognizable to his family and friends, and it wasn't until he lay dying that he told anyone who he really was. What Waldo took from this story is that the true path to salvation is to sacrifice everything in this life.

FACT

Some say that the troubadour's song was actually acted out as a street play. One way or another, it was the story itself that started the Waldensian movement and changed Waldo's life forever. He took his riches and put them in the hands of Christ. One of the ways he did this was to commission a French translation of the Bible.

Waldo was so inspired by the song that he sent his daughter to a cloister (secluded monastery), gave his wife a good deal of money, and became a mendicant (or traveling) preacher, much in the way that Christ and his apostles had done. Waldo was a fresh, new mind in the world of Christianity and had no real understanding of the scriptures. When he began to read the scriptures, he was troubled by the fact that what he knew from life experience in the church was not even referenced in the Bible. So immediately Waldo eradicated these external "truths" from his thinking and preaching.

The Waldenses

Soon a group that called itself "The Poor Folk of Lyon" caught on to Waldo's teachings. The group was already established, incorporating both men and women who read the scriptures and preached to the common people in a way in which they could relate to and understand. Within just a few years, "The Poor Folk" began calling themselves Waldenses, and one of the earliest "reform" movements was underway.

The movement did not last, however. While the pope gave them permission to preach, they were to do so only at the request of a bishop. When Waldo broke this rule, he and the Waldenses were excommunicated and banished from Lyon. Some of them stayed and continued to preach, others returned to the Roman Catholic Church, while still others were executed as heretics during the Crusades. The movement grew and spread through Europe, but it endured centuries of persecution and execution at the hands of the church. Their "back to the Bible" philosophy, however, served as an inspiration for future reformers.

Albigenses (Cathari)

The Cathari, or "pure ones," were from the region of Albi in France—which is why they were later called Albigenses. The Cathari began as a small movement in the early eleventh century and believed in the concept of a constant struggle between good and evil. According to them, all things material—matter and the human body—were products of an evil power. That was innocent enough, but one belief—the belief that Christ was only of a divine nature with no human element—was like a battle cry to the Roman Catholic Church.

QUESTION?

How did the Cathari manifest their beliefs?
The Cathari believed that the soul is trapped in the evilness of the human body and lived in a state of self-denial. They did not marry or engage in sexual relations; they did not own any material possessions; and they did not eat meat.

Albigenses and Duality

As you already know, the issue of Christology (the nature of Christ) caused some trouble for the early church. While the Council of Chalcedon declared Christ's two natures (human and divine) to be unmixed and inseparable, the Cathari, like the Gnostics, believed that it was impossible for Christ to be human in any way—he was only divine.

They believed that Christ was a life-giving spirit and a divine being who led people to God. They also believed he could not have died on the cross for the salvation of humankind because he was not human. The church was not about to let this kind of heresy resurface and spread at this point in time—as far as the church leadership was concerned, that issue had been settled and "legalized" years ago.

Persecution and Execution

When the Albigenses received protection from the prince of Toulouse (a province of France), allowing their movement to expand at a rapid pace, the church wanted to get rid of them. There were three options: diplomacy (talk them out of their beliefs), death by Crusade, or to hand them over to the Inquisitor (trial by torture; you'll read more about that in Chapter 10).

ESSENTIAL

There is a difference between a heretic and a reformer: A heretic will offer a dissenting viewpoint that challenges church doctrine, while a reformer will operate from within the church structure to try to improve it by bringing it back to its original meaning and purpose.

Mysticism

Let's leave behind the heretics and persecutions, and focus on some of the more peaceful aspects of the early Renaissance. A divinely inspired way of thinking had started in the twelfth century in Europe. It had everything to do with Scholasticism and the return to the Bible, but it was also more introspective and reflective.

The mystics devoted themselves purely to Christ, but this was by no means a new movement. Think back to Augustine of Hippo, Thomas Aquinas, the desert hermits, and countless others—these were the original mystics, the ones who turned to the roots of their spirituality in reflective study. The mysticism of the pre-Reformation was a revival of that and so much more.

Cistercians

A group of twenty Benedictines from the abbey of Cluny started their own strict religious community near Cisterium in France. They became known as the Cistercians and their order still exists today. Bernard de Clairvaux (later to be known as St. Bernard) became a Cistercian because he appreciated its structure and opposition to materialism.

Bernard de Clairvaux

Bernard de Clairvaux became one of the most powerful monks in the history of Christianity. He taught that a Christian does not receive salvation based on the good works he or she performs in the earthly life, but on the love of God. According to him, to love God was to be exposed to the love shared by the Father, Son, and Holy Spirit—this love is the mystical union between God and the Christian. Bernard also stressed the human weaknesses of Christ in an effort to help people relate to and understand his message.

FACT

During the fourteenth century, the Black Plague ravaged Europe and Asia Minor for four years. It killed off 88 percent of the population of Constantinople. People became so fearful and paranoid that they wondered if they were facing the wrath of God. The plague subsided by 1350, after the pope counted almost 24 million dead—one-third of the European population.

Hildegard de Bingen

Hildegard de Bingen was a medieval woman who achieved magnificent heights well before her time. As an author, musician, preacher, artist, and abbess, she was admired by popes and bishops alike. As a child, Hildegard experienced visions that she would later document in her book *Know the Way*. The bishop of Mainz, Germany, tried to discredit her visions, but the church praised her, and in 1400 made her a saint. Hildegard's music is still performed today by medieval choristers.

Here are a few other important and notable mystics of the era:

1. **Meister Eckhart (1260–1327):** A mystic from Germany, a theologian and teacher, who is most remembered for his teachings of God's closeness to humanity.
2. **Johann Tauler (1300–1361):** A student of Eckhart, Tauler was a preacher who emphasized the nothingness of humankind in relation to God.
3. **Catherine of Siena (1347–1380):** This Italian, Dominican mystic and preacher helped to return the pope to Rome by writing a letter to Pope Gregory XI in Avignon.

Devotio Moderna

Devotio Moderna (or "Modern Devotion") was a movement rooted in Holland, northern Germany, and Italy, which espoused that Christians should live their lives according to Jesus' life and teachings, including loving all of mankind. The *Devotio Moderna* movement emphasized the following four practices for Christians:

1. Reading the scriptures
2. Personal reverence of God (a direct spiritual connection)
3. Prayer and meditation
4. Religious education

The Franciscan Friars

St. Francis of Assisi (1181–1226) is one of the best-loved and notable mendicant preachers in Christian history. Born Giovanni Francesco de Bernadone, St. Francis started a group that later became the largest order of monks in the Catholic Church.

Francis was the son of a wealthy merchant of Assisi, Italy, but he renounced his father, his money, and his name after returning from military service. He then took on a life of poverty, begging, and the life of a traveling preacher. His message of love was so powerful that by the end of the thirteenth century, the order was 35,000 strong—including the female branch called the "Poor Clares," named after their founder, Clare Schifi. Francis' goal was not one of reform, but rather it was simply to follow Christ, which is why in 1214, Pope Innocent III sanctioned his mission.

ESSENTIAL

After Francis died, the church made an attempt to control the Poor Clares, by ordering them to no longer listen to monastic preaching and to stop leading a life of poverty. Clare decided that if she, and her order, could no longer take in their spiritual food, she would refuse to eat physical food and went on a hunger strike. In 1247, Pope Gregory IX gave in and approved the order.

The Dominican Friars

The church leaders called upon Dominic Guzman (1170–1221), a Spanish man, to talk the Albigenses out of their train of thought. The Albigenses had grown in size and so had their "heresy." Pope Innocent III feared their growth and called upon Dominic to go into their midst and change their ways. Ironically, Dominic would use the principles of the Albigenses to form his own monastery. Although his beliefs were different than those of the Albigenses, he admired their strict adherence to their practice and their ability to organize. Dominics saw these two factors as the driving forces behind the growth of their movement.

Dominic agreed to see what he could do to change the mindset of the Albigenses. What he saw as a major obstacle to converting them was the blatant hypocrisy in Rome. While the scriptures taught that people should live humble lives, the Catholic Church leaders were living in the lap of luxury. As long as this was true, there was no way the Albigenses would take him or his mission seriously.

So, Dominic decided to show them rather than tell them. He went off on his mission of conversion as a poor monk with distinctly Roman Catholic beliefs to show that one does not have to be a hypocrite to adhere to church traditions and beliefs. Dominic and his missionary companions did make some headway with the Albigenses, but it was not fast enough for the pope, who then declared war in the south of France—putting an end to Dominic's work and leaving him stranded in the chaos. This, however, did not stop Dominic from preaching and attempting to open small missions around the country. These were the building blocks of what would become one of the largest monasteries in Europe—the Dominican Order.

FACT

In 1220, only one year before Dominic's death, the pope officially approved the Dominican order. They were referred to as "brothers," rather than monks, because they lived amongst people, not isolated in a monastery.

Gerhard Groote

Gerhard Groote (1340–1384), the son of a wealthy merchant, is often referred to as the father of *Devotio Moderna*. He studied abroad and led a life of luxury and decadence. At one point in his life, Groote had a drastic transformation and converted to Christianity. He became a traveling missionary preaching that true Christianity was about love and worship of God, not about taking church office. He criticized the church for materialism, immorality, corruption, and the sale of church offices (known as "simony" and named after the attempt by Simon Magnus to buy the power of the Spirit). The church was not pleased and banned him from preaching. Groote appealed to the pope and won, but it was too late. He died as a result of the plague in 1384.

Groote's philosophy was a precursor to the leaders of the Protestant Reformation, especially in terms of his teaching of justification by faith—Groote said that human beings are justified (or morally correct) in God's eyes, not by the work they do, but the faith that goes into that work. In other words, a Christian's salvation depends on faith and not upon good and evil.

Groote believed that everyone should have access to the scriptures, because it is only through them and the purity of one's heart that a Christian can build a personal relationship with God. In order for everyone to have access, the Bible would have to be accessible in all languages. Groote translated portions of the Bible to his native tongue, which was Dutch.

Practical Mysticism

A mystical group called the Brethren of the Common Life was also referred to as the "practical mystics," because their devotion to God was demonstrated by their service to humankind. The movement, with its roots in Germany and The Netherlands, quickly swept across Europe. Christians practice this ministry of service to this day. The female branch was called The Sisters of the Common Life.

Here are some of the practices stressed by the Common Life movement:

- Poverty
- Chastity
- Obedience to God
- Bible reading
- Prayer

Thomas à Kempis

Thomas à Kempis (1380–1471) was a German monk who was one of the best-known students of the Common Life school of thought. It is widely believed that he was either the author or an editor of a popular devotional handbook, *The Imitation of Christ,* the most influential document of the *Devotio Moderna* movement. In addition to teaching, Thomas spent most of his life writing and copying manuscripts in the convent of St. Agnes near Zwolle, Germany.

The Imitation of Christ

This widely circulated handbook was actually four books—with each book containing anywhere from twelve to fifty-two chapters. The books emphasized the importance of spiritual contemplation and the belief in and love of Christ. *The Imitation of Christ* and many of Thomas' other writings defined the *Devotio Moderna* movement as well as many others that followed, including the Protestant Reformation. Ⓔ

Chapter 10

Protestant Inspiration

What Scholasticism had begun, the Protestant Reformation finished. The years 1400–1600 marked the world's ascension from darkness to the Renaissance. During that era, artistic geniuses, such as Michelangelo and Leonardo da Vinci, launched their careers, and the height of the persecution of heretics began, in the form of the Inquisition. In the middle of it all came Martin Luther—the man credited with changing the church forever.

What Was the Reformation?

The Reformation is the name given to the dramatic upheaval in the Catholic Church, which occurred between 1500 and 1625. It's hard to put an exact date on the era, since reformation had been going on well before Martin Luther came on the scene; however, historians generally refer to the dates as being between 1500 and 1625. You've seen the seeds planted in the early reformers of Peter Waldo and Arnold of Brescia. The mystics like the Franciscans added to the flavor of change with their inspiring words and deeds, but are not really considered reformers.

The Reformation began with the return to the scriptures highlighted by the great scholars, such as Peter Abelard, who supported the ancient Greek teaching and learning method. Although the church tried to halt the growth of the movement, the Reformers took the questions asked by the generations of church-labeled "heretics" and asked them again—in a time when questioning the church meant almost certain death.

"In all the disputes which have excited Christians against each other, Rome has invariably decided in favor of that opinion which tended most towards the suppression of the human intellect and the annihilation of the reasoning powers."

—FRANCOIS-MARIE AROUET DE VOLTAIRE (early eighteenth century playwright, poet, essayist, and historiographer)

The Inquisition

At the Fourth Lateran Council in 1231, Pope Gregory IX established the "Inquisition" as a means to put the Christian "heretics" on trial. During an inquisition, the person on trial had to prove his or her innocence without an attorney and without knowing his or her accuser. The official punishment for one's guilt was death by fire—being burned at the stake. The inquisitor was both prosecutor and judge. In 1245, the pope granted the inquisitor the right to absolve any of the assistants to the inquisition—persons inflicting torture on the accused.

Other punishments for heresy included the following:

- Confiscation of personal property
- Excommunication
- Excommunication for those protecting a heretic and complete forgiveness of sins for those cooperating in acting against a heretic

Torture

In 1252, Pope Innocent IV authorized the use of torture as a means to force a heretic to confess to his or her crime. Since clergy members, according to canon law, were not permitted to kill, their role was to torture and interrogate. Once the heretic confessed, he or she was turned over to local law enforcement for burning at the stake. These trials were far from judicious.

When Pope Gregory IX gave the duty of the Inquisition primarily to the Dominican monks—taking it out of the hands of the bishops—other monastic orders also became involved. By the end of the thirteenth century, inquisitions had become instituted all over the Christian world.

FACT

At the request of Pope John Paul II, the Dominican friars held a council in 2002 to re-examine their role in the practice of inquisition. They concluded that their role in the Inquisition had been greatly exaggerated: "We are tired of the propagation of errors which make us out to be the Inquisition's founders, the authors of massacres and the only ones responsible for persecution."

John Wyclif

Martin Luther may get the credit as the first Protestant reformer, but without the work of scholars, such as John Wyclif (1330–1384), it's hard to know how far Luther's ideas would have gone. Wyclif and the other reformers set the stage and Luther took the bows.

Historians will admit that they know very little about the Englishman and influential reformer, John Wyclif. What they do know is that he was an Oxford University graduate and one of the most outspoken reformers of his time.

Wyclif's first attack was on the corruption of the papacy. He wrote that it was the duty of the English government to stop the activities of corrupt officials, to correct church violations, and even to seize the property of church leaders who violated their offices. Wyclif was one of the lucky ones—he had friends in high places and was spared the ruthlessness of the Inquisition, despite the fact that his teachings were condemned by Pope Gregory XI.

Even though Wyclif died of natural causes, he was later declared a heretic and his body was disinterred and burned.

What about Jesus?

John Wyclif lived during the years of the Great Schism. He saw the papal rift as a tragedy and set out on a mission to reveal the papacy as corrupt and invalid. According to Wyclif, the true church was not about popes, priests, and sacraments, but rather about faith in Jesus Christ. Here is a list of Wyclif's disputes with the state of the Catholic Church:

- **Church accumulation of wealth:** The pope should live as the true pope, St. Peter, in humility and humbleness—in other words, the pope should live in apostolic poverty.
- **The sale of indulgences:** The sale of indulgences was nothing more than papal bribery.
- **Christ is the true head of the church:** If the pope did not adhere to the scriptures and the teaching of Christ and his apostles, he was not a true Christian and, therefore, could not be a church leader.
- **The doctrine of transubstantiation:** Wyclif denied this sacrament, claiming that the bread and wine did not physically transform into the body and blood of Christ—it remained bread and wine, but the Holy Spirit was present.

Breaking the Barriers

Up to this point in time, most Christians had been distanced from God by the church leaders: the sacraments, indulgences, papal corruption, political in-fighting, and salvation only as ordained by members of the clergy. Wyclif was one of the pre-reformers to break the barriers between the Christian Church and God. He suggested two ways to do so:

1. Translate the scriptures into all languages so that Christians could connect directly to their faith through the inspired words of God
2. Educate the common people so that their relationship with God would have nothing to do with the current state of the church and everything to do with Jesus Christ

The Lollards

After his death, a group of Wyclif followers, known as the "Lollards," spread the teaching of Christ all over Europe and beyond. In 1388, Wyclif's translation of the scriptures was complete and the Lollards set out to distribute the text as far as it would go.

FACT

Wyclif's beliefs were the forerunner to the future reform movement of Martin Luther. Historians refer to Wyclif as the "Morning Star of the Reformation"—in other words, he was the one to set the ball in motion.

The Lollards proved very successful in their teaching. By the end of the fourteenth century, their message took hold mostly amongst the lower classes—something that did not please the king of England at the time, Henry IV. He ordered the execution of the Lollards, and there were mass hangings and burnings at the stake. The Lollards then went into hiding, and in the sixteenth century merged with the Protestants.

The Lollards defined their philosophy in a text called *Conclusions*. Here are some of the points it adhered to:

- Denial of transubstantiation
- Condemnation of the sacraments
- Rejection of spoken confession
- Labeling clerical celibacy and the chastity of the nuns as "unnatural"
- Criticizing war

These were the sentiments echoed many years later by Martin Luther who began the Protestant Reformation.

Martin Luther

At last we reach the era of Martin Luther (1483–1546), whose dramatic spiritual journey and transition had a lasting impact on the future of Christianity. The sixteenth century was full of inspired religious leaders—people of great courage who put forth dissenting opinions to challenge the church. To the reformers, the "truth" was still the most important factor in a Christian's relationship with God, and they were willing to adhere to this truth and face the executioner if need be.

In the wake of Waldo, Wyclif, and Hus (and others) came Martin Luther—the man who initiated a movement that revolutionized Europe in every respect, including religion, politics, and culture.

> "If it were an art to overcome heresy with fire, the executioners would be the most learned doctors on earth."
> —MARTIN LUTHER (to the Christian Nobility of the German State, 1520)

Luther's Education

Martin Luther was the son of Hans and Margaretha Luther. Hans Luther was a miner by trade and a devoted parent. A strict disciplinarian, he was determined that his eldest son Martin receive the best possible education. When the time arrived for Martin to attend a university, Hans Luther wanted him to attend the university at Erfurt and to become a lawyer.

At the university at Erfurt, Luther received a liberal arts education. He studied classic Greek literature, rhetoric, logic, philosophy, physics, and Latin. Through his studies, he also developed a love of music and learned to sing and play the lute. Luther also dedicated himself to his strict Catholic upbringing and attended Mass on a regular basis.

To please his father, in 1505, Martin enrolled in law school, even though his previous education and his heart were leading him to the monastery.

His Own Damascus

That same year, Martin Luther had a terrifying experience. While traveling from Mansfield to Erfurt, Luther was struck by lightning, echoing Paul's experience with the Holy Spirit on the road to Damascus. As he was lying on the road, Luther prayed to St. Anna, promising to become a monk if she would help him survive the experience. He did survive and true to his word, he entered an Augustinian monastery in Erfurt. While in the monastery, Luther memorized most of the Old and New Testaments and mastered Greek and Hebrew.

A Troubled Soul

Despite his decision to enter the monastery, Luther was not happy. His religious studies led him to not only question the God of the scriptures, but also to his own personal relationship with God. Luther struggled to reconcile his own sinfulness with God's judgment and ultimately his own salvation. Through the process of self-examination and further studies, he became depressed.

Repentance

Luther became so troubled that he completely threw himself into repentance. He felt compelled to cleanse his sins in order to find favor with the God of the Bible. He attended confession regularly (sometimes for six hours at a time); he fasted, prayed, meditated, and practiced flagellation (beating oneself as punishment for sins). In his writing, Luther later referred to the days in the monastery as his "martyrdom." He believed that if penance was truly the road to heaven, he had earned it.

Disapproving Father

In 1507, Luther was ordained into the priesthood, but his turmoil did not subside. He became overwhelmed by the responsibility of being a priest, wondering if he was really up to such a task. He doubted himself because he never felt that he was worthy enough.

Through Luther's own writings, historians believe that his torment had much to do with his father's opposition to his chosen path. Hans loved his son and never turned his back on him, but insisted that Martin did not "honor his mother and father" as stated in the scriptures. Disappointing and disobeying his father was a huge source of torment for Martin, but he stayed on his spiritual course nonetheless.

Disillusionment and Discovery

Martin's troubled mind was eased slightly when he befriended the Roman Catholic scholar Johannes von Staupitz. Martin found him to be intelligent and inspiring, and listened carefully to what he had to say. Staupitz told Luther to remember Christ's death on the cross as proof of God's love for all sinners. Luther took these words to heart, but something was still not right for him. However, he continued to teach and continued his desire to understand how a sinner like him could ever receive God's grace—the love of God for all sinners as demonstrated by Jesus' death on the cross.

Despite Luther's later break from the Catholic Church, he and Staupitz remained friends. Staupitz's influence led Luther to claim, "I have received everything from Staupitz," and "If it had not been for Dr. Staupitz, I should have sunk in hell."

A Trip to Rome

In 1510, Martin Luther traveled to Rome because he wanted to see the seat of the church. He was happy when he got there, but his happiness was short-lived. Luther discovered that Rome was a city of corruption and materialism, with a religiously indifferent population. He also felt that for such a spiritual man of conscience and integrity, the state of the Holy City was a horror show. Luther left a very disillusioned man. He returned to Germany and continued his studies and teaching at Wittenberg University, where he received his doctorate in theology.

Personal Enlightenment

Through his theological studies and even more so through his teaching, Luther finally found the answers he was looking for, which were always right there under his nose. Luther realized that, like the pre-reformers before him, the truth is in the Bible—the inspired word of God. He then turned his attention away from the tradition of the Catholic Bible study to personal interpretation of the scriptures.

Chapter 11

The Lutheran Movement

Despite the fact that Martin Luther had studied the scriptures so intensely, he could never quite reconcile his own lack of self-worth with his relationship with God. Once he managed to face his inner demons, he began to understand what having a relationship with God really meant and decided to help others find the same enlightenment. His famous *95 Theses* were just the beginning that would pave the way of renewal for all of Christendom.

By Faith Alone

As Martin Luther scoured the scriptures to find the meaning that would quell his concerns about his relationship with God, he came across Paul's letter to the Romans. Luther wasn't the first to examine the letter, or the first to elaborate on "justification by faith," but the experience profoundly changed his understanding of his own spirituality, and his relationship with the Catholic Church. So how did his message take hold? It's hard to know for sure, but here are some interesting facts:

- He was in the right place at the right time. He followed on the coattails of some renowned heretics who got the ball rolling.
- Luther worked hard to reconcile his relationship with God, and his struggle was noted by his contemporaries. Perhaps his solution seemed more plausible within the German scholarly communities.
- The development of the printing press allowed him to publish his writing and spread it among the Christian community.
- When the inquisitor came knocking on his door, he was given protection by a German duke.

Luther believed that people achieve salvation by faith alone. If they believe in God through Christ's sacrifice on the cross, they are absolved of sin and will receive God's grace—and this has nothing to do with doing good deeds or donating your life savings to rebuild St. Peter's church. Through this discovery, Luther started the reformation of the church.

"I began to understand that this verse means that the justice of God is revealed through the Gospel, but it is a passive justice, i.e. that by which the merciful God justifies us by faith, as it is written: 'The just person lives by faith.' All at once I felt that I had been born again and entered into paradise itself through open gates."

—FROM LUTHER'S *TOWER EXPERIENCE*

Church Indulgences

By this time, the church had managed to convince Christian communities that the way to salvation was through good deeds, which had mainly to do with how much money one gave to the church. Good Christians supported their churches with their hard-earned cash, and in return for their donations, they received salvation. This had been a practice for so long that no one really questioned it, until Luther came along and demanded a change.

What about Penance?

During the Crusades, the church guaranteed automatic salvation to all Christians who went off to fight. In essence, they bought their seat in heaven. This practice continued throughout the Crusades and, according to the reformers, grew to be nothing more than religious blackmail. However, Luther's biggest concern was not so much the granting of salvation, but that one didn't have to do any penance to receive the indulgence. Luther claimed that if you didn't do penance, you were not in a relationship with God, since to repent meant to acknowledge one's sins in the eyes of God. The final straw in the indulgence debacle was the preaching of a Dominican named John Tetzel.

FACT

Luther elaborated on the concept of "faith alone" in successive scholarly works, letters, and other pieces of writing. As a result, this devout, albeit frustrated, Catholic scholar and priest turned his back on the church as an organization and devoted the rest of his life to the "true meaning" as indicated in the scriptures.

Overindulgent

In 1517, Johann Tetzel was on a mission from Rome to try to raise funds for the rebuilding of St. Peter's basilica. Tetzel was a highly persuasive preacher, who supposedly made a fortune for the church in his travels. In his preaching, Tetzel promised that the Christians who donated their money to this venture would be given an indulgence, which consisted of granting the pardon for past sins without penance, the release from purgatory of loved ones, and the pardon of sins that have not yet been committed. An indulgence granted a Christian the right to sin because if you had the money to buy yourself out of it, you would still be granted salvation.

Martin Luther, who had come to terms with—and solidified—his own belief system, set out on an all-out attack on the church. His three major arguments with the church by this time were:

1. The church had no say over your salvation, and only God could grant salvation.
2. The church was taking advantage of Christians (especially the poor) for its own material benefit, which had nothing to do with God, the scriptures, or the well-being of Christians.
3. A Christian was not given salvation for good works, but a good Christian automatically did good works.

God's Grace

Luther believed in the demonstration of God's love (grace) directly from God to the individual. An individual has a direct and personal relationship with God, and God will grant grace to the deserving. God's grace is demonstrated most profoundly through Christ's death on the cross. Luther came to believe that Christ made a sacrifice for our sins, so in his death, he took away the sins of the world. Those who believe that Jesus died for their sins and accept Jesus as their savior are "saved" through this sacrificial grace.

ESSENTIAL

The "doctrine of predestination" states that God is not interested in the good works done by human beings. God alone chooses who will be saved, based on faith. If an individual turns to God, confesses his or her sins, and truly seeks to find the truth through the Bible, he or she will be assured salvation. According to the doctrine of predestination, not all will be saved; some will perish.

The *95 Theses*

In 1517, Luther's answer to church indulgences and Tetzel's fund-raising mission was to write his *95 Theses* and nail them up on the Wittenberg University's Castle Church door. This act marked the official start of the Protestant Reformation.

FACT

It was customary in Germany at this time to debate local church leadership about spiritual matters. One of the practices in Wittenberg was to write out your challenges and nail them to the Castle Church door, which was considered the University of Wittenberg's bulletin board. A debate was held once a week to discuss the issues. The challenges were called "theses."

Luther's Explanation

After nailing the *95 Theses* to the church door, Luther also sent a copy to the archbishop with a letter explaining his actions and his reasons. What Luther explained was that he was not trying to be disrespectful of the church in any way, but simply wanted these issues debated like any other Wittenberg debate.

The key elements of the *95 Theses* were:

1. Luther agreed with most of the beliefs and practices of the Catholic Church, including offices of leadership and the sacraments.
2. He did not disagree with the pope's right to grant indulgences, but disagreed to the extent to which the indulgences were granted: Indulgences cannot relieve a person of guilt; cannot apply to purgatory; and cannot be granted without penance.
3. He defended the pope's writing and leadership, and warned that the exaggerated preaching of those granting indulgences on behalf of the church could damage papal authority.

Challenged to a Debate

Luther's *95 Theses* did not go over well with the church leadership. The Dominicans were the first to declare Luther a heretic, and a Vatican scholar offered his own counter-theses, which in essence said that anyone who criticized church indulgences was a heretic.

However, in 1519, Luther got his debate in Leipzig, which lasted eighteen days, during which Luther demanded scriptural proof that he was wrong in his criticism of the church. At the end of the debate, theologian John Eck compared Luther to the notorious heretic, John Hus, and condemned him as one. In his series, "Address to the Nobility of the German Nation," Luther set out to gain the support of his nation and requested the nobility to break from the corrupt leadership of Rome—and in essence, form its own national church.

ESSENTIAL

Luther had written his theses in Latin, rather than German, which historians believe reflects the fact that he was not trying to start a religious uprising. If he had written the *95 Theses* in German, more local people would have been able to understand them, and that would have been seen as provocative.

The Meeting in Augsburg

The word of Luther's ideas started to spread across Germany, and Pope Leo X ordered Luther to appear in Rome to explain himself. However, Luther knew he was walking on thin ice with Rome, and that if he made such a journey, his life would be in jeopardy.

Therefore, Duke Frederick the Wise got involved and arranged a meeting in Augsburg, Germany. When Luther arrived in Augsburg in 1517, he was surprised to receive a hero's welcome. Many Germans were on his side and a lot of political maneuvering was done to assure his safety. Luther fully expected to be tried for heresy, but instead he met with Tommaso de Vio Gaetani Cajetan (known as St. Cajetan), who was charged with trying to dissuade Luther from his mission.

Who is St. Cajetan?
Born of Venetian nobility, he studied law in Italy and later sought a religious vocation and was ordained when he was thirty-six years old. Interestingly, Cajetan was aware of the need for church reformation, but was not willing to take it nearly as far as Luther.

Although Cajetan agreed that reforms were necessary, he told Luther that the church could not rely on the scriptures alone because, as divine leaders, they had access to knowledge not available in the scripture. Luther stood his ground and said that if it's not in the scripture, it is irrelevant to Christianity. Nothing was resolved in Augsburg, and Luther received even further notoriety throughout Germany.

Disputation of Leipzig

In 1519, a debate was held between two universities in Leipzig: the Wittenberg University and the University of Ingolstadt. On the side of Wittenberg was Andreas von Carlstadt (one of Luther's colleagues) and John Eck represented the University of Ingolstadt. The debate became known as the "Disputation of Leipzig."

The sparring began on the issues of free will and divine grace, but it wasn't long before Luther jumped in to debate his own points. The debate was heated and highly controversial: They argued over indulgences, penance, and purgatory. However, the most heated debate was centered on papal supremacy.

Luther argued several main points:

1. If Christ is the head of the church, why do Christians need a pope?
2. If it is a heresy to deny papal supremacy, then all the early Christians were heretics. There were no popes in early Christian times.
3. Christ had already done the work to reconcile Christians with God, so why do they need any further mediation by church leadership?

Throughout the debate, Eck compared Luther to John Hus and condemned him as a heretic. Luther admitted there were indeed similarities between his ideas and those of John Hus, and added that Hus was right and should never have been condemned. Eck may have won the debate, but Luther's drive had hit an all-time high and he was not going to quit now.

Andreas von Carlstadt (1480–1541) is considered one of Wittenberg's more radical reformers. He was highly supportive of Luther's work and presented his own theses asserting salvation by faith alone and denying free will. John Eck (1486–1543) was a German Catholic theologian and an opponent of Lutheranism. He was also one of the leading theologians at the Diet of Augsburg, responsible for presenting Luther with Pope Leo's Bull of Condemnation.

Heretic or Hero?

Spurred by his devotion to the truth that he had spent half a lifetime discovering, Luther was on a mission of reformation. Despite pressure from Rome and the threat of death at the hands of the inquisitor, Luther continued to write furiously against the church. In two highly controversial documents: "The Babylonian Captivity of the Church" and "The Freedom of a Christian Man," Luther, however, pushed the envelope just a little too far, causing a huge ruckus in Rome.

Here are some of the controversial assertions that Luther made in "The Babylonian Captivity of the Church":

1. The sacraments held Christians captives of Rome.
2. The papacy denied Christians the right to a personal relationship with God through the mediation of clergy.
3. A sacrament must be instituted by Christ (not invented by the church) in order to be valid.

Lutheranism Is Born

In "The Babylonian Captivity of the Church," Luther dismantled the idea of the church hierarchy and instead focused on the idea of a Christian community. Luther's point was that all Christians are "priests" responsible for making spiritual sacrifices to God. In "The Freedom of a Christian Man," Luther set forth his views on Christian behavior and salvation, saying, "Good works do not make a man good, but a good man does good works." These two works, along with Luther's "Address to the Christian Nobility" collectively became the cornerstone of Lutheranism.

However, the more he wrote, the more trouble he got into with the church. In 1520, Luther wrote "On the Papacy at Rome" in which he referred to the pope as the "Anti-Christ." The Anti-Christ is "the beast" who, in the scriptures, appears shortly before the apocalypse.

Papal Bull of Condemnation

By 1520, Luther had pushed Pope Leo X to issue a papal Bull of Condemnation called "Exsurge Domine," declaring Luther a heretic and ordering the burning of all his writings. The pope then gave Luther sixty days to recant his beliefs and to turn away from his heretical path. Luther waited until the deadline, and on the last day, staged his own bonfire in Wittenberg, where he burned the bull and the book of canon law. The pope then excommunicated him.

QUESTION?

How did Luther manage to avoid the inquisitor?
Luther had the protection of Germany—both the people and its leadership. His beliefs had become widely popular and perhaps the secular leaders saw this as a way to gain more control over Germany. With the church leaders out and the nobility in, the secular officers would have more authority over the nation.

The Imperial Diet of Worms

The church ordered Luther to attend a legislative meeting (or diet) in the city of Worms, Germany. Emperor Charles V promised him safe passage to the diet, and even though Luther feared for his life, he was not deterred. In 1521, at the Diet of Worms, Luther refused to recant any of his beliefs or writings—a decision which led to what historians call one of the most important events in Western Civilization.

The Edict of Worms

Emperor Charles V then signed the Edict of Worms, declaring Martin Luther a heretic and an enemy of the church. He placed Luther under an imperial ban—which meant that no one in the empire was permitted to communicate with him—and ordered all of his books to be located and burned. The emperor also ruled that if any person or government offered Luther physical protection, they too would face the wrath of Rome.

Kidnapped to Safety

On his way home to Wittenberg from Worms, the German Elector Frederick the Wise arranged Luther's kidnapping and placed him in the Wartburg Castle in Germany, where he stayed for about a year. This was done for his own protection, and no one, except the German nobility, knew where he was or what had happened to him. To hide himself from gossip or enemies, Luther disguised himself as a knight named George. During this time, he managed to translate the Bible from Latin to German, so that all German-speaking Christians could have direct access to God through the scriptures.

The printing press was Luther's greatest ally in the Bible translation project—5,000 copies were printed, and the demand outweighed the power of the printer.

The Movement Continues

The Lutheran movement did not lose its momentum, despite Luther's disappearance. Von Carlstadt (the same man that debated John Eck in the Disputation of Leipzig) was another dynamic force, and he stepped in when Luther was absent. Luther knew of Von Carlstadt's activities at Wittenberg and grew concerned that he was putting too much emphasis on external church service reformations and not enough on the most important principle: justification by faith alone. German Christians in Wittenberg were not completely comfortable with Von Carlstadt's efforts, and word got back to Luther. He left Wartburg Castle, defying the papal edict against him, returned to Wittenberg, and picked up where he left off. (E)

Chapter 12

Protestant Reformation

Martin Luther was a brave pioneer who stood up for his beliefs. He was passionate about his newly found truth and took his work of reform both seriously and literally. While the severity of his stance helped his beliefs take hold across Europe, it wasn't long before the Protestants, like the Catholics before them, faced some trying times.

Lutheranism in Germany

While Martin Luther stayed in Wartburg Castle, the reform revolution accelerated beyond Rome's control. Radical reformers (more radical than Luther) popped up all over the empire, but especially in Germany. German nobles, dukes, princes, and electors defied Rome's condemnation of Luther and chose to back the reform movement.

Secular leaders abandoned the Catholic Mass; ministers abandoned celibacy; and Luther abolished the office of the bishop. He also declared that the Christian Church needed pastors, not religious dignitaries.

The Augsburg Confession

With Martin Luther condemned as a heretic, his movement within the empire was limited, but his work was not. In 1530, Emperor Charles V, seeking to regain Christian unity despite the reform movements and condemnation of heretics, called for a diet to be held in Augsburg, Germany. Luther, as one of the condemned, could not attend, so he stayed in Wittenberg, where he could remain under the protection of Duke Frederick the Wise of Saxony. However, his friend and colleague, Philip Melanchthon, did the legwork. He actually drafted the Augsburg Confession—the official Lutheran statement of faith (a statement indicating the beliefs of the Lutheran movement)—but the words and teaching behind the document belonged to Luther.

ESSENTIAL

It was critical for Charles V to attempt to show unity within the empire. Although he wanted all subjects of the empire to remain true to Catholicism, he also had to show possible invading armies (like the Turks) that there was still a unified Christian front. In an attempt to show his willingness to, at least, listen to dissenting opinions, he directed the diet reform attendees to draft a statement of what they believed.

The Confession Outlined

The Augsburg Confession was read out loud at the diet, and seven princes and two representatives of independent cities signed it. It contained twenty-eight articles: The first twenty-one established Lutheran teaching, while the last seven rejected Christian corruption.

Here are the main points that the Confession upholds in relation to Lutheran reform:

- Teaches the Trinity
- Discusses the meaning of original sin
- Explains the humanity and deity of Jesus Christ
- Addresses the sacrifice of Jesus for all human sin
- Explains justification by faith alone without good deeds
- Discusses the gospel, baptism, and the Lord's Supper as tools to create and sustain faith

Here are the church abuses outlined in the Confession:

- False ideas and practices of the Lord's Supper
- Celibacy of church leaders
- Church hierarchy as divine authority
- The misuse of confession and absolution

The Augsburg Confession cautiously attempted to divide the reformist principles from Catholicism. The Catholics were not at all happy about the Confession and offered their own "Confutation at Augsburg," rejecting the Lutheran document. Charles V accepted the Confutation, rejected the Confession, and reinstated the Edict of Worms. The emperor's interest in seeking Christian unity failed and the conflict continued.

The Augsburg Apology

In 1531, one year after the reading of the Augsburg Confession before the emperor, Melanchthon wrote the Apology (defense) of the Augsburg Confession. The apology was an attempt to explain and uphold the Lutheran doctrine of faith as indicated in the Augsburg Confession. Both the confession itself and the apology are published in the Lutheran *Book of Concord*.

The *Book of Concord* contains the Lutheran confessions of faith and outlines all factors of Lutheranism. The largest document in the *Book of Concord*, its longest chapter, is devoted to the most important truth of the Lutheran faith: the doctrine of justification by grace alone, through faith alone, in Christ alone.

Handbook Helpers

Martin Luther knew that he had to outline the basic truths of Christian faith for both the laity and the clergy, since there had been a lot of arguing going back and forth. Did the people really understand what Luther and the other reformers were trying to say? To be sure, he published two handbooks to help pastors and communities understand the truth about faith. These handbooks were called "The Small Catechism" and "The Large Catechism"—the former outlines the Lutheran doctrine in a nutshell, while the latter is a little more in depth. The books focused on the Ten Commandments, the Apostolic Creed, the Lord's Prayer, baptism, confession, and the Lord's Supper.

Peasant Uprising

While the princes, nobles, and clerics of Germany were reaping the benefits of Martin Luther's work, there was one group in particular that wanted to share in the same kind of newly found freedom. The peasants were not quite so concerned about their religious freedom, as with their right to live a decent life.

"The people are everywhere restless and their eyes are open . . . They will no longer submit to oppression by force . . . it looks to me as though Germany will be drenched in blood."
—MARTIN LUTHER, written in 1522 from Wartburg Castle

The Twelve Demands

The peasants wanted social, economic, and political reform, and they were fed up with working as serfs with all their hard-earned fruits of labor going to their lords. In 1525, they put together their own demands in writing (The Twelve Articles) and began distributing pamphlets. They based their demands on Lutheran principles, but Luther did not support the revolution. Even though he understood their complaints, he felt the peasants were misguided in taking the principles of Christ and applying them to temporal matters. But the peasants didn't see it that way. If the Lutherans could get what they wanted, why couldn't they? The peasants spelled out twelve demands:

1. **Choosing a pastor:** Each community should choose its own pastor and that pastor should teach the scriptures to the community.
2. **Tithes:** Some forms of tithing (church taxes) should be eliminated, but the peasants would be willing to pay the fair "tithe of grain" as indicated in the scriptures.
3. **Serfdom:** Serfdom is unfair and restrictive, and should be eliminated.
4. **Hunting and fishing:** Peasants should have the right to hunt and fish freely, unless the rights to do so had been sold.
5. **Building materials and firewood collection:** Peasants should have the right to freely collect building materials and firewood from the village forests, unless the rights to do so had been sold.
6. **Work load:** Lords should stop imposing oppressive work loads.
7. **Payment:** Peasants should only work according to what is "just and proper" according to an agreement between the lord and the peasant.
8. **Income:** The lords should appoint a person to fix affordable rents and make sure the peasant is not paying out more than he or she earns.
9. **Justice:** They want equal justice—they should be judged fairly and in accordance with the committed crime.
10. **Land:** Some community property has been unfairly taken over by landowners, and if the land has been fairly purchased, there should be some agreement on the division of the property between lord and peasant.

11. **Death tax:** The fee referred to as "Todfall" (a death tax) should be abolished.

12. **Scripture:** The peasants conclude that if any of these articles does not adhere to the word of God as per the scriptures, or is found to be unfair in anyway, it can be scrapped.

The Revolution

The princes of Germany did what they could to negotiate with the peasants, but the peasants failed to come to an agreement and violence began. Feeling somewhat responsible for indirectly prompting the uprising, Luther traveled to the city of Thuringia to attempt his own negotiations with the peasants and ask for the assistance of Frederick the Wise. He knew that not only was this uprising a threat to Germany, but to his own cause of reform as well. However, he was too late. The revolution was well underway and by 1526 had consumed at least one third of Germany.

The peasants were expected to turn as much as a third of their holdings before handing their "wealth" to the lord of the manor, which left them with very little of what they originally had.

Enough Is Enough

The leaders in Germany were not going to stand by and let Germany fall to its knees, so they crushed the revolution in almost one sweeping motion. One example of the ruthlessness of the German rulers was the battle of Frankenhausen, where more than 6,000 peasants were slaughtered. By the end of the war, 100,000 peasants were dead. To make matters worse, the peasants who survived felt their efforts were for naught as their lives did not improve one bit after the war.

The revolt also negatively impacted Luther's efforts, as he lost the backing of the lower classes. As a result, the peasants (especially in the south) turned their backs on Lutheranism to join more radical reform movements. With the peasant uprising abruptly halted, German rulers and the reformers were able to get back to business in orchestrating their own national church in Germany. Rome, however, was not going to make their road a smooth one.

The Diets of Speyer

Determined to crush the Lutherans once and for all, in 1526 Emperor Charles V called another meeting in the city of Speyer. At this diet, he asked each state to choose between Roman Catholicism or Lutheranism. The emperor may have thought this was a gesture of conciliation and an effort to bring some stability back to the church, but the edict of 1526 did not hold, and Charles became nervous that Lutheranism was beginning to spin beyond the borders of Germany. This was more than Rome was willing to tolerate, so in 1529, Charles V called another diet in Speyer and revoked his 1526 edict.

The Schmalkaldic League

Charles V continued his rampage against Lutheranism and was willing to go to war in order to stop it. In response to such a threat, in 1531, several Lutheran princes called a meeting in Schmalkalden, Germany, and came to be known as the Schmalkaldic League. The League was a defensive alliance against the Roman aggressor, as the princes agreed to take up arms in defense of one another if the emperor's army invaded one of their territories.

QUESTION?

Why was the reform movement called "Protestantism"?
While several German territories complied with Charles' revocation of the 1526 edict, there were some provinces that protested. The reformers who did not adhere to the 1529 edict at the diet of Speyer came to be known as "Protestants." Since then, Lutherans have been called Protestants, and the name applies to future Christian reform movements as well.

The Emperor Gets Side-Tracked

Charles never invaded as the League had expected. The Turks were threatening to invade Austrian territory, and the emperor needed all the help he could get from Catholics and Protestants alike. So Charles promised not to attack German territories, at least until a council meeting could be held to iron out the conflict. This unwritten and unsigned agreement between Rome and the German princes was called the Peace of Nuremberg. The Protestants decided to trust the emperor to uphold the agreement, and in turn agreed to help Charles defend the empire from invading Turks.

Treaty of Frankfurt

Philip of Hesse, a German nobleman, was one of the founding fathers of the Schmalkaldic League. He also helped the League grow throughout Germany. In response, Charles V formed the "Catholic League" in 1538. The two groups prepared for war, but the battle was again temporarily averted with the Treaty of Frankfurt, drawn up in 1539. During this lull in the rising tensions, Charles made yet another attempt to resolve the conflict peacefully. But he failed again, and war became inevitable.

The Schmalkaldic War

The Schmalkaldic League could not beat the empire, even though its force was larger than the emperor's army, and the Battle of Muhlberg in 1547 gave the emperor his ultimate victory. The Schmalkaldic leaders were arrested, and twenty-eight German territories were stripped of their independence from Rome.

The Peace of Augsburg

The Schmalkaldic War ended in 1555 with a treaty known as the Peace of Augsburg. The treaty gave the princes of Germany the right to choose the religion of their liking, as long as it was Catholicism or Lutheranism. All religious opinions were considered the property of the princes, and all beliefs had to be those dictated by them. If bishops converted to Lutheranism, they were forced to forfeit all their property, and all property held by Catholic bishops was considered the property of Rome. What the Lutherans gained from these tumultuous times, however, was the declaration of Lutheranism as a state religion, which soon broke through German borders into Scandinavia.

The Peace of Augsburg introduced the concept of "religious toleration," and although the treaty itself was weak, it brought increased stability. However, only Lutheranism was declared a tolerated religion during that time.

The Anabaptists

Other Protestant reform groups started appearing in Europe during the same time that Lutheranism was finding its grip on Germany. One such group was the Anabaptists, who sprang from the peasant uprising of the early sixteenth century. Feeling betrayed by their princes, Rome, and Martin Luther, some of the peasants took a deeper look at their faith and formed their own paths.

At the forefront of Anabaptism was the issue of baptism itself. The Anabaptists did not see the mandatory baptism of babies in the scripture. What they did see was St. John the Baptist baptizing believers—adult believers. They saw the day of the Pentacost, where thousands were baptized after discovering the message of Christ. Therefore, the Anabaptists believed that a person should be baptized once he or she has realized and accepted his or her spirituality.

The Anabaptists saw themselves as Christians, but they were also reformers. They were not revolting against the Catholic Church, rather they revolted against the Protestant reformers. While Calvinist and Lutheran in the roots, they did not feel that these reformers took reform far enough. They too turned to the scripture to find the true meaning of God's word.

The Anabaptists spread their beliefs through preaching (like the apostles and certainly like Paul). As a result of their travels, their message spread through Switzerland, Holland, and German-speaking regions of Europe.

Return to Scripture

The Anabaptists, like members of the neo-apostolic movements from which Lutheranism sprang, turned to the scriptures to find their faith. In doing so, they took the Bible very literally. The Anabaptist Protestants held intense Bible study classes where they analyzed every inch of the scriptures. In this sense, the Anabaptists set out to take a deeper step into the frightening abyss of what the Catholics called heresy. The Lutherans, however, had timing, Martin Luther, and the power of princes behind them, while the Anabaptists only had the scriptures and their own determination.

Grebel and Manz

Conrad Grebel and Felix Manz are considered the forefathers of the Anabaptist movement, which began in Zurich, Switzerland. In 1525, the Council of Zurich demanded that Grebel and Manz call an end to these Bible study classes and make sure all babies were baptized within eight days of their birth. Anyone who did not comply would be banished. Grebel and Manz held a meeting with other believers to decide what to do. Instead of giving in to the demands, they baptized each other to confirm their commitment to their faith in Jesus Christ—in the way they chose to believe, not in the way that was mandated to them by church sacraments and law enforcement.

Quakers, Mennonites, Baptists, Hussites, and the Old Amish Order are all branches of Anabaptism. Only the Amish adhere to strict living with no fringe benefits of modern technology, however. The Mennonites adhere to an austere lifestyle and consider themselves a peace-loving society in the tradition of Christ's message.

Separation of Church and State

The Anabaptists believed in the separation of church and state. They saw it as a conflict of interest, and it simply did not exist in the scriptures. In their intense examination of the New Testament, the Anabaptists discovered that not only did the state have nothing to do with Christianity, but discovered that the Christian community was just that—a community of people who believed and followed Jesus Christ. Despite the fact that Lutheranism was considered revolutionary reform, the Anabaptists did not accept it because it was still an organized religion with clergy and strong connection to the state—in this sense, it was no different than the Roman Catholic Church.

Return to Apostolic Christianity

The idea of returning to apostolic Christianity was not a new one. The monks and the mystics both headed in that direction as the pre-reformers. But the Anabaptists took it a step further. They believed that every Christian is a disciple of Christ and is part of a community of saints. All believers in Jesus Christ are saints, not just those canonized by Rome.

The Anabaptists wanted radical reform in terms of strict adherence to apostolic values. As a result, they refused to be part of a society that did not share these values or one that was founded on organized, nonscriptural Christian doctrine. They fought this point to the death, but it was difficult to do so with the refusal to take up arms or to take any political offices.

The Anabaptism movement split into three different branches:

1. The Swiss Brethren (with Grebel and Manz)
2. The Hutterites in Moravia (a Czech region)
3. The Mennonites in northern Germany and The Netherlands

Like all other reformers, the Anabaptists suffered their fair share of persecution. There had never been a peaceful path for "heretics," but Lutheranism did, unintentionally, help pave the way for other reformers. Ⓔ

Chapter 13

E Protestant Globalization

Martin Luther's journey and accomplishments are remarkable in that a new, established church organization began from his hard work, but what about the other reformers? There were many contemporaries of Luther who don't seem to get the same kind of credit for demanding similar, profound change. Well . . . you'll read about them here.

Luther's Later Years and Death

Martin Luther, without a doubt, led a passionate life. From his early days as a monastic scholar with his passion turned inward, to his attack on the church, to achieving his goal of a return to the "true" Christianity—every ounce of his being was behind his efforts. However, historians later reflected that perhaps Luther was a little too passionate and toward the end of his life became extreme to the point of being radical.

The Radical Luther

In the beginning of his reform efforts, Luther wrote about brotherly love and religious tolerance, but near the end of his life, he became impatient and disgruntled. Many of Luther's writings on Judaism became anti-Semitic, and scholars believe this was due to his disappointment that Jews were not converting to Christianity after the church reform had taken hold. He naively believed that once the Jews saw that Christianity did not have to exist in the corrupted form of the Roman Catholic Church, they would begin to convert and accept Jesus as the Messiah. This didn't happen, and Luther felt somehow betrayed, as reflected in his essay "The Jews and Their Lies" (1543).

ESSENTIAL

Martin Luther married a former nun, Catherine von Bora. Protestants saw nothing in the scriptures that said church leaders should not marry—in fact, quite the opposite: "Let deacons be married only once, and let them manage their children and their households well." (1 Tim 3:12, NRSV)

Coming Full Circle

In 1546, Martin Luther returned to the place of his birth in Eisleben, Germany, to help the nobles settle a land dispute. Just a few days after his arrival, he died. He was buried at Wittenberg's Castle Church—the very same place he had hung his *95 Theses* several years before. He unwittingly began a movement that picked up momentum and changed the course of history. After his death, Lutheranism spread quickly within the region of Scandinavia.

Reform Spreads to the Western World

Under the leadership of Swedish brothers Olaf and Lars Petri (both students of Luther and Melanchthon), Lutheranism became the official religion of Sweden by 1527. The Swedish subjects, like those in many other nations, were under the iron-fisted rule of the Catholic Church, and the country was in a state of poverty and decay. The citizens had no access to the Bible in their own language, so they were dependent on the church for spiritual guidance.

FACT

While the church went after Olaf and Lars, like it did with every other powerful reformer, King Gustavus Vasa of Sweden put equal energy into protecting them. The king wanted to reform both the church and state of Sweden and welcomed the work of the Petris in leading the country's reform.

Reform in Finland

A German-educated Finnish preacher named Peter Särkilahti spread the Lutheran message in Finland, which was in possession of Sweden. Therefore, the Petri brothers also had an impact on the establishment of Lutheranism in that region. Michael Agricola, a Wittenberg scholar, contributed considerably in Finland by translating the New Testament into Finnish (1548). He also translated portions of the Psalms and the Old Testament (1551).

Reform in Norway

Under the encouragement of King Frederick I, Hans Tausen led Denmark (and Norway, which was a province of Denmark at that time) into reformation. Ironically, Tausen, a peasant with obvious passion that was recognized by church leaders, was educated by the Catholic Church. He was given the opportunity to study anywhere he wanted, except in Wittenberg.

But Tausen got hold of Luther's writings and attended Wittenberg anyway. When he returned to Denmark, he quietly preached Lutheran beliefs. However, the church soon heard what he was up to and began watching his every move. By 1524, Tausen had cut ties with the Catholic Church, was appointed court chaplain by King Frederick I, and the Protestant Reformation swept the nation.

Reform in Iceland

Oddur Gottskalksson was the father of the Reformation in Iceland (also a Danish province). He studied Lutheranism in Germany, translated the Bible into Icelandic, and brought the Reformation home with him. Unlike other reforming nations, the Icelanders rejected Lutheranism at first, perhaps because it was mandated upon them by force, between 1539 and 1551. Eventually, a man named Bishop Gudbrandur Thorlaksson helped the people accept it.

ESSENTIAL

When the Reformation reached Iceland, Catholic poetry was discarded and attempts were made by the first Lutheran bishops to replace it with hymns translated from Danish and German. The Bible was translated into Icelandic during the Reformation by Gudbrandur Thorlaksson, who was also Bishop of Holar for fifty-six years.

Reform in Switzerland

Under the guidance of a Swiss priest name Ulrich Zwingli, Switzerland experienced a different kind of Reformation. Switzerland was (and is now) divided into different regions (called "cantons") that speak different languages: German, French, and Italian. Zwingli led the Reformation to the German-speaking populace. However, the movement did not take hold in Switzerland the way it had in Scandinavia and Germany—in other words, it did not unite religion and politics—and Switzerland was thrust into religious warfare.

Ulrich Zwingli

Ulrich Zwingli was the leader of the reform movement in Switzerland. Born to a middle-class family in the town of Wildhaus, he studied at the

University of Vienna, where he discovered the teachings of the humanists, including one of the most famous humanists of all—a German scholar named Desiderius Erasmus. In the year 1506, after receiving his master of arts degree, Zwingli was ordained and began his priesthood in Glarus, Switzerland.

Through his studies, Zwingli began to have some serious concerns about the practices of the Roman Catholic Church. Like Hans Tausen in Denmark, he tried to quietly incorporate some of his newly found knowledge and his humanist studies into his preaching. His main concerns about the church were the same as Luther's in some ways—the biggest gripe being that the church had strayed too far from the scriptures. Zwingli also added that the church put too much emphasis on the worship of saints and adoration of relics, and was not a fan of the indulgences either.

Like some of his reformist predecessors, Zwingli gained in popularity amongst the German-speaking Swiss and, surprisingly, maintained the favor of the pope. In 1519, Zwingli became the priest at the Great Cathedral in Zurich ("Grossmunster" in German) and soon afterward it became the Wittenberg of Switzerland. People came from all over Switzerland to listen to his preaching, despite the reformist undertones of his services. In his days at the University of Vienna, Zwingli memorized Erasmus' Latin translation of the Bible, but preached from the original Hebrew and Greek versions. To Zwingli, the Bible in these languages was the closest to the original scriptural text.

FACT

Zwingli defied the church and its law regarding the clergy and celibacy by secretly marrying Anna Reinhart Meyer. The marriage did not become public until 1524, when Zwingli picked up the pace with his sermons against celibacy. Anna was a widow with three children of her own. Her marriage to Zwingli added four more children to their ready-made family.

The Humanist Influence

Humanism was cultivated by intellect and culture. It began in Italy in the fifteenth and sixteenth centuries and spread throughout Europe.

Desiderius Erasmus was the most influential humanist in Europe. He is said to have used his pen for peace, seeking understanding and peaceful solutions to explosive situations. He was against war and could not fathom the idea of Christian fighting Christian. Erasmus' most famous piece of writing "The Praise of Folly" (1511) satirized all humankind and the crazy times in which they lived.

Zwingli's Pamphlets

Zwingli got his hands upon a printing press in the year 1519 and was able to spread his pamphlets throughout Zurich. He was a huge fan of Martin Luther's work, and by the time his message was working its way around Switzerland, the Lutheran message was already on the move. That same year, Zwingli became a victim of Europe's worst enemy: the plague, but his life was spared. By 1520, Zwingli was able to convince the Zurich Council to ban any religious teachings that were not directly biblical.

Among the issues of contention with the church that Zwingli preached and wrote about were:

- Fasting
- Celibacy of the clergy
- Confession
- Monasticism
- The Mass celebration
- The use of images and music during services

The Zurich Council

In 1523, the Zurich Council called a meeting (The Zurich Disputation) to discuss matters of religion. At the meeting, Zwingli presented his *67 Conclusions* (also referred to as "67 Articles" or "67 Theses" like the 95 of Martin Luther). He did not have to nail his Conclusions on a church door but had to present them to the representatives from Rome.

Here are ten of the Conclusions presented to the Zurich Disputation:

1. The Bible is the only source of faith.
2. Jesus Christ is the sole mediator between humankind and God (not the clergy).
3. The Mass is a commemoration—not a sacrifice.
4. Monasticism should be abandoned (there are no monks in the Bible).
5. Celibacy should not be mandatory practice among the clergy.
6. Christians should obey their governments unless their governments disregard the scriptures.
7. Only God can forgive sins, not the church.
8. There is no such thing as purgatory.
9. The tradition of fasting should be rejected.
10. The grace of God grants human beings the ability to do good works.

When many people think of the Renaissance, they think of the growth of art, music, literature, and thought—this was the humanist movement. Humanism, in fact, was the force that spurred the Renaissance and the Reformation.

The council accepted Zwingli's Conclusions and banned all preachings that did not originate from the Bible. The Reformation—Zwingli style—had begun in Switzerland.

The effects of the council's decision included:

- Music and religious images were removed from churches.
- The clergy were permitted to marry.
- Communion became a commemorative celebration and not a Christian sacrifice.
- Monasteries were converted to hospitals.

Church's Dilemma

The Catholic Church was on a lifelong mission to create Christian unity through the ages, but Luther showed up and threw wrenches in everything the Catholics thought had been set in stone by virtue of their various councils. Lutheranism certainly broke any Catholic attempts at unification, and created further turmoil in the church.

When Zwingli appeared on the horizon with more "radical" opinions, the church had no choice but to let Germany break away—it had too many other problems to worry about on other fronts. However, Emperor Charles V was not about to let the church disintegrate before his very eyes.

QUESTION?

Why is Zwingli's theology often referred to as "simple"?
Zwingli's theology was based on a single principle: If it's not in the Old or New Testament, then no Christian should believe or practice it. This was the basis of his critique of indulgences. In 1522, Zwingli protested against the Catholic fasting at Lent. He argued that the New Testament says absolutely nothing about fasting at Lent.

Protestant Unity

In response to the growing armies of Charles V, the Protestants had one choice: to unite and prepare for attack by Catholic armies, or give in. The princes of Germany were getting a little uneasy at the thought of Charles turning his attention from France to the countries adopting Protestantism.

In 1529, Philip of Hesse, the Duke of Saxony, called upon the Protestants to attend a meeting at his castle in Marburg, Germany. The point was to try to unite Lutheranism with the growing Zwinglian reform movement in Switzerland. With Rome breathing down their necks, they could not afford to have disunity among the Protestants.

The Marburg Colloquy

Zwingli was happy to attend because he wanted to see the unity of the Protestants for both religious and political reasons. Luther, however, was not so enthused. He felt that the colloquy was simply a way for the

Protestants to prepare for war against the Catholics. Not only did he not believe in such a war, but he also did not want to make waves with the Catholics. Hoping for a peaceful solution, Luther, accompanied by Philip Melanchthon, gave in and went to Marburg.

Luther put together fifteen topics of Protestant dissension that were discussed at the Marburg Colloquy. The topics included the Trinity, the Incarnation (Christ as a human), Christology (the nature of Christ as both human and divine), original sin, justification by faith, baptism, good works, confession, and the Lord's Supper. These were the key issues of contention for Luther.

The Marburg Colloquy was, by and large, successful in terms of the discussion of spiritual matters. The attendees agreed on everything but, of course, the Lord's Supper—specifically in what manner Jesus was present during communion. That's not really surprising, given that most of the other issues could be pin-pointed in the scriptures, but Christ's words: "Take; this is my body . . . this is my blood of the covenant, which is poured out for many" (Mark 14:22–24, NRSV), which could very well have been a metaphor. Zwingli and Luther could only agree to stop attacking each other on the topic. While they may have agreed on many issues, the colloquy did not bring the unity the Protestants needed to defend themselves against Roman troops. There would always be a division between the Lutherans and the reformed Protestants (Zwinglianism).

FACT

Luther and Zwingli agreed on most of their reform ideas, but disagreed on the issue of the Last Supper. Luther believed in "consubstantiation"—meaning that Jesus' physical body was present in the bread and wine. Zwingli, on the other hand, believed that what Jesus meant at the actual Last Supper was that the bread and wine represented his body and blood.

Zwingli and the Anabaptists

Reformed Protestantism took hold in the German-speaking cantons (or states) of Switzerland, but it stopped there because the Anabaptists put a stop to its growth into other regions of Switzerland. The Anabaptists did not think that Zwingli took matters of reform far enough, and they wanted more radical changes.

However, the Anabaptists were not the only obstacles to Zwingli's movement. There was a group of Swiss militants from various cantons, still loyal to the Roman Catholic Church, who were willing to combat the spread of this "heresy." The cantons from where these militants came became known as the "Forest Cantons."

Anabaptist Persecution

In 1526, the Council of Zurich decided that anyone discovered "re-baptizing" (referring to the assumption that these adults had already been baptized) would be put to death. The means of execution? Drowning. The council's theory? "If they want water, we'll give them water!"

In 1527, Feliz Manz became the first Anabaptist to be executed by drowning in the Limmat River, which flowed through the city of Zurich. With this execution and several more to follow, the Anabaptist movement fled Switzerland and became virtually nonexistent there by 1531. The Diet of Speyer (1529) officially declared the Anabaptist movement illegal, and more than 4,000 Anabaptists were burned, drowned, and beheaded.

The Anabaptists had four issues that they documented in their Schleitheim Confession (1527):

1. **Discipleship:** Christians should live their lives as disciples of Christ.
2. **Love:** Christians should lead a life of pacifism and love.
3. **Congregational view of church authority:** The congregation of believers is both priest to each other and missionary to the nonbelievers.
4. **Separation of church and state:** Faith is a gift from God that has nothing to do with civil or church governments.

QUESTION?

After fleeing Switzerland, where did the Anabaptists settle?
In an effort to find a safe haven, the Anabaptists moved north to Moravia, where they found sympathetic princes willing to take them in. In Moravia, the Anabaptists formed their own community called the "Bruderhof." The communes were organized by Jakob Hutter and these groups of Anabaptists became known as the Hutterites—still in existence today.

Anabaptist Women Reformers

It is important to note that there were many active Protestant women reformers—many in the noble ranks as well as the wives of notable reformers. But some of the most famous and most persecuted were the Anabaptist women. They distributed the sacraments, taught Bible classes, and debated theological issues. They would die like many of their male counterparts by drowning or by fire.

Here are just some notable Anabaptist women:

1. **Elisabeth Dirks:** Latin scholar and Bible teacher who was arrested and suffered death by drowning in 1549.
2. **Margarette Pruess of Strasbourg:** The daughter of a printer, and author of many Anabaptist writings.
3. **Anna Salminger and Veronika Gross:** Known for their preaching and contributions toward the establishment of an Anabaptist congregation in Augsburg, Germany.
4. **Argula von Grumbach:** Ecclesiastical writer.
5. **Goetken Gerrits:** Composer of hymns.

Religious Civil War

The Swiss cantons were not religiously united. While several of the provinces had converted to Protestantism, there were five cantons that remained strictly Roman Catholic (these were the "Forest Cantons," mentioned earlier). As a result, war broke out in Switzerland between the Protestants and the Catholics. In 1529, there was one minor breakthrough with the signing of the "First Peace of Kappel," which permitted the Forest Cantons to remain Catholic. But war did not stop there. In an act of desperation, Zurich added fuel to the fire by imposing sanctions against the Forest Cantons, which deprived them of the necessities for survival. As a result, the Forest Cantons attacked the city of Zurich in 1531.

Zwingli is often referred to as the forgotten reformer. He is usually mentioned only after Luther and Calvin in terms of his importance in the Protestant Reformation. But Zwingli paved the way for future reformers like John Calvin, who, in turn, made profound changes upon Protestant reform and ultimately upon Western Civilization.

Death of Zwingli

In 1531, Zwingli himself took up arms to fight for the cause that had originally fallen under his leadership, but was wounded in the Battle of Kappel. When the Forest Canton troops found him, they killed him, and then they quartered and burned his body for added insult.

The Next Generation

However, Zwingli's death did not signify the end of Reformation Protestantism. Zwingli's son-in-law, Heinrich Bullinger, took over where Zwingli left off, but later transitioned into the leadership of John Calvin. John Calvin was a preacher from Geneva, located in the French-speaking region of Switzerland. At first, Calvin was a die-hard Zwinglian, but in time, he developed his own theology and broke away from many of Zwingli's beliefs. Ⓔ

Chapter 14
Calvinism

John Calvin is another famous name in the history of the Protestant Reformation. Calvin was a powerful reformer, whose ideas were influenced by both Luther and Zwingli, but his own theology led future reformers into a whole new realm of reform, and eventually to Presbyterianism. These new reformers assisted in changing the face of European religion forever.

John Calvin

John Calvin (Jean Cauvin) was a Frenchman, born in the town of Noyon outside of Paris in 1509 to a relatively prestigious family. John's father, Gérard, was a notary in the city of Noyon and his mother, Jeanne le Franc, was the daughter of a wealthy local innkeeper. When John was fourteen years old, his parents sent him to the Collège de la Marche, where it was expected that he enter into the priesthood.

Later, Calvin continued his studies at the Collège de Montaigu, the same university at which Desiderius Erasmus studied. Calvin's father then changed his mind and thought an education in law might be the way to go for his son. Many historians believe that Gérard's motivation for this change of heart was his own legal troubles at home. John did change his course of studies to law but went back to theology after his father's death.

The need to translate Calvin's name into various languages is a good example of how Calvinism spread throughout the Western World. Each translation establishes him as the leader of a movement in a particular region of the world. For example, although Calvin's name is actually Cauvin, his name was first translated to Latin, "Calvinus," and then later abbreviated to a more English-sounding name, "Calvin."

Educational Reform

Even though he did not choose law as his profession in the end, Calvin's time in law school at the universities of Orléans and Bourges was not lost. He studied the humanities, learned Greek, and devoured the New Testament. After his father's death, Calvin returned to Paris, where he studied the ancient classics and Hebrew.

In the end, Calvin received what many refer to as a "Renaissance education." He learned a lot about almost everything, but especially about the value of the human condition. Unlike Luther, whose spiritual reform came from deep inner self-examination, Calvin's spiritual reform came from his education. Through his studies, he came to the conclusion that the common human being should have a say in religious and political policies that govern his or her life. This should not be up to the church and state without the consent of the populace.

Questioning the Church

Like many students of his time, Calvin's studies led him to question the current practices of the Roman Catholic Church. Sometime after his father's death in 1531, John Calvin experienced his own "enlightenment" (or what he called his "unexpected conversion") that changed his life forever. After Calvin's friend and the rector of the university, Nicholas Cap, made a Protestant address, which caused quite a stir, Calvin was forced to leave Paris. He fled to Basel, Switzerland, where hordes of other Protestants had been going for some time. In 1536, while living in Basel, Calvin wrote one of the most famous and influential Protestant documents of all time: *Institutes of the Christian Religion*.

The *Institutes of the Christian Religion* is an epic work that Calvin revised at least five times during his lifetime. It is one of the most widely read statements on belief, and is still read to this day. It is the foundation of Calvinism.

The *Institutes of the Christian Religion*

In the *Institutes of the Christian Religion,* Calvin stated the basic principles of his reformist beliefs, which were based upon the complete sovereignty of God. According to Calvin, God is perfect and good while human beings are completely sinful. Human beings cannot do anything to be absolved of their sin except seek forgiveness from God through faith in Jesus Christ.

The first step is for a person to acknowledge his or her innate sinfulness, the second step is to have faith, and the third is to spend a lifetime in repentance. Calvin claimed that even then, it is up to God as to whether or not the sinner will be saved. So a Christian, in Calvin's theology, will not know if he or she has attained salvation until death.

Calvin's Reform Principles

In addition to the complete sovereignty of God, Calvin's *Institutes of the Christian Religion* also set forth Calvin's other Christian principles. Some of his ideas jived with those of Luther and Zwingli, but there are a few more radical ideas that set Calvin apart from other Protestant reformers.

Predestination

Calvin and Luther shared the opinion that only God can determine who will or will not be saved. Predestination asserts that after the fall of Adam and Eve, human beings have been stripped of "free will" and are automatically marked for eternal damnation. Luther ascertained that a Christian stands a good chance of salvation through faith: "No one can come to me unless drawn by the Father who sent me; and I will raise that person up on the last day." (John 6:44, NRSV)

"We call predestination God's eternal decree, by which He determined with Himself what He willed to become of each man. For all are not created in equal condition; rather, eternal life is foreordained for some, eternal damnation for others."
—JOHN CALVIN, from *Institutes for Christian Religion*

Free Will

Free will is the opposite of predestination in that it assumes that all human beings are saved automatically by Christ's death on the cross. This is a gift that was bestowed on them by Christ's sacrifice. Human beings can either accept this gift or reject it—free will. Calvin did not believe in free will.

Communion

Calvin rejected the ideas of both transubstantiation (Catholic) and consubstantiation (Lutheran). However, he did believe that the body and blood of Christ are received during the Lord's Supper, but only in a spiritual manner, not in a physical one. The Lord's Supper is how Christ communicates to Christians—a reminder of their faith and acceptance of him. In other words, both Luther and Calvin believed that Christ is present during the sacrament, but the question was—in what manner?

Another issue of contention was whether or not to serve leavened or unleavened bread. When Christ was alive, the bread he shared at the Last Supper would have to have been unleavened, since it was the Judaic season of Passover and leavened bread (with yeast) is symbolic of sin. Unleavened bread, for Christians, became symbolic of Christ's sinlessness, and therefore unleavened bread would be served during communion.

Original Sin

The fall of Adam and Eve (Adam disobeyed God by taking a bite of the forbidden fruit handed to him by Eve) is referred to as the "original sin." Since Adam and Eve were God's first human creations, they were pure and good, and lived in an earthly paradise. But, by disobeying God, they damned all future human beings to a life of sin. Calvin believed that this sin was not erasable by any earthly works, and that God alone would determine who shall be saved in the end. Protestants were sticklers on this point, while Catholics tended to believe that through good works a person would be given salvation.

Church and State

Calvin wanted to see a unity between church and state. Recalling St. Augustine's *City of God*, Calvin claimed he wanted to build a "City of God" in Europe. He wanted to see the church and state working alongside each other to create a better society. Calvin believed that the government should support and protect the church by upholding standards of morality as per the scriptures.

Calvin believed that the scriptures dictate that Christians must obey the lawmakers whether they were corrupt or not. God would judge the corrupt officials in the end. The only time Calvin objected to obeying the law was if the law did not coincide with the law of God.

Calvin and Geneva

In 1536 after completing and publishing the *Institutes of Christian Religion*, John Calvin decided to travel to Strasbourg (a city on the border of France and Germany), where he wanted to lead a quiet life and continue his studies. He had to take a detour, however, because of the war between Emperor Charles V and King Francis I of France.

He decided to stop in Geneva until the coast was clear. Calvin hoped it would only be for one night, but a man named William (or Guillaume) Farel had other plans in mind for him. Calvin's introduction to William Farel not only changed his life, but it changed the life of many Christians as well. In the long run, the Geneva side trip had a profound effect on the future of Protestantism. Calvin was only about twenty-six years old at this point in time.

William Farel

William Farel was another reformer working his beliefs into Geneva society. He started his preaching in homes throughout Geneva and finally took his message to the streets. He became very popular with the people of the city, but not with the lawmakers. When the council members called for his execution in 1533, Farel fled the city but continued his preaching from the outside. He even sent in other reformers to continue preaching Protestant ideas. These Farel-appointed reformers made great strides in Farel's absence, and many in Geneva began to turn from Roman Catholicism. In 1535, the Geneva Council officially converted the city to Protestantism.

Farel and Calvin

The Genevans paid little attention to the council's new rules, and continued to march to their own collective drummer. Farel knew he needed help to institute the changes and began to think John Calvin was just the man. Farel was a tremendous admirer of Calvin and when he heard that Calvin was in Geneva, he set out to find him and convince him to stay. Later in his writings, Calvin said that Farel was a persuasive and fiery individual who did everything to convince him to stay. Calvin refused repeatedly until Farel became desperate and threatened him with the wrath of God. He was so passionate in his threat that he convinced Calvin that he could very well be right, and so Calvin unpacked his bags and stayed in Geneva.

QUESTION?

What were some changes that occurred under Farel?
Under Farel, the Mass was abolished; religious relics were removed from churches; daily sermons were given; the sacraments were given according to the scriptures; and laws were passed banning gambling, dancing, and drunkenness.

Declaring a Strict Moral Code

Although Calvin was a reformer, he was perhaps a reluctant one in some ways. He didn't really want to get into politics and religious reform. He was never very healthy and he longed for peace, quiet, and a place to study. Farel, on the other hand, with his fire and energy, contrasted with Calvin's steady pace. Since Geneva was already on the path to reform with the declaration of Protestantism as the official religion, what Farel wanted was to see the people of Geneva change their sinful ways. Calvin had a strong propensity toward a strict morality as indicated in the scriptures, and Farel needed his knowledge to establish and uphold a moral standard of living for Geneva.

21 Articles

The people of Geneva gambled, partied, swore, and engaged in sexual relations outside of wedlock. They were, what we might call today, rather free-spirited. To Farel and Calvin, however, this was a society of immorality and decay. The only way to even glimpse the slightest chance of salvation was to change their evil ways. Calvin started slowly by preaching from Paul's letters. Eventually, Calvin, with the help of Farel, began to work on the "21 Articles," which indicated the principles of Christian faith, as well as the implications for citizens who did not adhere to those principles. The Geneva Council adopted the articles (also known as *Articles Concerning the Government of the Church*) as the law of the land. The punishment for disobeying these "morality" laws ranged from excommunication to banishment.

Here are just seven of the rules outlined in the articles:

1. Ban on gambling
2. Ban on dancing
3. Ban on singing songs considered "obscene"
4. Ban on drunkenness
5. Ban on cursing
6. Pub hours were shortened and a 9 P.M. curfew enacted
7. Punishment for those who did not attend services regularly

The Libertines

A "free-spirited" people, Christian or otherwise, are not going to take well to being told how to conduct their lives. At first they just ignored the rules, and when law enforcement stepped in, they saw it as invasive. The opposition grew into an organized party called the "Libertines." When they demanded that the council revoke the ridiculous code of conduct, the council banished them from the city. But the Libertines had picked up too much momentum to be silenced, and in 1538, they were elected to the majority of the council. That was the voice of the people of Geneva telling their leadership what they could do with their ideas on morality. The Libertines told Calvin and Farel to stay out of law and stick to the pulpit.

ESSENTIAL

The doctrine of predestination would seem to refute the fact that Christ died on the cross to save humankind. If Christ died on the cross for human salvation, how can human beings be automatically damned? Calvin believed that Christ is "seated at the right hand of the father" helping him make the selection of who deserves salvation and who does not.

An Issue of Bread

Calvin and Farel did not care what kind of bread was used during the Lord's Supper. If it wasn't specifically in the scriptures, it was a nonissue. However, it was a huge issue for the Libertines. As Easter approached in 1538, the Libertines began to wreak havoc in the streets of Geneva over the issue of the bread. They fired guns in the streets and created a general state of chaos.

When Easter Sunday finally arrived, Calvin and Farel stood inside the church refusing to give communion at all. Calvin and Farel told the congregation that communion was a sacrament not to be given to those engaging in immoral conduct. The Libertines did not back down, and the two men barely escaped with their lives.

Forced into Exile

Calvin and Farel were exiled from Geneva that Easter Monday. The Geneva Council could not see any reason to keep them around when all they seemed to do was evoke the wrath of the citizens. Calvin and Farel fled to Basel and then went their separate ways: Calvin finally made it to Strasbourg, whereas Farel continued his preaching in Neuchâtel, in a French-speaking canton of Switzerland.

FACT

Calvin would later refer to his years in Strasbourg as his happiest. In 1540, he married Idelette de Bures, a widow from Belgium with two children of her own. They had a happy marriage with one major tragedy, the birth of a child who lived only a few days. Idelette died nine years after their marriage.

Calvin Returns to Geneva

Calvin returned to Geneva in 1541. The city was in a state of decay, and when the Roman Catholic Church invited Geneva to return to the church, the council was torn. It despised the church, but it craved a return to order. Council members weren't fans of Calvinist thought, either, but the new council consisted of many of Calvin's friends, who thought maybe this time they could make it work.

So, partially out of desperation, the council urged Calvin to return. Calvin had no desire to return to the city from which he had been forced to flee, but he saw an opportunity to implement his ideas, so he went back. However, he agreed to return only if the council enacted his major reform principles. The council approved and Calvin went back. He was only thirty-one years old and already incredibly influential.

Religious Leadership

Four offices were established in Geneva to govern the church. They consisted of pastors, teachers, deacons, and elders. From these offices, the Consistory was formed—a body of government established to enforce Calvin's 21 Articles. The Consistory "consisted" of twelve elders of the council and the ministers. It was their job to keep an eye on immoral conduct. The opposition continued to grow, but so did Calvin's following as more and more persecuted Protestant refugees fled to Geneva.

Big Brother

The Consistory was nothing more than a "Big Brother" system. It spied on those suspected of not adhering to the strict moral code initiated in Calvin's "21 Articles." It questioned children about the conduct of their parents. Citizens were also punished for everything from playing cards, family squabbles, not attending church services, to other behaviors considered Calvinistically immoral.

QUESTION?

What were the punishments for violating the 21 Articles?
More serious crimes, such as adultery, witchcraft, and heresy
were punished by banishment or even death. Fifty-eight
Genevans lost their lives between 1542 and 1546 as a product
of these strict times.

A Safe Haven for Reformers

With persecution of the Protestants running rampant across Europe,
including the slaughter of 10,000 Anabaptists, many Protestant refugees
sought shelter in Geneva, which had come to be seen as the European
safe haven for Protestants. Throughout this time, Geneva was seen as the
standard-bearer of perfect Christian living.

However, that didn't mean everyone was safe. Calvin saw that the city
was growing with refugees from all over Europe and took pride in the fact
that the city had become renowned as a center of Christian truth. Given the
influx of "believers," Calvin developed the city into a center of ministerial
training and eager students from all over Europe (including John Knox,
whom you will read about later) came to live in the one place considered
the nirvana of apostolic truth. Calvin knew that when these students went
home, they would take the "truth" with them, and he was right.

The Growth of Calvinism

Calvin spent the rest of his life working for the citizens of Geneva. He
preached seven days a week, every other week. He tended to the sick and
the poor. He opened hospitals and supported the improvement of the
infrastructure of the city. He supported the growth of industry as a way to
make money, and taught that hard work was an important virtue—and
should the hard work be rewarded with a successful business, that was a
gift from God. Many scholars attribute the philosophy of capitalism to
Calvin's promotion of commerce.

Calvin died in Geneva in 1564. He had battled long-term illnesses his entire life and it's remarkable that he lived as long as he did. He is buried in an unmarked grave in Geneva.

Calvinism is interesting in that its spread across the Western World morphed into many different forms. Calvinist philosophy spread to France, The Netherlands, England, and eventually to the New World (the Americas).

The French Calvinists became known as the Huguenots; the Dutch Calvinists became known as the Dutch Arminians; and in England they were known as the Puritans. The Puritans were among the first Europeans to set foot on American soil, and they would carry Calvinist thought with them. Basically, Calvinism became known as a strict adherence to a moral code of ethics.

Chapter 15

Presbyterianism

Calvinism spread from Switzerland to Germany, to The Netherlands, then on to Scotland and England. The Catholics spent more time trying to combat Protestantism than they did on their own church leadership, but they soon learned that they were in a no-win situation on the Protestant front.

The Scottish Reform Movement

To avoid persecution, the Protestants fled to Geneva and then headed for the even more distant shores of England and Scotland. Ironically, by trying to halt reformist ideas, the Catholic Church actually spread the "heresy" far and wide. With the aid of Patrick Hamilton, George Wishart, and John Knox, in the middle of the sixteenth century, the roots of Calvinism took hold in Scotland.

Early Scottish Reform Efforts

The Protestants, however, were not the first reformers to land on Scotland's shores. In the fifteenth century, the Lollards (the followers of John Wyclif) attempted to escape persecution in England by crossing the border to Scotland. However, on the other side they faced arrest and execution at the hands of Scottish authorities.

FACT

Paul Crawan, a Bohemian Hussite and a follower of John Hus, landed in Scotland after traveling the world and learning reformist ideas. He was summoned to St. Andrews (the seat of the Catholic Church in Scotland), where he was found guilty of heresy because he practiced Lutheranism. In 1528, at the age of twenty-five, he was burned at the stake.

Perhaps the new era of reformers thought they stood a better chance, and they weren't entirely wrong. But like any of the reform efforts before them, they faced a long road ahead.

George Wishart

While serving the church, John Knox, the man who became known as the forerunner of the Scottish Reformation and the founder of Presbyterianism, came in contact with reformer George Wishart who, although influenced by Zwingli, had actually studied with Martin Luther. Wishart, a Scot, had to flee to England to escape being arrested for heresy. However, he later returned to Scotland and continued his reformist teaching. Knox was so impressed with Wishart that he was said to have been his bodyguard—and Wishart certainly needed that kind of protection as he began preaching against Roman Catholicism.

Under Arrest

Persecution of heretics was still taking place in Scotland (1527–1558) and the pope was getting word of Wishart's activities. Wishart knew that the authorities would eventually get the better of him, but that didn't stop him from preaching. He was arrested while preaching in a small village in Scotland. Knox was with him at the time and wanted the authorities to take him along with his friend, but Wishart told him to go home and spare himself. George Wishart was taken to St. Andrews and was burned as a heretic in 1546.

Revenge

John Knox was not Wishhart's only friend. He had a large following who wanted to avenge his death and while they were at it, end the rule of the Catholic rulers. Wishart's death and the actions taken by his followers signified the beginning of the Scottish Reformation. Just three months after his execution, sixteen of his followers stormed Cardinal Beaton's castle in St. Andrews, murdered him, and hung his body on the castle wall.

The place where George Wishart died is marked by the letters "GW" in cobblestones outside the castle, and commemorated by a plaque. He is also recorded on the Martyr's Monument at St. Andrews, and in a painting by John Drummond entitled "George Wishart on his way to Execution Administering the Sacrament for the First Time in Scotland after the Protestant Reform."

John Knox

The death of Patrick Hamilton and then of his friend, George Wishart, had a tremendous influence on John Knox. Very little is known about

Knox's early life, not even the year of his birth. Some say he was born in 1505, while others seem to feel it may have been as many as ten years later. He may have been about sixteen years old when he attended Glasgow University. In 1530, he became a Catholic priest.

Dangerous Friendship

Knox became close to Wishart, and as a result his life was in danger. Friends encouraged him to seek refuge in St. Andrews Castle, where many other reformers were hiding, but the refuge did not last. The Catholic Scots joined forces with the French and took St. Andrews. When Knox and his reformist friends tried to escape, they were seized and sentenced to hard labor aboard French ships. Knox was a slave to the French for two years before King Edward VI of England (and a Protestant) intervened. In 1549, Knox was freed in a French and English/Scottish prisoner exchange.

Knox in England

Once freed from French captivity, Knox went to England, where he preached against Roman Catholicism for several years. Knox was later appointed as one of the chaplains in the court of the king. During this time, he met and married a young woman named Marjorie Bowes.

QUESTION?

What were Knox's views on women?
Knox and Calvin were both known for being outspoken misogynists. They both claimed that women had a purpose in society as wives and mothers, and their roles should not extend any further. To both Calvin and Knox, the existence of a queen as the ruling monarch could only be the result of God's wrath.

Marjorie Bowes was the daughter of Richard and Elizabeth Bowes. Richard Bowes was the captain of Norham Castle in England and raised Elizabeth as a devout Catholic. However, Elizabeth became disillusioned by church corruption and converted to Protestantism. The one Protestant issue she struggled with, however, was the doctrine of predestination and she turned to Knox for help. They began to correspond by letters and developed a friendship. Elizabeth wanted Knox to marry her daughter, but Richard Bowes was against it. However, Knox married Marjorie despite her father's disapproval.

Bloody Mary

Mary Tudor (Mary I, or "Bloody Mary") was the daughter of Henry VIII and his first wife, Catherine of Aragon. Born in 1516, she was raised a strict Catholic and suffered from ill health her whole life. Mary was constantly under pressure to turn from the Catholic Church to the Protestant faith. She married Philip II of Spain in 1555 and they never had a child. When Mary took over the throne after her brother Edward VI's death, her first mission was to repeal Protestantism as the religion of the land and reinstate Catholicism.

As long as Mary reigned over England, Knox knew his life could be in danger if he remained in England. He then made the decision to flee to France, the very same nation that had imprisoned him just a few years before.

Mary's bloody years lasted through the last four years of her reign until her death in 1558, but when she first became queen, she seemed willing to compromise. She allowed Edward to be buried in Westminster Abbey in a Protestant ceremony, but behind the scenes she was holding consultations with the pope to try to reinstate Catholicism as the official religion of England.

Mary wanted to institute the changes gradually, but pressure from Rome forced her to take more drastic measures. Parliament reinstated the act that allowed the burning of heretics and the stakes were set alight once again in 1555. It is believed that Mary became paranoid as she realized that there were more devoted Protestants than she thought. Conversion back to a church that many believed to be corrupt would not be an easy task. The burnings didn't help her cause, either. In fact the "heretics" were seen as martyrs and this only caused more support for Protestantism.

Mary's nickname, "Bloody Mary," became commonly used by seventeenth-century Protestants. But Mary was not the only monarch to burn the "heretics." Her father, Henry VIII, had done the same before he changed the official religion of England to Anglicanism. What Mary did that horrified the masses, however, was burn the heretics without offering the chance to recant. Under her reign, 300 Protestants were burned at the stake.

Knox Goes into Hiding

Many of the Protestants, including John Knox, fled England and Scotland while they had the chance. Mary did nothing to stop them because she was happy to see them go. However, she did dispatch spies to keep track of their movements and activities abroad—another sign of her paranoia.

But her fears were not entirely neurotic or unfounded because, as we have learned from history so far, the message of the heretics was no longer contained within a nation's borders. With the freedom of movement and the invention of the printing press, there was no way to stop the spread of other ideas. When Knox was exiled, he unleashed his wrath on Mary by publishing documents and letters condemning her reign.

The Attack on Mary

Knox did not stop in France, however. He decided to move on to Geneva to consult the eminent Protestant John Calvin, the man whose opinions he shared. Even though he hated the idea of a queen, Calvin did not advise disobedience. He believed that the scriptures upheld the idea of obedience to government authority. Disappointed with Calvin's advice, Knox traveled on to find other Swiss Protestant authorities. Finally, while back in France, he began to publish pamphlets advocating rebellion against Mary I. His pamphlets made their way to England and were certainly not lost on the queen.

Book of Common Prayer

At the urging of John Calvin, Knox went to preach for an English Protestant community in Frankfurt, Germany. But while there, he found himself in the middle of an academic battle regarding the use of the *Book of Common Prayer*. Knox believed in the scriptures as the only reference for Christian faith. The English Protestants were in favor of the *Book of Common Prayer*, while many other Protestants were of the same thinking as Knox, Calvin, and Luther: If it's not the Bible, it's not Christian. Knox got tired of the dispute and returned to Geneva—familiar religious turf.

The *Book of Common Prayer* is a collection of ancient and "modern" prayers used to this day by English Protestants (Anglicans in England and Episcopalians in America). The book contains portions of both Old and New Testaments and is meant to be a prayer reference for a congregation.

Back to Scotland

The Scottish reform movement was floundering without leadership, and the reformists called for Knox to return to Scotland to help. Knox had his reservations, but Elizabeth Bowes talked him into going back in 1555.

Here are some of the issues Knox tackled upon his return to Scotland:

- The Catholic tradition of fasting during Lent should be eliminated.
- Church tithes should be banned (since Knox believed the money wasn't going to the poor).
- The word "Mass" should not exist, and services should be referred to as "Communion" or "The Lord's Supper."
- The doctrine of transubstantiation should be banned (since Knox did not believe in it).
- Religious images, relics, music, and colorful, clerical robes should be eliminated.

The argument on these issues became heated, and the Scottish monarchy became nervous that if tempers were unleashed, civil war would be inevitable. So, Mary de Guise, queen regent for her young daughter (later to be known as Mary, Queen of Scots) and a devout Catholic, protected Knox from persecution. Knox saw this as an opportunity to convince the queen regent of the evils of Catholicism. However, all he managed to do was make her angry, and so he was forced to flee to France and then on to Switzerland in 1556. He sent Elizabeth and Marjorie ahead of him.

In 1559, Knox once again returned to Scotland, where the Catholic and Protestant disagreements were leading the country to the brink of civil war. Knox did not do anything to calm the waters, either. Instead, he launched his attacks on the Catholic Church, which included preaching against the Mass, equating it with idolatry (the worship of icons and relics).

FACT

John Knox wrote an article on the evils of female monarchs entitled *The First Blast of the Trumpet Against the Monstrous Regiment of Women.* It was aimed at Mary, but it did not slip past Queen Elizabeth I of England (Mary's half-sister and another daughter of Henry VIII), who was well aware of Knox's feelings toward women.

Civil War

Legend has it that the civil war in Scotland began with a little boy who threw a rock during a Mass and broke a church relic. The onslaught to follow the event led to the destruction of church property throughout the country. Churches were looted, monasteries destroyed, and religious images, statues, and relics vandalized.

Knox may not have approved of these acts, but nor did he do anything to stop the chaos. The French were still in the region, at the request of the Scottish Catholic monarchy, to help the Scots stamp out the Protestants. The Scots not only wanted freedom from Rome, but freedom from the French, so they looked to an unlikely source—England.

An Unlikely Alliance

Queen Elizabeth I gave Scotland the support it needed, but her motives were not unselfish. By teaming with the Scottish, she had a better chance of beating the French off British soil, so the Treaty of Berwick, between England and Scotland, was signed in 1560.

A second treaty was signed in 1560, after the death of Mary de Guise. It was the Treaty of Edinburgh, which called for the withdrawal of French troops from Scotland; the ban of any Frenchman from holding political office in Scotland; and the upholding of Scotland's future as a Protestant nation.

John Knox used this opportunity to implement some lasting changes in Scotland and prepared the *Scottish Confession of Faith* (not unlike Luther's Confession of Augsburg). Knox got help in putting together this twenty-five-chapter document from John Winram, John Douglas, John Row, John Willock, and John Spottiswoode. This group is known as "the Congregation," and its aim with the *Confession* was to put forth the goals of the Scottish Reformation and set the foundation for lasting change. Scottish Protestantism had arrived.

The *Confession* dealt with many issues, including the doctrine of the Bible, the character and structure of the church, and the definition of the only two sacraments.

The goals of the *Confession* were to abolish Roman Catholic doctrine that was not supported by the scriptures; restore methods of worship according to the Book of Acts; support the poor; promote education; and provide revenue for the Protestant clergy.

The Birth of Presbyterianism

When Knox and the Congregation presented the *Confession*, they gave the Scottish people the right to criticize the outline for faith. If the people found the document to be flawed, their complaints would be reviewed. This inclusion of the people in decision-making was one of the earliest signs of an organized religion we now know as Presbyterianism.

Calvin was the first to set the tone of Presbyterianism, and Knox was the one to lay the foundation. But the stones were not set until the *Westminster Confession of Faith*, which was presented in 1647—a more comprehensive version of Knox's Confession.

FACT

Presbyterianism is the governance of worship and faith by assemblies referred to as "presbyteries." You remember reading about the early church leaders called "presbyters" or "elders?" Scottish reform attempted to adhere to this old system with the election of church leaders—groups of church leaders from various regions upholding church doctrine on behalf of their congregations.

Discipline and Order

The Church of Scotland had always been referred to as the "Auld Kirk" which, in Scottish, meant the "Old Church." Knox, however, set forth to create the new Church of Scotland that he would simply refer to as the "Kirk." Ironically, the original plan for Scotland was to return to the early church method of electing church leaders, which is indicated in the New Testament, but it actually evolved into something very different—out with the old, and in with the new, seemed to be the inevitable outcome of what was to follow.

Knox outlined his goals for the church in 1560 with the publication of *The First Book of Discipline.* The purpose of the book was to establish organization and to understand the Protestant Reformation in Scotland. While parliament never approved the document, it was commonly accepted within the presbyteries.

The First Book of Discipline dealt with the following topics:

- The act of the sacrament of baptism as a public event.
- The celebration of communion (four times a year).
- The recognition of five church offices consisting of a minister, an elder, a deacon, a layperson, and a superintendent.
- The election and approval of ministers (elected by the congregation of ministers, but approved by the church congregation—the public).

Book of the Common Order

All this was new to the Scottish populace, and it needed leadership. Without guidance and structure, everything the Scottish reformers had toiled for could fall apart. So, with the help of his colleagues, Knox drew up an instruction guide for the understanding of this new form of Scottish worship. He called it the *Book of the Common Order.*

The Scottish government approved the *Book of the Common Order* in 1564, and the book came to be seen as the structure of the Presbyterian Church for generations to come. It outlined the Protestant practices of performing religious ceremonies, like marriage and funerals; instruction on the election of church officials, and the discipline and behavior of the congregation and its ministers.

Presbyterianism in a Nutshell

Presbyterianism is a system of faith that is similar to a democratic government. The power is in the hands of its people, providing a balance between clergy and laity. Protestants sought to bring Christianity back to the people, where they felt it rightfully belonged.

In Presbyterianism, the people have the power of electing officials and they turn the guidance to their church representatives, who have a responsibility to uphold the needs and desires of their electorate. There is even a larger checks-and-balances system within the Presbyterian structure. In an effort to stay true to the course of their faith and to create unity within the religion, each presbytery belonged (and belongs to this day) to a synod (a larger general assembly of church leaders).

The Return of a Queen

With Mary de Guise off the throne, Knox and his followers had time to iron out plans for Scottish reform, but the reprieve saw a ripple—Mary's daughter was on her way home. Mary, Queen of Scots was returning to her homeland and brought Knox to trial for denouncing both her mother and herself.

Mary was a Catholic, like her mother, but she did not really have an interest in returning Scotland to its Catholic roots. She had her eye on bigger things—like the English throne. But she did want to silence the arrogant leader of the Scottish reform movement. Mary reportedly laughed at Knox all the way into the courtroom, saying, "That man once made me weep . . . I'll see if I can make him weep." Nevertheless, the Scottish nobility unanimously acquitted Knox. That, however, was only the beginning of Mary's worries. Setting her sights on the English throne would be her ultimate downfall. Ⓔ

Chapter 16

Reformation in England

The English Reformation was one of the most political reforms and a source of never-ending documentation in plays, books, and movies. Henry VIII and the drama over his six marriages and the succession of the English throne, were the elements that made for this dramatic period. The English experience was not so much an issue of faith as it was of self-interest, political motivation, and the lust of a king.

The English Experience

The translation of the scriptures into native languages was obviously a very powerful piece of the Reformation picture. The pre-reformers wanted to see this happen to enhance Christians' personal relationship with God—one that bypassed clerical mediation. As more and more Christians were being educated in the cathedral schools, this became a more likely possibility with the growth of literacy and, of course, the invention of the printing press.

But it was rather a scary prospect for Catholic leaders. For centuries they had had almost complete control over what Christians believed, because many were not able to read the scriptures. In other words, church leadership had a great deal of control over a person's faith. Over the centuries, the church was witnessing its own deterioration with the Protestant Reformation and knew that one of the key dangers was Bible translation.

William Tyndale

While Luther, Zwingli, and Knox were taking charge of reforming their native lands, William Tyndale was a reformer in England. What Tyndale wanted, and accomplished—the translation of the scriptures into English—was what many reformers before him had wanted in their own nations and languages. Tyndale was a firm believer that every English subject should be able to read the Bible. But Bible translation in England was still illegal at that time. So Tyndale picked up where Wyclif had left off. Wyclif managed to translate portions of the Vulgate into English, with his Lollard followers finishing the rest, but there were inaccuracies in this version. What Tyndale wanted to give the people of England was one solid, complete, reliable translation.

In 1526, Tyndale's New Testament was the first ever printed in English. In the 1530s, he also translated the first fourteen books of the Old Testament. He thus became the first man to translate anything from Hebrew into English—as Hebrew was virtually unknown in England at that time.

The Church's Point of View

The Catholic Church thought there was no reason to translate the scriptures into any other languages. St. Jerome's Vulgate was the church's main source of scripture and that was good enough for the Catholic leadership. The church believed it should be the only voice of the scriptures because, after all, the Bible in the hands of common people would just cause chaos. The Catholic Church didn't believe the average person would be able to understand it anyway, and that the translation would just lead to misinterpretation and confusion.

The church also faced a crisis and it couldn't afford to lose any more control than it already had. It is clear that there is power in knowledge and if the common persons could access the scriptures, they would be able to interpret them for themselves and draw their own conclusions. If the church remained the sole voice of the scriptures, then it had the ultimate control over the faith of the Christian commoner. However, English church leaders were not able to stop an English version, and the Bible was popping up in various languages all over Europe. Tyndale had to be silenced.

"There is no work better than another to please God; to pour water, to wash dishes, to be a cobbler . . . or an apostle, all are one; to wash dishes and to preach are all one, as touching the deed, to please God."
—WILLIAM TYNDALE, *A Parable of the Wicked Mammon* (1527)

Seeking Approval

Tyndale, an ordained priest educated at both Oxford and Cambridge universities (England's most prestigious universities to this day), really didn't have any desire to break the law. He wanted the law on his side, so in 1523 he sought the approval of the Bishop of London, Cuthbert Tunstall. Tyndale knew that Tunstall was a scholar himself, and more significantly, a friend of humanist Desiderius Erasmus (another supporter of Bible translation). Tyndale thought that if he could get the bishop's approval, the bishop could help him get permission from Rome. What Tyndale did not anticipate, however, was that Tunstall, as a newly appointed bishop, was not likely to want to make waves with Rome. Needless to say, Tyndale did not get any support for his project and left the meeting with his tail between his legs.

Exile

While in London, Tyndale befriended a wealthy merchant named Humphrey Monmouth, who agreed to finance Tyndale's translation and allowed him to work out of his house. Word of Tyndale's work spread through London, and the Catholic Church leaders wanted him stopped.

Monmouth was not powerful enough to pull Tyndale out of this mess, so with the help of other merchants and Protestant sympathizers, Tyndale left England for Germany. He wasn't necessarily much safer in Germany because England had spies all over the reformist nations where English subjects were seeking refuge from religious persecution.

Spreading the English Word

Tyndale completed his work and made arrangements for his Bible translation to be secretly printed in Cologne, Germany. The printing process was underway when word of the project got out. A powerful antireformist named Johannes Dobneck (or simply Cochlaeus) planned a raid to stop the so-called heretical print job. However, Tyndale had enough supporters and was tipped off to the raid. He took the existing printed copies and fled to Worms, where he was able to complete and publish his version of the New Testament in English.

Tyndale arranged to have his Bible smuggled into England in large quantities. Church officials tried to stop any future smuggling operations, but it was too late. The English Bible was everywhere.

Smuggle That Book!

Tyndale had many supportive friends in England. He certainly had the reformers behind him and even though England was a Catholic country at the time, there were enough reform rumblings going on to make a difference.

The Archbishop of Canterbury was on a mission to stop the distribution of the English translation within the country, so he approached a merchant and offered to purchase all his copies of the Bible. The merchant took the archbishop up on his offer. In fact, the merchant told him that he'd be happy to buy as many Bibles as he could get his hands on and sell them to the archbishop to destroy at his leisure. The archbishop thanked him profusely for his assistance. What the archbishop did not know was that the merchant was a friend of Tyndale and used every penny of the money to finance the printing of more Bibles. If he was caught, he knew he could say that the Archbishop of Canterbury helped finance the printings.

E

FACT

While it would seem like any good humanist would be pro-reform, Johannes Dobneck was not. He wrote under the name Cochlaeus, which is how he is most commonly known. He wrote pamphlets against Luther, Melanchthon, and Zwingli. He was not as literate as the reformers, however, and his pamphlets reflected this in addition to his bitter temperament.

Even though many of the Bibles were burned, so many had been printed that the church had to concede that to try to stop distribution was pointless. Finally, the Christians of the English-speaking world could now read the scriptures for themselves and develop personal faith extending beyond the voices of the church.

Tynsdale's Death

Despite the fact that Tyndale had friends in England and Germany, in the end he was betrayed by someone he thought was a friend. Tyndale longed to leave Germany and go home to England, but it was too big of a risk. Even living in Germany, he had to remain in hiding to avoid the English spies. A man named Henry Phillips befriended Tyndale, but little did Tyndale know that this man was no friend. Phillips turned Tyndale in to the authorities and he was imprisoned in Brussels. Tyndale was executed in 1536 and his last words were rumored to be "Lord, open the eyes of the King of England."

William Tyndale may be known as the "Father of the English Bible," but it was Miles Coverdale (1488–1569) who actually completed the English translation in 1535. Coverdale was a Catholic, but was also one of the earliest supporters of the English Reformation. In 1539, King Henry VIII ordered that every parish in England must make a copy of the Bible available to all parishioners.

The Legacy

Before his death, Tyndale was working on an English translation of the Old Testament as well. He was able to translate the first five books: Genesis, Exodus, Leviticus, Numbers, and Deuteronomy. His New Testament translation was not actually a complete translation but one that would work for the everyday use of the common person. He dreamed of completing the New Testament, but died before he got that chance. Tyndale's translation was considered so faithful to the original text that almost all of his work is in the *King James Bible*, which was first published in 1611. This version is still used by the Church of England today.

Henry VIII

While most people dabbling in history may think that the English Reformation began with Henry VIII (1509–1547) and the second of his six wives, Anne Boleyn, they are only partially correct. He was certainly the catalyst to launch England into "reform," but in fact, there had been reformers speaking out all over the nation for quite some time. While most of them were burned, including Wyclif and Tyndale, the movement existed everywhere.

It's a little tricky to get your head around all the wives and maneuverings of Henry VIII, but it makes a lot of sense as to why Henry wanted to take control. To put things in perspective, here is a list of Henry VIII's wives:

1. **Catherine of Aragon (1485–1536):** She was the daughter of King Ferdinand and Queen Isabella of Spain and was married to Henry VIII from 1509–1533.
2. **Anne Boleyn (1500–1536):** She was a lady in waiting to Catherine of Aragon; she married Henry in 1533 and bore him one child—a daughter who became Queen Elizabeth I; after a miscarriage of a son, Henry accused her of adultery and incest; she was then put on trial and beheaded.
3. **Jane Seymour (1509–1537):** Henry married Jane just twenty-four hours after Anne Boleyn's execution; she was the only wife to be buried in his tomb and was the mother of Henry's long-awaited son, Edward VI.
4. **Anne of Cleves (1515–1557):** Anne of Cleves was Henry's political marriage—an attempt to gain a political alliance with Germany and other Protestant countries; the marriage was a disaster and was annulled just six months after it began.
5. **Kathryn Howard (1521–1542):** She was the first cousin of Anne Boleyn; Henry married her in 1540, and then executed her after learning she was cheating on him; she was buried next to Anne Boleyn.
6. **Katherine Parr (1512–1548):** Katherine Parr married Henry in 1543; she bore him no children, but was a positive influence as stepmother to his children; she was accused of associating with Protestant heretics, but before Henry could even think about another beheading, he died, and Katherine was safe.

FACT

Henry VIII had personal motives for wanting church reformation. The reason why Henry VIII needed to break away from the pope wasn't about religion, but rather about church laws and how they affected both his monarchy and his love life.

Desperate for an Heir

Catherine of Aragon, the widow of Henry's deceased brother Arthur, was Henry's first wife. The marriage lasted eighteen years, and in that time Catherine gave birth to five children. However, only one of the children lived into adulthood: Mary, also known as "Bloody Mary." When Catherine turned forty, Henry became concerned that he would never have a male heir to the throne.

A king wanted to hand his rule on to his male prodigy so that his lineage and name would be continued into the next generations. This was a way for the king to carry on his own reign, giving him a false sense of immortality.

Turning to Rome

Without a son, Henry's masculinity and immortality were up in the air, so he turned to the Catholic Church to be granted an annulment from Catherine—basically saying that the marriage never existed. But it wasn't that easy. Henry had fought the church to marry Catherine in the first place because she had been married previously to his brother, Arthur.

According to the Catholic Church, it was considered incest to marry your brother's wife. The church excused this rule and let Henry marry Catherine. If the church agreed that this same marriage never existed, it would be an embarrassment, since it had repealed another church law validating it. To say the marriage was now null and void would be admitting it had made a mistake with its first decision. To make matters worse for Henry, Pope Clement VII was not going to ask Emperor Charles V to nullify this particular marriage because the Emperor was Catherine of Aragon's nephew. There was no way that he was going to let this insult happen to his aunt, so Clement was not going to push the matter.

Thomas Cranmer

Things did not look good for Anne and Henry. Henry was in love and wanted to marry her—especially after she became pregnant in 1532. His hopes were high that the child would be a boy and his heir. Therefore, he had to find a quick answer to this whole marriage problem, because an illegitimate child (born out of wedlock) could not legally take the crown. In March of 1533, Henry secretly married Anne. The one problem was that he was still married to Catherine.

FACT

Henry VIII had once enjoyed a good relationship with the papacy and considered himself a defender of the Catholic faith. That's exactly what the pope thought, too, and gave Henry the special title of "Defender of the Faith." The English monarch still holds that title today. This favor was bestowed upon Henry after he offered a counterattack on Luther's rejection of the seven sacraments.

And that's where Thomas Cranmer (1489–1556) came into the picture. Thomas Cranmer was a friend of Anne Boleyn and put the idea into Henry's head that he didn't need Rome to get his annulment. There was another way.

Henry appointed Cranmer to the position of Archbishop of Canterbury. As an archbishop, Cranmer annulled the marriage himself, without the go-ahead from Rome. He also declared the marriage of Henry and Anne to be valid despite the fact that Henry married her before he was divorced.

Rome was enraged and threatened Henry with excommunication if he took this false marriage any further. However, Henry had no qualms about it and had his new wife crowned as queen. He took it even further than that by having the Act of Supremacy passed in parliament, declaring the King of England as head of the English Church. With this major slap in the face to Rome, the Protestant Reformation in England took center stage.

Controversy and Upheaval

It doesn't really sound like much of a reformation, now does it? This is not the shape that other reform movements had taken over the years. This was about a man and his desire. Then it became about the pride of a king. In fact, what Henry had was a major temper tantrum that shook the entire kingdom.

Had there really been any reform? Yes, in a different way and not like we've seen so far in other parts of Europe. Henry VIII had declared himself supreme ruler of the church, which then merged the church and state in England. But the people of England were still Catholic and loyal to Rome. Many wanted to see church reform, but they didn't want to break away from the church altogether. As a result, Henry confiscated land from those who remained loyal to the Roman Catholic Church, and violence soon wracked the region. If anyone rejected Henry's "reforms," they were accused of treason and executed. And Henry was not picky: He executed friends, noblemen, and bishops—you weren't safe whoever you were.

The story of Lord Chancellor Thomas More (1478–1525) has taken on legendary proportions since his execution in 1525. A martyr and now a saint, More, as a pious Catholic, did not approve of Henry's marriage to Anne. After refusing to swear an oath accepting the marriage, Henry executed him. The stage-play and the 1966 movie *A Man for All Seasons* tells this sad and dramatic tale.

Reform or Control?

Henry wanted the church to stay Catholic, but wanted the laws to be in his hands, not in the hands of Rome. He learned his lesson when he couldn't get what he wanted for himself because of papal control. His goal was to establish the Church of England versus the Church of Rome. The religion would not be changed, however.

Henry upheld the principles of the Catholic faith by instituting his "Six Articles." The articles insisted on the continuation of certain Catholic practices such as clerical celibacy, confession, and private Mass. The only two real differences regarding issues of faith had to do with the closing of the monasteries and the installation of the English version of the Bible in every church.

One of the reasons Henry closed the monasteries was to get their money and replenish the funds of his monarchy. He also managed to get on the good side of some of the nobles, whom he offered the chance to purchase these valuable pieces of property. What happened to the monks? Initially, when Henry shut down some of the smaller monasteries, he offered the monks the chance to go to another monastery or go back into their communities. Surprisingly, most of them chose the latter.

QUESTION?

What happened to Anne Boleyn?
Henry's devotion to Anne was short-lived. He grew concerned that he had been cursed by the Catholic Church for his insistence on marrying Catherine, and then on an annulment. What Henry didn't realize was that his wife had just given birth to one of England's greatest and most powerful monarchs, Queen Elizabeth I. Later, Anne was beheaded on charges of adultery and incest.

King Edward VI

It is said, in hindsight, that Jane Seymour was Henry's greatest love, perhaps because she was the one to finally bear him the son he so desperately wanted. However, Henry died when Edward (1547–1553) was just ten years old. Since he was too young to rule England, a group of advisors was appointed to rule in his stead.

As a baby, Edward was betrothed to Mary, Queen of Scots. It seemed like a good way to merge the two nations, but the marriage never took place due to a rift in relations between England and Scotland. Edward, however, would never have seen his wedding day anyway, because he died when he was just sixteen. As it turns out, the advisors raising the young boy—and, in essence, running the country—were Protestant sympathizers and England was heading toward a new era of reform. Here are some of the steps taken to change the Church of England to Protestantism:

- Henry's *Six Articles* were repealed.
- Cranmer's *Book of Common Prayer* replaced the Latin service.
- Cranmer defined the new faith of the Church of England along Protestant lines with his *Forty-two Articles*.

Mary I

You read a great deal about Mary in the previous chapter, so there's no need to go into great detail about her here. Edward VI's life was very short, as was this brief period of Protestant reform. Cranmer was executed and Mary reinstated Catholicism as the law of the land. Mary may have been the most pious English monarch, but she made a lot of enemies. With the reinstatement of Catholicism, England saw a return to the governance of Rome, and that did not please a country that was happy to be free of Rome's corruption. When Mary married Philip II of Spain, that was the straw that broke the camel's back for the English subjects. They saw her as a great betrayer of her kingdom. Mary led an unhappy life and died an unhappy monarch.

FACT

As you know, several books and movies have been written and made based on this era of history, and here's just one example: Mark Twain's 1881 novel *The Prince and the Pauper* is a fictitious tale of two boys who discover they look exactly alike: one is Prince Edward of England and the other is a poor boy from the streets of London. They decide to change places to experience the other's life.

Elizabeth I

After the death of Mary, Anne Boleyn's daughter, Elizabeth (1558–1603), became Queen of England. She had quite a task ahead of her in order to get the religious state of England under control. Given the back-and-forth from Catholic to English-reform to Protestant and then back to Catholic, Elizabeth was going to have to think on her feet and find some kind of compromise. England's church was still under the supreme head of the English monarchy, but Elizabeth chose to tone it down a little. She changed her title from "Supreme Head" of the church to "Supreme Governor." It sounded a little more modest and perhaps her humility gave her efforts more weight amongst her subjects.

Enter the Puritans

Elizabeth established the Anglican Church (or Church of England) by enacting her "39 Articles." Although her reform smacked of Protestantism, she worded her changes in her articles in such a way as to not offend either group: Protestant or Catholic. The articles upheld only two sacraments: baptism and the Holy Eucharist. The liturgy (or public worship) remained the same as that of the Catholic Church, as did church leadership.

Elizabeth was later heralded for her brilliant reform efforts, which were made subtly and peacefully. Some of the returning exiles were not so happy, however. They saw Elizabeth's reforms as a lame effort and not strict enough. These former exiles later became known as the "Puritans." They saw themselves as the preachers of righteousness. They were amongst the first settlers to step foot on American soil. Their strict adherence to their faith still has an impact on the United States today. Ⓔ

Chapter 17

(E) **The Church of England**

The Reformation had found its way across the English Channel and the changes that took place soon affected the New World (the Americas). But there were still more changes to face and decisions to make about the future of English faith. The English weren't the only ones focused on change—the Catholic Church knew that if it didn't clean up its act, its days could be numbered.

Mary, Queen of Scots

Mary, Queen of Scots (1542–1587) was first a princess of Scotland, then queen of France, and finally queen of Scotland. She was related to the Tudor family (the English monarchs) by marriage, making her a first cousin of Elizabeth. She was considered a threat to the English monarchy first as queen of France and then as queen of Scotland. Because of her family tie to the English monarchy, Elizabeth feared that as Queen of France, the French could try to take over the English throne.

When Mary returned to Scotland after the death of her husband, Elizabeth offered her a new spouse: Robert Dudley, a nobleman with little power or influence. If Mary married this nobleman, Elizabeth could be a little more assured that Mary would not attempt a coup upon the English throne.

Marriage Complications

It is believed that Robert Dudley was Elizabeth's ex-lover, so it was a big scandal when Elizabeth tried to match him with her cousin. Even though she raised his status to Earl of Leicester—to make the marriage more appealing to both Mary and Dudley—Dudley felt he had been made a laughingstock. Elizabeth believed that due to his affection for her, Dudley would never be a threat to the throne as Mary's husband. Dudley was hurt. Mary was insulted. And in the end Elizabeth did not have it her way. Instead, Mary married Lord Henry Darnley, her English Catholic cousin, who also had a claim to the English throne. Elizabeth was furious.

Since Elizabeth had no intention of marrying, and, therefore, of producing an heir to the English throne, she had to be very wary of claimants to the title. If Mary had married Dudley, Elizabeth would have recognized her as the rightful heir to the English throne after her death. It was while she was alive that she was fearful of Mary.

Mary's marriage to Lord Darnley was not a happy one, but they did manage to produce a son in 1564, who later became King James VI of Scotland and King James I of England.

Mary's Abdication and Execution

Mary was forced to abdicate the throne of Scotland and was arrested for plotting to kill her husband. Her supporters freed her and she fled to England. Her baby son became king of Scotland, and James Stewart, Mary's half-brother, was regent. Elizabeth was concerned that Mary's presence could cause a Catholic uprising, and after all the work she had done to stabilize the Church of England, she couldn't afford to see this happen.

Mary was "imprisoned" in the home of the Earl of Shrewsbury and watched carefully for the next twenty years. Rumors of plots to put Mary on the throne of England were present on and off during the time she was in England. Elizabeth's advisors urged her to execute her cousin, but she refused, believing one monarch does not murder another. In 1587, after Elizabeth received word that Mary was most certainly involved in one of these plots, she reluctantly agreed to execute her cousin.

Elizabeth I and Rome

It is understandable that the pope was not happy with Elizabeth on the throne of England. In an effort to punish Elizabeth for leading England away from Rome yet again, Pope Pius V attempted to excommunicate her and remove her from the throne. This failed, however, because the English subjects did not accept it. Pope Gregory XIII allowed anyone to get rid of Elizabeth if they so chose, and between 1581 and 1584 several attempts were made on her life. In another attempt to thwart the queen, the Catholic Church also set up schools with the intention of educating Catholics as missionaries to England.

FACT

Mary, Queen of Scots was executed at Fotheringhay Castle in Northamptonshire on February 8, 1587. She was buried in Peterborough Cathedral, but in 1612 her son, James, had her body exhumed and placed in the vault of King Henry VII's Chapel in Westminster Abbey. Ironically, Elizabeth I is buried just a few feet away from Mary.

The Catholic Church underestimated the English, however. They loved their queen and they were quite content with their religious autonomy. They did not want any outside interference in their state of affairs, whether political or religious.

As result, there was quite a reversal in the religious climate. Instead of the Protestants facing persecution, the Catholics were singled out. Catholic Masses were banned, and fines and arrests were imposed if anyone was caught practicing Catholicism. Also, any Catholic missionary who attempted to spread the word of Rome was ousted from the country. The English had no intention of turning back to Rome. It was not just a question of faith, but also a question of national pride.

The Puritans

The Elizabethan Settlement (1563) established Anglicanism as the official religion of England (otherwise known as the Church of England). But despite Elizabeth's peaceful attempts at quiet reform, like the Catholics, the Puritans did not let her off so easily. The exiles were on their way home to England, sensing a cooler climate of tolerance. And they came home with a vengeance.

The Puritans believed that a Christian's faith relied on spiritual awakening and growth—a pure, uncorrupted, uninterrupted relationship with God. The church leaders could support this and guide this, but they could not control it. One's connection to God through Jesus Christ is not mandated by church organizations, but by faith alone.

The Puritans were certainly conservative and in the eyes of Anglicans and Catholics alike, a little too radical in their reformist persistence.

The Puritans believed that there is no need for pomp and circumstance like music, relics, and fancy robes—these things have no place in the church—they were not in the scriptures and were nothing but distractions from pure faith.

Anglican–Puritan Conflict

The Puritans made several attempts to purify the Church of England under four different monarchs. The first time they attempted reform was during the reign of Elizabeth I, when they tried to implement Calvinist reforms. Elizabeth was quite tolerant, but watched that they didn't get out of hand. The second was during the reign of James I, and then Charles I, when they were pressured to stop their reform efforts and accept the high-church style Christianity of the Anglicans. They had one more chance at seeing any real progress in their reform during the English Civil War (1642–1660), when Oliver Cromwell ruled the nation. They bungled this attempt as well, due to their own disorganized leadership.

Purifying the Church

The Puritans wanted to eliminate anything that reeked of Catholic influence, including the Anglican Mass. It was just too close to the Catholic rituals. The Anglican–Puritan conflict began with rather a simple matter, which had to do with the vestments worn by the clergy during religious services—vestments mandated by the queen. The Puritans didn't approve, and the issue became known as the "Vestiarian Controversy" (1563) and marked the beginning of a long patch of Protestant conflict in England.

The Puritans also objected to other aspects of the Anglican Church:

- Kneeling during communion
- The use of organs in churches
- The observance of too many "holy days" (or "feast days")
- Using the sign of the cross during baptism

As far as the Puritans were concerned, these practices were as Catholic as they come. It's true that the Anglican service (even today) is not much different from that of the Catholic Mass, and this was not lost on the more radical reformers. Not only did the Puritans not want the traditions of the Catholic Church, but they did not want to use the Protestant-based scriptures either. In other words, the Anglican Church was not "true" reform in their eyes.

QUESTION?

Is Puritanism considered a religion?
Puritanism was a movement, not a religion. The name "Puritan" applied because they were trying to take away all the glitz and showiness and get back to the basics of faith.

Admonitions

By 1572, they were organized enough to arrange and attend a Puritan conference in London. Led by Thomas Cartwright, a Fellow at Trinity College in Cambridge in England, the Puritans released their statement on church leadership. There were two documents that the Puritans called "Admonitions." The First Admonition called for the elimination of the post of bishop and the installation of democratically elected ministers—so chosen by the congregation of each parish. The Second Admonition had to do with the structure of church leadership in the big picture. The reforms they were looking for were very similar to those of the Presbyterians. The Puritans believed that strict adherence to scripture would allow any society the ability to provide structure within the home, the church, and the government.

Puritans and Separatists

Thomas Cartwright was a reformer, but he had no intention of separating from the Church of England: he simply wanted to make changes from within. There were many Puritans, however, who did want a complete break, and they became known as the "Separatists." Robert

Browne was the leader of the Separatist movement. Browne advocated that the Church of England was influenced by Rome, and true Christians should have nothing to do with an institution influenced by the corruption of the Catholic Church. True Christians should pack their bags and leave Roman Catholicism—and that is exactly what some of them did. Browne's followers (called "Brownists") joined forces with other Puritan groups and later became known as "Independents."

Congregationalism

Robert Browne is also known as the founder of Congregationalism. He founded his first Congregationalist church in Norwich, England. The idea behind the principle of Congregationalism is that the congregation, and not a bishop, runs the church. The idea was to move beyond the hierarchy of the Roman Catholic Church system, the Anglican system, and even the Presbyterian system that the Puritans found only deterred a Christian from having that direct covenant with God. They didn't need mediators, they simply needed mentors—those mentors would be the ministers as elected by the congregation. In Browne's church, the congregation would govern itself.

ESSENTIAL

Episcopal is a type of church government used by Catholics and Anglicans (and later by the United Methodists), in which bishops govern the congregations. Many reformers rejected this kind of church leadership, but it was the major driving force behind the Puritan Separatist movement and eventually the Congregationalist Church.

Robert Browne was eventually forced to recant and was appointed to an office in the Church of England. His experiment in church leadership did not die, however—rather it became the inspiration behind the Baptist, Unitarian, and Christian (Disciples of Christ) Churches.

Silencing the Separatists

The Separatists became the ammunition that broke the quiet tolerance of the queen. Elizabeth didn't mind if rabble-rousers complained and held conferences, but when there was talk of forming a new and separate church, Elizabeth had to act. If this kind of reform movement continued to grow, it would threaten every compromise she had put in place after her coronation and, therefore, would shake the foundations of England and the monarchy. As "Supreme Governor" and queen, Elizabeth had no choice but to keep her subjects under religious control.

Archbishop Whitgift

The Puritans had it pretty easy under Elizabeth's first two archbishops of Canterbury, Matthew Parker and Edmund Grindal. Archbishop John Whitgift, however, was not as lenient. Upon taking office, he made it his first priority to put a stop to the Separatists. One of his first acts was to produce his six articles in 1583, which demanded that all English subjects submit to the queen on matters of religion and government, or face arrest and imprisonment (Elizabeth wasn't all that big on burning heretics).

FACT

The office of Archbishop of Canterbury began with St. Augustine, and his role was to oversee the governance of the Church of England in the southern portion of the country. Although this office has played a significant role in the politics of England, perhaps more so than in its faith, its role was supposed to be the senior Christian spiritual voice of England. There is still an Archbishop of Canterbury to this day.

His edict, however, was not effective, and 200 Puritan ministers were suspended from preaching, and hundreds of Puritans were imprisoned or fled to Holland. The Separatists did not stop their efforts. Their movement kept its momentum right into the seventeenth century. Elizabeth failed to bring peace between the Anglicans and Puritans during her reign. The climate only became more and more hostile.

Books and Bibles

While exiled in Geneva, a group of reformers, including Miles Coverdale, who officially completed the English translation of the Bible that William Tyndale had started, produced the *Geneva Bible*. This was a user-friendly Bible that provided numbered verses for easy reference, clear prose, and marginal notes. It became the most popular Bible in England and the one that the Puritan pilgrims used in America.

The *Geneva Bible* was replaced in popularity by the *King James Bible* (1611), but it is important to realize here that these user-friendly Bibles, along with John Foxe's *Book of Martyrs*, were the most influential books in English society. They set the standard for the English psyche and the Puritan movement.

Puritans were the first pilgrims to arrive in America, and their beliefs helped shape the American psyche. The Puritans wanted to form a disciplined society of Christians. Some of the evangelical movements of modern times stem from the Puritanical structure.

Book of Martyrs

John Foxe, also exiled in Geneva, wrote a book that had a huge impact on English Christians. The *Book of Martyrs*, as it was called, detailed the suffering and deaths of Christians who died in the name of God. The book was so powerful that for generations to come, many English read their Bibles and viewed history through the eyes of Foxe and these martyrs. This is especially true for the Puritans.

The Puritan Covenant

One of the fundamental principles behind Puritan thought developed from the reading of the scriptures and the admiration of the martyrs depicted in Foxe's book. The principle was that of the "covenant." A covenant is a sort of spiritual contract that a Christian has with God. The most important of these contracts is the covenant of God's grace—the spiritual contract that links a Christian to God. While the Puritans believed in the sovereignty of God to pick and choose who will be saved (predestination), they also believed that through faith there is redemption. The scriptures are the foundation on which one builds the covenant of grace, and the covenant obliges a Christian to follow the scriptures and the word of God. The Puritans took this as their major discipline.

FACT

John Foxe is the first to have coined the nickname for Mary I: "Bloody Mary." The *Book of Martyrs* depicted the persecution of Christians that took place under Mary's rule, earning her the title, and therefore, the reputation that lasted into modern times. There is even a modern-day cocktail named after her, the base of which is tomato juice.

King James I of England

Born James Charles Stuart to Mary, Queen of Scots and her husband Lord Darnley, King James I became the heir to the English throne after the death of his mother. He was King James VI of Scotland but also the first James to rule England. Despite the fact that his mother was a Catholic, James was raised a Protestant.

Protestant, Scholar, and Monarch

James was crowned king of Scotland after the execution of his mother in 1567. Since he was only a year old, he was raised by the Scottish regent and a handful of humanists. James was also a scholar, with a love of literature inspired by several different tutors. Because he lived during the time when Knox was making waves throughout Scotland, James was raised distinctively Calvinist.

When he was thirty-six years old, James also became king of England. His Scottish subjects felt betrayed by this move, but James was the rightful heir as indicated in Elizabeth's will. It was a powerful position, and James saw an opportunity to do great works for both nations.

One of the principal theories of kingship upheld by James I was the "Divine Right of Kings." This meant that some kings were chosen by God to rule a nation, and James I believed he was one of those selected.

Guy Fawkes

You can imagine that a Protestant on the throne may not have been a welcome addition to the Church of England. Although the Anglican Church floated somewhere around the periphery of Rome and the Protestant movement, James was aware that it could cause him some problems and spent the first few years of his reign ducking the assassin's sword. The most famous attempt on his life occurred on November 5, 1605, when a man named Guy Fawkes plotted to blow up the Houses of Parliament when the king was in attendance. Fawkes was caught and burned at the stake.

Guy Fawkes has always been considered England's most notorious traitor, and while some countries commemorate their heroes, the British in their infinite wit, have made November 5th a day of great celebration: "Guy Fawkes Day." Bonfires are lit and a handmade dummy called "the guy" is burned as people cheer and fireworks ignite the skies.

King James Bible

King James I made his mark on history on two counts: He is the monarch that united England, Scotland, and Ireland into what is now known as "Great Britain," and the creator of the most influential Bibles of all time. The *King James Bible*, still used in the Church of England today, has long been heralded as the most significant literary work of religious history. It is not only considered to be the most complete and encompassing translation of the Bible, but also the most beautifully written.

Hampton Court Conference

Being a scholar and perennial monarch, James I knew that the best way to unite all the different variances of Christianity was to hold a conference. But this time, James did not limit the conference to a specific group of Christians; rather, he invited all Christian leaders to contribute their thoughts on the current state of Christianity in the kingdom. He was surprised to hear that the English Bible translations were inaccurate. It was, ironically, a Puritan named John Reynolds who stood up in the conference and insisted that England needed a new Bible. James liked the idea.

The New Bible

James enlisted fifty-four of the greatest scholars and linguists from all over the world to write the new Bible. He had a vision in mind and was determined to see it come to fruition. Although the Catholics had serious objections concerning this project, James was not deterred. The end result was the creation of the *King James Bible*, which to this day, is the best-selling book of all time.

James and the Puritans

Like his predecessor, James did not give much credence to the Puritans. Thinking they might stand a better chance with a more Protestant-minded ruler, the Puritans did attempt to tackle some of their issues with him. They wanted James to relax some of the rules and standards enforced by Elizabeth during her reign, especially in terms of the services and ceremonies. But James felt that the very rites and rituals to which the Puritans objected were the very things holding together Christian unity in England. Ⓔ

Chapter 18

Counter (Catholic) Reformation

While European nations worked out their religious crises, the Roman Catholic Church did not sit idle. Much of the energy of the church was spent on fighting off the reformers, but when it became clear that it was not going to win the battle, it was time to start looking in the mirror.

The Counter Reformation

The people who complained about the corruption of the Catholic Church were not just the ones who wanted to break away and get back to basics. There were many Catholics who wanted to stay Catholic but wanted the church to change its ways. The groups that may have had the biggest impact on internal reform were the mystics and the humanists.

FACT

In an attempt to unify the church and establish some needed reforms, several councils were held between 1215 and 1545. The councils worked out how to manage certain church issues but did little to enforce any kind of change in church abuses.

Counter or Catholic?

So which is it? The Catholic Reformation or the Counter Reformation? Well, it depends from whose perspective you're seeing. For Catholic theologians, it was a matter of reform from within. It was the Catholic Church's attempt to work within its own boundaries through self-examination and change. For other scholars, this reformation was an opportunity for the Catholics to "counter" and thwart the Protestant movements, thus the term "Counter Reformation."

However, it is really both. The church knew it had to clean up its act when it came under the scrutiny of Protestant eyes. The Catholic mission was two-fold: clean up from within and prove the truth of its own doctrine.

Conscience and Questioning

You've read a great deal already about the mystics and humanists in previous chapters, but it's important to note how significant these two groups were to the Counter Reformation: the mystics, because they were the spiritual conscience of the church, and the humanists, because they were the students and teachers who helped formulate opinions through the concept of questioning. Before there were universities and scholars, Christians only had the ability to believe what the church told them to believe, but with the growth of education and development of thought, a whole new world was exposed.

The Mystic Influence

One of the most influential Catholic reformers of the sixteenth century was a Spanish nun and mystic named Teresa of Avila. At the age of twenty, Teresa entered the convent after being inspired by the letters of St. Jerome. While in the convent, she became seriously ill and was partially paralyzed. It is believed that Teresa became frustrated after her illness and wasn't sure whether or not she wanted to continue on at the convent. She did leave briefly and returned with a new vigor for prayer and study. During this time of intense introspection, Teresa said that she was seeing visions. She began seeing images of heaven, hell, and the Holy Spirit. This experience marked the turning point for her and she intensified her commitment to her career and to her relationship with God through devotion to Christ.

St. Teresa established many new convents, which she continued founding up to the year of her death. The order of nuns that inhabited these convents came to be known as "The Carmelites of the Strict Observance." St. Teresa also left a significant legacy of writings, which represent important events in the history of Christian mysticism. Her works include the *Way of Perfection* and the *Interior Castle*. She also left an autobiography, the *Life of Teresa of Avila*.

The Humanist Influence

While the mystics took care of the soul of the Christians, the humanists took it upon themselves to take care of the mind. Both groups, however, affected lasting changes on the Christian Church. In addition to some of the humanists you've already read about—such as Sir Thomas More and Desiderius Erasmus—there were a few new and different humanists on the horizon.

Oratory of the Divine Love

The Oratory of the Divine Love started in Rome in the year 1517. The group was comprised of about fifty individuals, mostly humanists, who gathered to meditate, pray, and discuss issues of Catholic reform. They weren't looking to separate from the church; in fact, what they discussed was how to make it work better. The most notable and influential name to come out of the Oratory of Divine Love was Gasparo Contarini, who became a cardinal under Pope Paul III.

First Step Toward Reform

In 1536, the pope appointed Contarini to head a special reform committee, the result of which was a report on the state of the papacy. Contarini filed an honest report, indicating that the major problems within the papacy and the Roman Catholic Church were materialism, secularization, and other church abuses. Pope Paul took action and started to implement some reforms, which included eliminating simony (the purchase of church appointments). He had a tough time, however, as he came up against opposition from some of his more powerful cardinals.

The Council of Trent

Unlike some of the other councils held by the Catholic Church over the centuries, one of the purposes in calling the Council of Trent was to try to find some sort of middle ground between the Catholics and the Protestants. One of the things Pope Paul III agreed to upon taking the office of the papacy was to call a council that would not only emphasize the need for reform, but also define Catholic doctrine.

The Council of Trent actually comprised three separate sessions and spanned from 1545 to 1563. The outcome was the pivotal junction of what is now called the Catholic Reformation.

It seems this had been done many times over the centuries and so it had. However, with reform movements on the rise and the Catholic Church the focus of such scrutiny, Emperor Charles V decided it was necessary to protect the Catholic faith with a final, definitive statement of doctrine. If it couldn't bring the Protestants into the fold, it could at least unify the Catholics within the existing fold.

The First Council

The first council (between 1545 and 1547) did not attract as many participants as the church had hoped, and much of the debate was focused on what should be debated. The first council brought together four archbishops, twenty bishops, and four monastic leaders. The meeting was not entirely fruitless for the church, however. It did come to several determinations that set the tone for future council meetings, including:

- Meetings should discuss both doctrinal matters, as well as issues of church abuses.
- A pronouncement that scripture, in addition to tradition (writings of the apostles, papal pronouncements, and church councils), were both valid in relation to faith and church government, thus rejecting the Protestant insistence of "justification by faith alone."
- St. Jerome's *Vulgate* was the authentic biblical text and the official scripture of the church.
- Only the Catholic Church had the right to interpret scripture—again negating the Protestant ideal of every Christian's right to formulate his or her own relationship with God through the Bible.
- The Protestant belief that humans were completely sinful after the fall of Adam and Eve was rejected.

The Second Council

The French decided to boycott the second council (1551–1552) and the Protestants were banned from attending. Emperor Charles V managed to convince Pope Julius III to allow Protestant representation, but they were not allowed to vote on any decisions. At this council, the

Catholic Church confirmed the seven sacraments were essential to salvation and could only be administered by church leaders. However, in the end, there were still many issues unresolved for the Catholics and the Protestants.

QUESTION?

What emerged from the Council of Trent?
The Council of Trent played an important role in determining the outcome of the Counter (Catholic) Reformation, and several assertions came out of it: the principle that the pope was supreme in the Catholic Church and that only the reforms passed through him were accepted; the improvement of bishops and clergy to give proper lead to the Catholic laity; and the clear definition of Catholic doctrine.

The Third Council

By the third council (1562–1563), the Catholics knew what had to be done. Pope Pius IV called the meeting and, in the end, it proved to be the most successful of all the councils.

The Catholic doctrinal issues resolved at the Third Council of Trent were:

- The doctrine of transubstantiation
- Justification by faith and works
- Affirmation of the seven sacraments
- Affirmation of the celibacy of the clergy
- Affirmation of the existence of purgatory
- Clarified practices surrounding seminaries (priest training schools)
- Affirmed indulgences but would take steps to curb abuse and corruption

The Catholic Church recognized the fact that there was corruption and abuse inside its ranks and knew that one of the main issues to be dealt with—thanks to Martin Luther for the most part—was the sale of indulgences. The Catholics were happy with the outcome and, in 1564, at the close of The Council of Trent, Pope Pius IV issued the papal bull called *Benedictus Deus*, outlining and affirming all council decrees.

In the end, the Council of Trent was quite productive for the church. It established Catholic doctrine, and lifted the position of pope to a level of respectability. What it didn't manage to do, however, was formulate any kind of Christian unity.

St. Ignatius Loyola

Born in the Basque region of Spain, Inigo de Loyola (1491–1556) was a philanderer, a gambler, a soldier, a monk, and finally a saint. Like many before him, Ignatius Loyola discovered his calling while recuperating from an illness. When he was a soldier, he fought in the army of Emperor Charles V against the French. During battle, he was hit by a cannon ball—one of his legs was broken and the other severely damaged. The French did not kill him, however. They saw something in him that they admired and took him back to their headquarters, where they nursed him back to health.

FACT

The process of being made a saint takes a very long time. In 1595, the Catholic Church began a review of the life of Ignatius Loyola and, in 1609, he was beatified (the first step to sainthood). In March 1622, along with Teresa of Avila and Francis Xavier, Loyola was canonized—meaning he was made a saint.

The story goes that during his recovery, Loyola had asked for some novels, but instead received a book about Christ and the lives of the saints. The book inspired him to look inward and reflect on his past life, as well as on what kind of life he wanted to have in the future. Because of the experience, Loyola dedicated his life to mysticism. He had no desire to develop a new religion, since his beliefs fell in line with Catholic doctrine, but he tried to administer changes from within the Catholic Church with permission from Rome. This is what made Loyola a significant participant in the Counter (or Catholic) Reformation.

The result of Loyola's introspection did not only change his life, but the spiritual repercussions of his journey reverberated throughout the generations and the world.

The Jesuits

When Ignatius Loyola was able to walk again, he decided to head for the Benedictine abbey of Montserrat. There, he turned to a life of poverty and prayer. He lived for a year in a cave near the small village of Manresa: he begged, he fasted, and he wore a barbed girdle (something worn under a cassock to cause discomfort to serve as a reminder of the monk's dedication to God).

During this time, Loyola also went through a personal spiritual struggle, which often left him frustrated and depressed. Finally, on the shores of the River Cardoner, Loyola had a vision of the Virgin Mary and baby Jesus. This was the beginning of his spiritual enlightenment.

After the experience, Loyola became a man on a mission— devoting his life to religious discipline and militaristic dedication to the pope. He was the founder of the Society of Jesus, which is more commonly referred to as the Jesuits. The Jesuits became the most powerful force during the Counter Reformation because their message was one that restored spiritual territory that the church desperately needed to reclaim. Their intention was to restore the Catholic Church to the power and spiritual influence it once had enjoyed in its youth.

"Teach us, good Lord, to serve Thee as Thou deservest;
To give and not to count the cost;
To fight and not to heed the wounds;
To toil and not to seek for rest;
To labour and not to ask for any reward
Save that of knowing that we do Thy will."
—St. Ignatius Loyola, *Prayer for Generosity* (1548)

The Birth of an Order

The Jesuits became the public relations officers of the Catholic Church. When Pope Paul III approved the new society, Loyola and his followers promised to go wherever the pope wanted them to go—which has earned them the nickname "the soldiers of Christ."

The Jesuits believed that human beings had the option to choose between God and Satan. With disciplined faith, a Christian's determination could be strengthened to make the right decision. This theory was in diametric opposition to Luther's belief that man cannot save himself—only God can do that.

Spiritual Exercises

When Ignatius Loyola was struggling to understand the meaning of life in Manresa, he came with up with ideas that he called "Spiritual Exercises." The exercises were a compilation of his own spiritual journey in the form of what could be described as an instruction manual. It prescribed four weeks of meditations, including on the subjects of sin, death, judgment, hell, and then Christ's life, death, and resurrection.

The exercises also gave the ingredients to the path of spiritual "perfection" through a thorough examination of conscience, releasing all feelings of guilt once one has been confronted with the forgiveness of God.

This work of Loyola became the spiritual guide for all aspiring Jesuits. The Catholic Church later accepted the exercises for its own training purposes in other areas of instruction in faith. The book *Spiritual Exercises* was published in 1548 and is used to this day as a training manual by the Society of Jesus.

For the Greater Glory of God

After his pilgrimage to Jerusalem, Loyola returned home and received his education at the University of Paris. During this time, Loyola had a small group of followers, who became the original members of the Society: Francis Xavier, Peter Faber, Diego Laynez, Alfonso Salmeron, Simon Rodriguez, and Nicholas de Bobadilla. Together, they swore an oath to celibacy, poverty, and a life devoted to God.

There were more than 13,000 Jesuits all over the world in the early seventeenth century. The motto for the Society became *Ad majorem Dei gloriam*, Latin for "To the Greater Glory of God" to reflect the high standards for which they stood.

Their first goal was to go to Jerusalem and convert the Muslims, but they only got as far as Venice. Their mission was thwarted by war with the Turks. But the group of seven stayed in Venice and continued to educate and recruit new members of the Society.

By 1566, there were 1,000 Jesuits living in Spain, Italy, and Portugal with scattered groups working in France, Germany, India, Brazil, and Africa.

Educated Missionaries

The Catholics welcomed Jesuits abroad, for the most part, but they didn't have it easy. The Protestants saw them as spiritual demons, missionaries of the corruption and decay that they saw in the Catholic Church. However, none of the criticism stopped Loyola from achieving his goal: to convert the heretics and the heathens.

Loyola developed strict standards for entry into the Society (these standards still exist today). Education was of the utmost importance, with the objective to educate as many young people as possible in the hopes of spreading and growing the Catholic Church. With education, the Jesuits believed that they not only instilled the Catholic doctrine in the areas in which they taught, but they helped spread the message to the rest of the world as well. These high standards for education garnered support for the Society from the elite, and the Jesuits became leaders in education throughout Europe.

Loyola died in 1556, but before his death, the Jesuits founded two colleges in Europe. By 1640, 100 years after the pope approved the Jesuit order, there were 500 colleges in Europe, and by the mid-seventeenth century, there were more than 650. Today, there are twenty-eight Jesuit colleges in the United States.

Catholic Missionaries

The Jesuits were instrumental in assisting the explorers to convert the "heathens" across the world. It was Columbus who made the most significant impact in terms of trade and exchanged knowledge between Europe and the New World (the Americas). The other explorers came and left, but the influence of Columbus affected a lasting change with new trade routes to the Far East and the establishment of European colonies throughout the newly discovered landmass. This was the beginning of the age of global expansion.

QUESTION?

What is a heathen?
In the eyes of the Catholic Church, a heathen was different from a heretic. While a heretic is one who strays from, or opposes, the doctrine of the Catholic Church, a heathen is someone who has not been educated in the Christian faith at all.

Columbus' interest in the New World was not strictly for the glory of a great adventure. It was a mission for God. After greeting the natives, when he first landed in the West Indies (in an area he named "San Salvador" meaning "Holy Savior"), Columbus realized that their conversion should be accomplished through love rather than force.

Explorer or Invader?

Historians refer to the era during the fifteenth and sixteenth centuries as the "Age of Discovery." During that time, European nations were packing their vessels and sailing to new lands to discover what resources were out there and also to expand the Christian faith. Aboard almost any sailing vessel was a Jesuit, a Dominican, a Franciscan, or an Augustinian. It was their task to convert the heathens in each newly discovered region of the world.

The Portuguese, the Dutch, the French, and the English all set sail for various undiscovered territories. In 1486, the Portuguese managed to reach the southern tip of Africa, and named it "The Cape of Good Hope." Later, they continued around Africa toward Asia, where they first spotted the Malabar Coast of India. The Portuguese used this region as home base for expansion into the Far East. The Spanish had made their way through America to the southern tip of South America, behaving more like fanatical crusaders than adventurers or explorers. They became knows as the "conquistadors," which translates to not just "conquerors" but "brutal conquerors."

FACT

"Ecomienda" is the name of the first policy the Spanish established toward the natives of their conquered lands. In exchange for an education in Christian faith, the natives were expected to work in the mines and on the plantations. They were, in essence, captives of their conquers, forced to convert or face death—with the extra implanted fear of damnation.

For example, Hernando Cortes made his way through Mexico and demolished the ancient Aztec culture and slaughtered tribal leaders. Other explorers forced the natives of each land to succumb to the ways of the Christian Church or face death and damnation. This is how some explorers made their way through the world, whereas others chose a more peaceful approach.

St. Francis Xavier

Francis Xavier (1506–1552) was one of the seven original members of the Society of Jesus and probably the greatest and most dedicated missionary next to Paul (the apostle). Xavier's mission was to convert the population of the Far East. He launched his mission as a papal legate (or messenger), under the commission of Portugal, from the Portuguese seaport of Goa, India. His work in Goa was brief, and feeling he was leaving the port in a state of moral well-being, he set his sights on the remote regions of southern India.

While there, the local village fisherman (Paravars) sought refuge with the Portuguese explorers from invading robbers who were making their lives impossible. The Portuguese agreed to help them if they submitted to baptism and the Christian faith. Out of desperation, they did, but it went no further than that. They had no idea what Christianity was and no one bothered to teach them until Xavier showed up. Xavier read to the villagers from the scriptures, helping them memorize the Ten Commandments, the Apostolic Creed, the Lord's Prayer, and the Rosary. Once they had sufficiently consumed the words and the faith behind the words, Xavier baptized them by the hundreds at a time.

Sitting on the perimeters of this Christian change, however, were the Hindus and the Muslims. While Xavier has been praised for his influence and ambition, he is criticized for his call for an inquisition to convert the heathen Muslims. The King of Portugal agreed and "the Inquisition" lasted in Goa until the early nineteenth century. In an effort to destroy all signs of heathenism, portions of India were leveled to the ground.

QUESTION?

What is the Rosary?
The Rosary is a series of prayers said in memory of events or mysteries applicable to salvation. The purpose of "saying the Rosary" is to thank and praise God for these events and mysteries. There are twenty mysteries divided into four categories: joyful mysteries, luminous mysteries, sorrowful mysteries, and finally the glorious mysteries.

The Japanese Experience

In 1538, Xavier arrived in Japan, where the Jesuits left a lasting legacy. Eager for change from their primitive feudal system to a world of prosperity and trade, the Japanese welcomed the outsiders. Upon arrival, Xavier was pleased that Buddhism was fading from the psyche of the people, so there was no state religion to combat.

The Japanese also changed Xavier's thinking about destructive imperialism. He was enamored of Japanese culture, and while he knew that they needed to accept the scripture and adopt the Christian faith, he saw no need to destroy the existing lifestyle. This was Xavier's first adaptation of religious tolerance—not a characteristic familiar to the Counter Reformation.

The Jesuits remained in Japan well into the sixteenth century, leaving behind 300,000 converts and two Jesuit colleges in the Jesuit-established town of Nagasaki. However, the glory of the Jesuit endeavors died off in the seventeenth century, when new rulers of foreign nations declared the missionaries to be foreign invaders and launched a policy of Christian persecution. Between 1614 and 1642, more than 4,000 Christians were slaughtered. Nagasaki collapsed and Christianity disintegrated in Japan.

The Chinese Challenge

Xavier almost managed to make it to China, but he died in 1552, just off the southern coast. After Xavier, another Jesuit, Matthew Ricci, undertook his missionary work in China. Ricci found that the Chinese were not nearly as welcoming as the Japanese. Confucianism had a strong hold over the Chinese, and the nation saw no need for the missionaries on their soil.

But Ricci was clever. He attempted to teach the Chinese that Christianity was not something new, but something they already had as their own faith—the belief in the "Lord of Heaven." Ricci taught that there was no difference between their God and the Christian God. Instead of bombarding his way with force and wrath, he learned the culture and language of the region and slowly made attempts to talk to Chinese leaders, honoring them with gifts and friendship. When Ricci died in 1610, there were 2,000 Christians in China.

Among the gifts Ricci gave to the Emperor of China during his stay in Peking (now known as Beijing) were two clocks. The emperor loved the clocks, but at one point they stopped working. Chinese experts could not figure out how to get them started again, so the emperor saw it fit to keep Ricci around—he was the only one who knew how to start the clocks and keep them going.

After Ricci's death, Johann Adam Schall took over and worked his way into the Chinese scholarly community. He won its commendation by accurately predicting the time of an eclipse of the moon. The Chinese were so impressed that they wanted him to stay so that they could learn even more. Schall agreed, and before his death in 1666, there were almost 300,000 Christians in China.

In 1692, China passed an edict of toleration, rewarding the service of the Jesuits. With this edict, the door was open for the growth of Christianity throughout China. But again, the Catholics proved to be their own worst enemy. When the Franciscans and the Dominicans witnessed how the Chinese were practicing Christianity, they reported their complaints to Rome. This started a quarrel in Rome, resulting in a decline in the spread of Christianity in China.

The Outcome

It's hard to say what the outcome of the Counter (or Catholic) Reformation was exactly because it depends on the perspective from which you perceive it. If you see this era of reform as the Catholic Reformation, it was highly successful. The Catholic Church managed to reestablish itself as a force to be reckoned with; it mended some of its corrupt ways (mostly in terms of the indulgences); and it managed to spread the Catholic faith throughout the world at the hands of missionaries, such as the Jesuits.

However, from the perspective of the Protestants and the use of the term "Counter Reformation," the Catholics had done virtually nothing to mend their misuse and abuse of power, nor did they do anything to appease the Protestant reform movement. So in that sense, the Catholic Reformation was a failure. Ⓔ

Chapter 19

The New World

The Catholics may have put to rest any issues concerning matters of faith within the Church and laid aside any Protestant threat to Catholic doctrine at the Council of Trent, but it was not over yet. The Thirty Years' War was on the horizon and the Protestants continued to spread throughout Europe and into the New World. This was a time of renewal and revival.

The Thirty Years' War

The Thirty Years' War was a dark time in history and is considered to be the last of the major religious wars to wrack Europe. It started as a religious war, but gradually became a tangled web of political mayhem. The Thirty Years' War is broken down into four periods in history (the names and dates of the periods will vary from historian to historian, but this is the gist of it):

1. The Bohemian Period (1618–1623)
2. The Danish Period (1625–1629)
3. The Swedish Period (1630–1635)
4. The French Period (1635–1648)

This was a war fought between the German Protestants and their allies (France, Sweden, Denmark, England, and other European provinces), and the German Catholic princes in conjunction with the Holy Roman Empire. It was basically a grand-scale war between the Catholics and the Protestants.

The Holy Roman Empire was trying to regain portions of Europe that were under the control of the Protestants. Germany had been under siege by anti-Protestant factions for quite some time before the war even began. The nation's churches were destroyed and restrictions were placed on the services. The violence then carried over to Bohemia, where the Emperor of Rome appointed the devoutly Catholic Ferdinand II to throne. The Bohemians were largely Protestants and were enraged by the placement of a Catholic king on the throne of their nation. When they protested, anti-Protestant groups attacked them, and the king did nothing to stop the violence.

FACT

The Thirty Years' War greatly impacted the social and economic well-being of Europe, especially Germany. But, even within Germany, there were regions that escaped the Thirty Years' War and suffered relatively little damage. Some city-states, such as Hamburg, Leipzig, and Danzig (currently located in Poland), actually profited from the war.

The Bohemian Period

In 1608, a Protestant nobleman named Heinrich von Thurn led a defensive Protestant alliance called "the Evangelical Union." This group often stepped in, as a small militia of radical protectors, when Protestants were on the defensive. In this case, they took action in Bohemia. Known as the "Prague Protestants," they stormed Ferdinand's palace and threw his ministers and secretary out the window. They fell into a moat 50 feet below and managed to swim to their safety. This incident became known as the "Defenestration of Prague" and was the event that led to a major uprising of Protestants within Bohemia and the beginning of the Thirty Years' War.

The Danish Period

The persecuted German Protestants asked other Protestant nations to assist them, and King Christian IV of Norway and Denmark came to their aid by invading Saxony. But the Danish army was poorly organized and suffered defeat at the hands of German Catholics. Under the Peace of Lübeck, King Christian was forced to stay out of German politics.

The Swedish Period

This period of the war was a little bit more successful for the Protestants, when in 1630, Gustavus Adolphus, King of Sweden, managed to enter Germany without almost any opposition. After the Battle of Breitenfeld, he won the Saxon provinces and the support of the Protestant princes of Germany. This victory boosted the morale of Protestant forces, pushing them on to win more battles. But by 1635, the battling army came to a standstill. The Protestants held southern Germany while the Catholics held the north, and there was no way that one army was able to overtake the other.

The Peace of Prague

Eventually, the people of Germany grew tired of all these years of endless bloodshed and called an end to it with the Peace of Prague, which was signed in 1635. This marked the end of the Swedish part of the war. Both Catholics and Protestants signed the treaty, and it seemed that Europe might have finally found the religious peace it needed after so many years of unrest. But there was still one more stretch of the war to go.

The French Period is also referred to as the "International Period" because of the effects this stretch of the war would have on all of Europe.

The French Period

The French had successfully managed to stay out of this war—for the most part—but they were forced into it when it became clear that this was no longer a fight about religion. The longer the war waged, the more political it became, with armies attacking one nation and then counter-attacking another—it became a matter of military prowess. In 1635, France declared war against Spain.

By the end of this phase of the war, and countless lost lives later, Europe was nearly destroyed and Germany was devastated. It is estimated that between 1600 and 1650, five million people in Germany alone had been killed—and it would take a century for the nation to regroup financially.

The Peace of Westphalia

The Peace of Westphalia was signed in 1648 in Münster, Germany, thus ending a war that shattered the European community for decades to come. It was not one treaty, but a series of treaties that outlined the terms of peace in relation to religion and political matters. The Peace of Westphalia was a turning point for all of Europe and unexpectedly marked the end of the Holy Roman Empire. Smaller systems of government throughout Europe began to form, rendering the Holy Roman Empire redundant and quickly obsolete.

The Peace of Westphalia proved to be even more powerful than that. What it did was allow autonomous governments to form by terminating the strong political influence of the pope. Pope Innocent X rejected the Peace of Westphalia but was ignored by both Catholics and Protestants alike. Both religious entities relished their newfound religious and political independence. The Peace of Westphalia also corrected something that the Peace of Augsburg did not acknowledge: the acceptance of Calvinism. This was a new autonomous Europe—divided by borders and by religion.

FACT

After the war, the nations that remained Protestant were Scotland, Holland, Scandinavia, England, parts of Germany, and parts of Switzerland. All other European nations remained predominantly Catholic.

Pilgrims of the New World

To escape religious persecution, the Puritans left Europe to find a new land where they could practice their beliefs in peace—there was nowhere in Europe to hide or find solace in order to practice one's faith. The Thirty Years' War scattered more Protestants, and many took advantage of the sailing vessels heading for uncharted waters to new lands. Both England and France were sending explorers to try to find the Northwest Passage to China, and many of those persecuted for their beliefs took the opportunity to be the first of the colonists.

At the expense of the London Company, in 1607, the first English colonists docked in Jamestown, Virginia, in what we now call the United States. This was a far cry from China, but it was the start of a New World. This was the beginning of an influx of frustrated Protestants to this region of the world. In 1620, the Pilgrims landed in Plymouth, Massachusetts, aboard the Mayflower, and between 1629 and 1642, more than 25,000 Pilgrims had docked in what became known as New England.

The Puritans weren't the only ones to head for the seas. The Quakers (a branch-off group of the Anabaptists) went to Pennsylvania, while Catholics went to Maryland and the Reformed Dutch settled in New York.

Other Protestants to head for the New World included:

- The Scottish Presbyterians
- The Baptists of England
- The French Huguenots
- The Swedish Lutherans

Jamestown

The London Company eventually changed its name to the "Virginia Company of London" and its rules were clear. It wanted to civilize Virginia by baptizing the natives, developing a community, and producing a commodity that would put money back into the floundering English economy. In the case of Virginia, the primary commodity would be tobacco.

Sir Thomas Dale, an Englishman, arrived in Jamestown as governor to oversee the colonization process. He forced regimented religious practice, adherence to scripture and law, and opposed the death penalty for theft as well as trading with the Native Americans. Another Englishman named Alexander Whitaker joined Dale in the New World. Whitaker's job was to go out and convert the natives, which, in the long run, proved no easy task.

Since the Jamestown colony was not terribly productive and money was not flowing in the way the monarchy had hoped, England decided to give Jamestown some autonomy. An assembly of local, secular, elected lawmakers was formed and, in an effort to curb Puritan control, the Church of England became the official religion.

No matter how hard Dale tried to inflict his iron-fisted rule, the settlement was failing, mainly due to unanticipated factors: The crops didn't grow because the tobacco seeds were bad; disease killed many of the settlers; starvation was rampant without decent food crops; and the Native Americans wanted nothing to do with Puritan plans for conversion. Instead of creating a paradise of new believers, the Pilgrims found themselves fighting a losing battle on many fronts.

African Americans

The first African Americans to land in the New World came aboard a ship called *Jesus*. The Puritans were firm believers in the hierarchy of human beings: God created the superior and inferior—Christians over pagans, believers over nonbelievers, the civilized over the uncivilized—and with the arrival of the ship *Jesus*, whites over blacks. There were about twenty men aboard the ship, who were sent to the New World to serve as slaves to the white settlers. These black men were forced to convert to Christianity, and this started the beginning of a new wave of Christianity that would grow in the coming centuries.

Colonization

While the colonists may have been thinking that their arrival in the New World was an escape from religious intolerance in their native lands— namely England, in the case of the first colonists—the English monarchy was far more concerned with what was in it for them. It was discovered that this new, rugged territory was full of natural resources, and despite the cold winters, was a highly survivable region where people and profits could thrive. The New World was a virtual gold mine.

Charters

The business ventures to colonize the New World were "chartered" ventures. A charter was a legal document that had to be obtained by a company in order to set up a business in the New World. The ruler of the "parent" nation basically gave that company permission to invest its money outside the kingdom. In essence, it gave the monarchs the ability to mandate certain laws that they could not necessarily oversee from thousands of miles away. The document not only stated the legal rules of the investment, but also indicated legal, religious, and social guidelines. Each company financing a trip to the colonies had its own charter, and no one charter was the same as another.

FACT

The London Company had a clause in its charter stating that while the colonists were in the New World, they must not only keep their faith as members of the Church of England, but it was their responsibility to convert the "heathens" (natives of the land) to Christianity. On board the London Company's vessels were devout religious settlers determined to live by that charter.

There was one major exception to the ideal of religious tolerance in the New World, which came at the hands of some frustrated Puritans. They saw the opportunity in the New World and dreamed of a perfect society—their own Garden of Eden—untouched, uncorrupted, and pure. They dreamed of a world with moral standards in strict adherence to scripture. They were idealists in every sense.

Visions of Perfection

Taking advantage of a gap in the English charter, which insisted that the headquarters of a company financing colonization be located in England, a group of Puritans looking to create the "Zion of the Wilderness" opened the Massachusetts Bay Company. They called themselves the "Congregational Puritans of Massachusetts Bay," and in migrating to the New World they took the charter with them. Because they had no affiliation to England—thanks to the gap in the charter—they became their own republic.

As a result, the strict and disciplined Puritans of the New World set out to create a world of religious conformity. If anyone strayed from regular services, denied the sacraments or Christ's resurrection, and did not adhere to scripture, severe punishments were delivered.

Massachusetts Settlements

Earlier, you read about the Puritan Separatists who were chased out of England under threat of persecution. They sought refuge in Holland and, in 1620, were granted a charter from the Virginia Company of London to set sail for the New World on the famous ship called the *Mayflower*.

The Dutch exiles made one stop in England to pick up other Puritan Separatists (and some non-Puritans) and then took to the Atlantic in search of a new life in Virginia. There were thirty-seven Puritans and sixty-five others aboard the ship. But they didn't quite land in Virginia. Instead, they landed in what we know as Massachusetts, on the now-historic site: Plymouth Rock.

ESSENTIAL

One of the most important symbols of the establishment of the New World is Plymouth Rock. This is the site where the *Mayflower* reportedly docked in 1620. Historians have debated whether or not the site that exists today is the actual landing spot. One way or another, the rock can still be seen by the waterfront in Plymouth, Massachusetts, where the *Mayflower II* is docked and remains a symbol of American colonization.

The Mayflower Compact

In order to create some sort of balance in this new colony, the Puritans put together a civil document called "The Mayflower Compact." It was a significant achievement that established a balance in government and law enforcement. It was the original philosophy of a "government for the people, by the people." It also established them as a permanent colony, something their charter seemed to omit. They wanted to ensure their place in the New World so that they could not be pulled back to England to face further persecution.

These settlers called themselves the "Plymouth Colony" and soon faced some trying times. The winter and rugged conditions proved too tough for these Puritan pilgrims, and over half of them died before the colony really got underway.

The Massachusetts Bay Colony

Back home in England, the Puritans were becoming increasingly frustrated with the religious climate. The non-Separatists (ones that chose to remain part of the Church of England) found that they were being ostracized from religious hierarchy. The Church of England saw the Puritans as a threat and was not about to allow them into the church ranks as equals. The church saw that as a recipe for disaster.

In 1629, a group of non-Separatists opened "The Governor and Company of the Massachusetts Bay in New England," and obtained a charter that permitted them passage to the New World. John Winthrop, a Puritan layman, was a clever fellow and managed to find a loophole in the royal charter that allowed them to not establish the company's headquarters in England. So off they went, charter in hand, to "New England," where the Puritan movement was thriving right up and down the eastern seaboard.

John Winthrop

John Winthrop (1588–1649) was born in Suffolk, England, to a wealthy family of merchants. The Winthrops were Puritans who believed that the Church of England should purify its practices and beliefs in accordance with the Bible. John had every intention of becoming a minister but instead chose to study law. This did not cause him to stray from his spiritual devotion, however. In fact, it may have brought him even closer to his faith, choosing to spend every nonworking hour in the church.

When the persecution of Puritans increased in the 1620s as England went through monarchial and religious turmoil, many chose to emigrate. So when the Massachusetts Bay Colony formed to settle America, John jumped aboard—literally. As governor, he joined 700 colonists aboard the *Arabella*, where he is said to have preached Christ's "Sermon on the Mount" to the anxious travelers.

John had also devised a plan that he called a "Model of Christian Charity," which called for very simple things like commitment to the Christian faith and an atmosphere of "brotherly love." Simple yes, but

John was determined and he held fast to his model. He wanted a Christian society—anything short of that was heresy. It was this kind of determination that led to the witch trials.

Puritan Life in New England

Once the Puritans got used to the conditions and climate of the new land, their communities began to thrive. They had their "perfect" society of believers; they had money, families, and freedom of religion. Their laws were strict and infractions were punishable by public flogging, hanging, or humiliation. Living in a town also made them less susceptible to attacks by the Native Americans.

FACT

The 1804 novel *The Scarlet Letter*, written by Nathaniel Hawthorne, depicts the harsh reality of life in Puritan Massachusetts during colonial times in the seventeenth century. It is a tale of a priest named Dimmesdale and the secret affair he has with a married woman named Hester Prynne. The affair results in the birth of a child and Hester is branded an adulteress and forced to wear a letter "A" on her clothing. The outcome is tragic.

Denominationalism

The practice of denominationalism came into being in the eighteenth century during the Evangelical Revival, but the idea started with the Puritans. The whole idea of denominationalism is a reaction to sectarianism. Sectarianism is exclusive, meaning that each sect of a religion believes that its way is the right way and that no other way is acceptable. Denominationalism as a concept is more inclusive, because it espouses that one particular Christian group is really just a part of a bigger religious community—the Christian Church. Denominationalism means that each subgroup is accepted and acknowledged, and no one group can represent the entirety of Christianity.

The reformers started this concept, but in actuality they did not practice denominationalism, because when new Christian factions popped up, the reformers made every attempt to crush them, rather than incorporate them into the whole.

The Congregationalists

You remember reading about the Congregationalists. They were the first group to put the power of the church organization in the hands of the believers rather than church leadership. The church leaders were elected and their role was to mentor the congregation but not mandate faith. Well, the Congregationalists of the seventeenth century made up a political group in England called the "Independents."

Dissension in Their Midst

The Puritans and Anglicans were not the only ones to set sail to the New World—the Baptists were right behind them. Before the Baptists arrived, however, a man named Roger Williams, a Separatist, rebelled against the idea of one established religion for a given territory. Massachusetts had become strictly Puritan, and Williams spoke out against it. As a result, he was banished from the Puritan Church in Massachusetts.

FACT

Roger Williams was an admirer of the Baptists. He relished the thought of baptism upon spiritual awakening. He became a Baptist for a brief time but in the end he found himself a "Seeker"— someone who stays on a path of seeking the true church, which ultimately is not part of the physical world.

Williams headed to the Plymouth Colony, where he hid himself amongst his fellow Separatists and then with the Narragansett Indian tribe. He finally made his way to Rhode Island, where he opened a refuge for persecuted Christians. All denominations were welcome. They arrived in droves: the Quakers, the Baptists, as well as a woman named Anne Hutchinson, a critic of the Boston Puritans. Because of this influx, the Puritans referred to Rhode Island as "Rogue Island."

Anne Hutchinson

Anne Hutchinson (1591–1643), a devout Puritan and spiritual leader, was not only a pioneer in the New World but also a pioneer within her faith. It was not customary for a woman to preach, but there was nothing in Puritan "doctrine" that stated it was not permitted. So Anne preached to about eighty people in her home on a regular basis.

She was becoming very influential and powerful, and the male leaders of the Puritan community did not like it. This was a patriarchal community and it didn't matter if Anne was a true defender of the Puritan belief system or not, nor did it matter how powerful her services were—that's not what the community leaders were seeing. They saw the woman as a threat to the system.

Anne, then, moved to Boston, where she also found herself in "hot water" for arguing that a human being's salvation was entirely in the hands of God and had nothing to do with free will. This thought in itself was threatening because such a belief, as we saw earlier, could lead to lawlessness. When Anne claimed that the Holy Spirit spoke from within her, she was practically branded a heretic and was forced to stand trial. The charges against her were dropped, but she was still excommunicated from the church and forbidden to preach.

Witches

These were the days of the infamous witch-hunts. While the Puritans thought it was a good deed to keep an eye on one's neighbor, behaviors were often misinterpreted and labels brandished. The New World brought together Europeans from cultures with different ethnic behaviors and folklore, and it was very likely that not all practiced the same social or cultural behaviors. This, however, created fear, paranoia, and superstition amongst the Puritans.

As a result, accusations of paganism and witchcraft were abundant and countless people were executed. Women were most often accused because they were believed to be more likely tempted by the devil as witnessed in the Garden of Evil—when Eve took the forbidden fruit from the serpent. The "witch burnings" have been examined and analyzed from all perspectives, and explanations of what happened abound.

QUESTION?

What were the Salem Witch Trials?
The Salem Witch Trials occurred in Salem, Massachusetts, between 1692 and 1693. The hysteria started when several girls fell sick, manifesting convulsions and bizarre outbursts. The Salem village doctor claimed the girls were under the spell of a witch. This resulted in twenty-five people being hanged and numerous others sent to prison for witchcraft.

Other Protestant Colonists

The Dutch Calvinists, who were in the ship-building business in Holland, began settling on Manhattan Island in the seventeenth century—they called it "New Amsterdam." Later, in the mid-seventeenth century, the Swedish settled in Wilmington, Delaware. They called the region "New Sweden" and were predominantly Lutheran. Outside of the Puritan colonies of Massachusetts and Virginia, where Quaker hangings and beatings of Anabaptists were the way of life, there was a growing culture of religious tolerance as more and more Protestants flocked to the colonies.

Pennsylvania is a good example of the atmosphere of religious tolerance that existed in some of the colonies. William Penn assisted the Quakers in settling in the region, and they accepted anyone of any religion as long as they believed in one God. In Germantown, Pennsylvania, the German Mennonites and the Dutch Quakers lived in one community.

In the last part of the seventeenth century, the Presbyterians, under the leadership of Francis Makemie (an Irishman educated in Scotland), settled in the Maryland area. Makemie was accused of preaching without a license and had to stand trial in a New York court where he, and Presbyterians in general, were upheld as defenders of freedom of religion. The first presbytery opened in Philadelphia—a logical choice due to its reputation as a safe haven for religious freedom.

While it may seem like prosecuting someone for not having a license to preach is an attempt at silencing freedom of religion, in actuality, one of the major problems in the New World was the inexperienced and ill-advised leadership of unlicensed preachers. The colony leaders were trying to get some control over the chaos, and what developed was the desire to create stronger local ministries.

Decline of Puritanism

Eventually, even the Puritans were forced to acknowledge and implement religious tolerance. England was putting pressure on them to stop enacting the death penalty against those of other religious orientations. But the English monarchy had to keep a handle on the colonies somehow—the profits were rolling in and it didn't want religious intolerance to slow any further growth. So in time, the Puritan intolerance quelled and evangelism took hold. When the Puritans allowed the "half-way" acceptance of baptized children into the church, they lost an element of their strict code. Between this breakdown, enacting the death penalty, and the burning and hanging of "witches," the Puritan order began to collapse.

E Chapter 20

The Great Awakening

I n the early eighteenth century, the New World went through a spiritual growth spurt. It was the birth of evangelism—an almost frantic renewal of religious fervor. As new leaders arrived and brought with them new vigor and a flurry of new ideas, the population of the Americas continued to grow. In Europe they called it "The Age of Reason." In the New World, it was known as "The Great Awakening."

The Age of Reason and Enlightenment

The centuries of religious intolerance in Europe had taken a toll on the psyche of its citizens. Burnings and hangings, excommunication, poverty, and warfare were enough to send anyone packing it up to a world across an ocean. Anything had to be better than what they were living with at home. As a result, there was a backlash against Christianity.

It seemed that being a Christian and having to conform to one religion or another or face persecution was a lot more dangerous than not being religious at all. What was worse? That was the question many of the scholars of the era between 1648 and 1789 began asking themselves. Another question on the table was what is more important: what you believe in or how you behave?

ESSENTIAL

The Age of Reason was not so much a rebirth, but a revival—an awakening of the mind with a fresh look at the world outside of religious boundaries. Reason replaced faith. People began to question why they were worrying so much about the afterlife and not spending nearly as much time appreciating the here-and-now.

Science

Scientific thought was always a spooky area for most Christians. It was nearly impossible to reconcile human-made scientific breakthroughs with scripture. How do you explain why things fall to the ground except to say that God made it so? How do you explain the existence of the universe except to say that God made it so? Well, there were plenty of great minds out there who weren't willing to accept what Christian thought determined as "truth."

Copernicus, a native of Poland, was one of many scientists and philosophers of the age to shake the law of creationism and other biblical "truths." Copernicus theorized that the sun, and not the earth, is the center of our galaxy, while Johann Kepler of Germany added to that by theorizing that the sun emits a magnetic energy that forces the earth and other planets to rotate on a course around the sun. Galileo, from Italy, then added the icing to the cake by inventing a telescope to examine the planets—thus offering proof of a scientific "truth." In 1687, Isaac Newton, an Englishman, summarized all these theories depicting the universe as one giant machine with each bit and piece working in tandem to make us what and who we are today.

Newton published a major scientific manuscript entitled *Mathematical Principles of Natural Philosophy*, in which he turned the world upside down with his theory on the law of gravitation. This presented an entirely new way of looking at the world without God's eyes.

Absorbing New Philosophies

This was an exciting time for the thinkers of the era. The scholarly community was eating up all this new information. It was a fresh way of thinking and an alternative to the only other theory out there as existed in the scripture. Society was disillusioned and looking for new answers, and these scientists, philosophers, and writers offered a renewed energy for understanding.

FACT

John Locke was one of the most influential philosophers of his time. He managed to strike that necessary balance between faith and reason in his *Essay Concerning Human Understanding.* In the essay, he argues that the existence of God is the most "obvious truth that reason discovers." Basically, Locke manages to rationalize the existence of God.

The world was captivated, but opening the world to a new perspective on what seemed to be a completely uncontrolled scientific environment stirred other kinds of fears. Isn't it easier to think that God is in control rather than a magnetic force field? Still others tried to reconcile faith and science. After all, isn't Christianity a perfectly reasonable answer to the laws of the universe? These philosophers tried to strike a balance by saying that the existence of God can be proven by the existence of the heavens, while the resurrection of Christ is a matter of faith as indicated in the scriptures. While this was a time of intellectual enlightenment, it was also an era of intellectual warfare.

The Great Awakening

While Europe was undergoing its Age of Reason and intellectual enlightenment, the New World was experiencing its own revival, otherwise known as "The Great Awakening"—an evangelical movement that whirled its way throughout the New World. Many historians claim its effects are comparable to the upheaval caused by such major events as the French Revolution. However, this revolution was more of a spiritual development that took place over a period of years. Here are some of the beliefs of most evangelical movements:

- Jesus died for the sins of humankind.
- Christ died to redeem humankind from its innate sinful nature.
- The scriptures are the inspired word of God and the absolute authority governing all earthly affairs.
- The church is the eternal body of Christ with a congregation of believers.

Life in the colonies was not easy, and sickness and death were everywhere. There were insects and fevers, animal attacks, floods, and poor nutrition. The colonists not only needed strong community leadership and doctors, but they need spiritual healing as well. In fact many of the ministers were community leaders and doctors. Unlike in their homelands, where public preaching was commonly outlawed, America offered a whole new world of evangelic opportunity to the colonists.

Preachers began to travel from region to region spreading Christian doctrine and keeping the people alive in terms of their religious fervor. They taught their congregations that in such perilous times it was imperative to be concerned with salvation. Without the forgiveness of God, they would preach, a soul could be damned to eternity. So spiritual food became as significant as the food they ate and the clothes they put on their backs.

As the population of the country grew, so did the fear of religious apathy. It was time to hit the road and reach as many people as possible so that they did not stray from God. The preachers took to the towns, to the streets, to the village greens. At first, they may have simply offered a diversion from the stress and boredom of the work-weary colonists, but those who really listened became divinely inspired. The personal awakening of the individual en-masse is what comprised the Great Awakening as an era in American history. The end result was powerful—pushing America toward a greater sense of national awareness and pride, which spurred its citizens toward the American Revolution.

Like Puritanism, evangelicalism wasn't so much a religion as a movement. The Puritans were focused on politics in the New World, trying to create a holy commonwealth that would allow the Puritans the control over community that they so desired.

Jonathan Edwards

Jonathan Edwards (1703–1758) is said to be one of the most influential forces behind the Great Awakening. He was born in 1703 in Windsor, Connecticut. He was one of eleven children. From the time he was a boy he was interested in science and spirituality, and he would study them both. He studied theology at Yale University, and, in 1727, joined his grandfather's Christian ministry in Massachusetts. When his grandfather died, John took over the congregation. He was said to have a monotone voice, lacking the vocal passion of many contemporary evangelists of his time. But he was a popular minister, nonetheless, because despite a lackluster presentation, his message came through loud and clear and spread throughout the country.

Edwards was able to combine his knowledge of philosophy and science with his strong devotion to faith, and successfully convey the resulting message to his congregation. He preached predestination and the dependence of a human being upon God's divine grace. He was a firm believer that grace alone would lead humankind to salvation.

In 1734, Edwards held a religious revival in Northampton, Massachusetts, which brought the Great Awakening to the New England region of the country. The revival resulted in the conversion of hundreds of people. But despite its success and Edwards' growing popularity, his congregation members found him to be far too staunch in his leadership, and expelled him from the congregation in 1750.

Edwards moved on to Stockbridge, Massachusetts, where he cared for a Native American mission and preached to a small, white congregation. In 1754, he completed *The Freedom of Will*, which discussed the many arguments involving determinism. In 1757, he was asked to be president of what is now Princeton University in New Jersey. Edwards died just a few months later from a smallpox vaccine, which actually gave him the disease instead of protecting him from it. Edwards and his wife had eleven children, and he spent an hour a night teaching them religious doctrine.

ESSENTIAL

Determinism is a philosophical theory that opposes the doctrine of free will. Those who espouse determinism believe that a human being's existence is based on pre-existing circumstances.

Historians have called Edwards the "last of the New England Calvinists." His focus on the personal relationship with God and the revival in Northampton led to the Great Awakening and is widely believed to have led to the growth and development of evangelical revivalism.

The Tennent Family

The Tennent family was Presbyterian and had settled in the region of Philadelphia, Pennsylvania. In an effort to put some fire in the bellies of the local congregations, William Tennent and his son Gilbert traversed the countryside and preached against religious complacency. The Presbyterian Church leaders were not pleased because the Tennents' words came across as an attack on orthodox doctrine and their style was positively irreligious.

But the congregations did not have the same reaction. The Tennents' words were so terrifying that they were causing people to cry and wail and break down into fits and seizures. The Tennents and later the likes of

George Whitefield were awakening sleepy-eyed colonial churches, encouraging enthusiasm and conversions that would take hold and form the future of American religion.

FACT

William Tennent opened a school in a log cabin in Neshaminy, Pennsylvania, which later would be known as "The Log College." Tennent taught his students to preach with the passion of the evangelist, and many became revivalist preachers during the Great Awakening.

The Methodist Revival

In many ways, the Great Awakening was to America what the Reformation was to the Catholics. It was a rebirth of sorts—going back to basics, opening the eyes of the complacent, and renewing the meaning of Christ in everyday life. There were many fanatics roaming the wilderness, but in the end the idealism of the colonists took center stage and renewed faith took hold. This was a new world, ripe and ready for anything.

John Wesley

The theological formation of two of the greatest eighteenth-century evangelists originated with a woman. John Wesley (1703–1791) and his brother Charles were the founders of Methodism—a Protestant branch of Christianity that was a late bloomer in relation to the Reformation, but took hold and grew to enormous proportions as a leading church in both England and America.

But what about that woman? Well, the story began in a little town called Epworth, England, in which John and Charles and seventeen·other Wesley children were born and raised. Their mother, Susanna Wesley, was not only their nurturer and caretaker, but their spiritual guide as well—which led the brothers to their destiny of methodical biblical study and religious practice. Their father, Samuel Wesley, was the pastor of St. Andrews Church, a parish of the Church of England.

Plucked from the Burning

When John was five years old, a fire broke out at the parsonage. All the Wesley children were accounted for except John. Samuel tried to run back into the house to get him but the flames were too great and there was no way to find the boy. As the fire raged, a neighbor saw John through the window on the second floor of the burning house and called to him to jump. One neighbor stood on the shoulders of another and the boy jumped into his arms to safety. John's mother, Susanna, considered John's rescue to be an act of God, and later wrote that her son was "a brand plucked out of the burning." Both Susanna and John believed that his daring escape from that fire was a sign from God that he was destined for life in the ministry.

Susanna not only raised her children so that they had food in their stomachs and clothes on their backs, but each week she took time to be their spiritual mentor. Even as a university student, John relied on the words of his mother and one day said that every hour she spent coaching her children and nurturing their souls "would be useful for correcting my heart as it was then for forming my judgment."

FACT

Susanna was a strong, intelligent, and spiritual woman without whom the Wesley brothers would not have developed their zest for religious vocation. For this reason, John Wesley was supportive of women in leadership roles in the Methodist Church, but being the product of his biased times, he did not believe that women should be preachers.

The Results of an Education

John was bright and very well educated. By the time he was eleven years old, he could read English, Latin, and Greek. Because of his mother's teachings, John was able to leave Epworth and attend, through a scholarship, the Charterhouse School in London. At seventeen, John was offered a scholarship to attend Christ Church College at Oxford

University—to follow in the long line of Wesley men that attended this college, starting with his great-grandfather. Despite the fact that Susanna was the inspiration behind the Wesley boys' spiritual and educational lives, there were many Wesley girls in the family who were not allowed to attend university due to eighteenth-century biased laws.

The Little Society

It was during John's Oxford days that the Methodist movement began. He was part of a group that met on a regular basis in order to encourage one another in the Christian faith. The group was called "The Little Society." Although John gets most of the credit for the onset of Methodism, Charles (also a prolific hymn writer) was very influential in the formation of this movement.

Evangelical Awakening

Europe went through its own Great Awakening, but to a much smaller degree than was experienced in the New World. Germany experienced it with the rise of what became known as Pietism, and the English experienced the new wave of religious fervor through the Wesleys' Methodism. Originally, Methodism was strictly part of the Church of England but espoused the principles of more regimented study and the application of religious practice in everyday life.

QUESTION?

Where did the term "Methodist" come from?
The term "Methodist" started as a sort of mockery—it was intended as a derogatory expression directed toward the regimented "method" of its followers. The "Methodists" held a strict adherence to biblical study, fasting, and prayer. Their dedication to scripture also led them into the communities to help feed the poor and help the imprisoned.

This is what the Methodists believe to this day:

- **Christian perfection:** A perfect, sinless life is attainable and should be the goal of Christian existence.
- **Universal redemption:** Jesus Christ died for all people and therefore all people can be saved.
- **Justification by faith:** A Christian is saved through faith alone by the grace of God and not by any good works.
- **The witness of the Holy Spirit:** Each Christian is a child of God, and God is at work in the life of the believer at all times; the Holy Spirit dwells within and calls Christians to witness the life of Christ by loving and caring for all people.
- **Falling from grace:** Even if a Christian had once accepted a life in accordance with Christ's teaching, he or she still can "backslide."
- **The sacraments:** There are only two sacraments: baptism and the Lord's Supper.

The Methodist Mission

In October 1735, John and Charles set sail for the New World. John had received an invitation from a friend to travel to Savannah, Georgia, and like many reformers before him, he was struggling with a restless soul. The work that he and The Little Society continued to do did not seem to be making any kind of dent. John and Charles had bigger ideals than that and were on an inner quest to understand what their purpose in life might be. The opportunity to sail to the New World enlightened their idealistic souls, and they saw an opportunity to make a difference.

The Church of England ordained John, who then served for some time as an assistant at his father's church. He, then, became the pastor of the Georgia settlers. He had dreamed of being a missionary to the Native Americans, and now it seemed there was a possibility of his wishes coming true. Charles shared his brother's vision.

The Singing Moravians

On board the ship, John was impressed by the simple faith of the Moravians (from a region of Germany), who were confident in the midst of stormy seas. John was scared and marveled at the way the Moravians bore the journey through faith and song. John felt that his faith was weak and pined to have such faith and assurance in his life. He was heartened to see that such faith did exist and even more amazed that it could bring such inner peace.

FACT

The Moravians were Pietists—a reform movement that began with the spread of Lutheranism in Germany during the seventeenth century as an "assembly of piety" (or devout spirituality). The Pietists were against secularization and wanted greater emphasis placed on social concerns and education.

Recipe for Disaster

John's Georgia experience was a complete disaster. He didn't elegantly maneuver his way into society; rather he bombarded his way in with his idealistic vim and vigor. But it's not like these settlers had just arrived and were floundering in a sea of religious confusion. Religion had taken hold by the eighteenth century and most communities were quite content within their religious stability and practice.

John was also far too pious for the communities of Georgia. He considered the colonists to be a bunch of "gluttons, thieves, and liars." He tried to prohibit the jewelry and fancy dress of the local women, and to preach his strict piety, but the congregations would have none of it. To make matters worse, John fell in love with a woman named Sophy Hopkey, who did not seem to return his affections and married someone else. John was hurt, and so he barred her from the rite of Holy Communion. This incensed her husband, so John was forced to flee the colony and decided to head back to England.

Lost and Found

By 1737, John was obviously dispirited and questioned his calling. Charles, who was also ordained by the Church of England, tried to help his brother, but John seemed to continue to flounder. He sought solace amongst the Moravians, remembering how they had inspired him aboard the vessel to the New World with the advice: "Preach faith till you have it; and then *because* you have it, you *will* preach faith."

Spiritual Enlightenment

On May 24, 1738, something dramatic happened to John at a meeting at Aldersgate Street in England. Upon reading Martin Luther's preface to the biblical book of Romans, John experienced a conversion. He later wrote, ". . . through faith in Christ, I found my heart strangely warmed. I felt I did trust in Christ, Christ alone for salvation: and an assurance was given me that he had taken away my sins even mine, and saved me from the law of sin and death." (From John Wesley's journal, dated May 24, 1738).

John knew he was saved and he had found his message—now the trick was to figure out what to do with it.

From this experience came the "Great Revival." Modern United Methodists still pay homage to Aldersgate and John's experience. In fact, many churches and other institutions are named Aldersgate after John's moment of epiphany.

Taking It Outside

John and Charles were still Anglican priests throughout the "Great Methodist Revival," but they were controversial in both their style and methods. The Church of England was a rather staid institution with certain laws and values firmly implanted. The rector at Epworth did not let John or Charles preach at the Anglican Church, and they were also censured by the Church of England due to their controversial ways.

Why would these two influential preachers be reprimanded? Well, they did what the Church of England frowned upon and that was open-air preaching. John preached everywhere and anywhere in order to spread the "good news" (or the teachings of the gospel).

George Whitefield

George Whitefield (1714–1770) also attempted to preach in the New World only to find an endless sea of trouble. He headed back to England, where he was ordained in 1738. Instead of taking to the limited audience of a pulpit, George decided that the best way to preach to the people was in the great outdoors. This was, however, outlawed by the Church of England—but that did not stop George.

In 1739, he went to Bristol, England, to preach to the miners who had little interest (or time for that matter) to bother attending church services. This was a tough audience, too. These men were hardened and tired, and there was no way to tell if any of these Bible teachings would hold any meaning at all for them. But George trusted his instincts and sure enough, he managed to renew their spirits and bring them back to church. Whitefield practiced the same revivalist preaching as William Tenent in the New World. Before he knew it, Whitefield was preaching to thousands of locals at a time, getting similar results with every sermon.

FACT

Wesley was on a mission. He preached to the prisoners, to travelers just passing through, in open fields, and on vessels crossing over to Ireland. Wherever there was an opportunity to spread the word, Wesley grabbed it. In fact, it is said that he once preached a sermon to hundreds while standing on his father's tombstone.

Whitefield tried to convince John Wesley to join him in Bristol, but John knew he was no match for Whitefield's style of preaching. Wesley was a stand-at-the-pulpit kind of preacher and didn't think he'd be adaptable to the outdoor method. But he went anyway and discovered something he never expected. He was really good at it. He had finally found his calling. He preached to thousands at a time and the "Methodist Revival" was officially underway as thousands converted to the church by virtue of his powerful sermons. He didn't have to travel to the New World to convert the "heathen," as there were enough of them right there on his own doorstep.

The Methodist Structure

It wasn't always easy for Wesley. Not only was he mocked as a Bible-thumping preacher, but every so often he was attacked by a barrage of sticks and stones and other such missiles. He was even beaten by angry mobs. But this would not deter him. He felt this was his calling and no amount of insult or violence was going to force him from his work.

In 1751, Wesley married a woman named Molly Vazeille. She tried to travel with him, but due to failing health could not keep up. Their relationship became rocky and she eventually left him.

Whereas Whitefield was an outstanding preacher, he lacked any kind of desire for organization. That's where Wesley stepped in. Wesley was a man of great administrative ability in addition to being an inspirational preacher. Although Methodist societies were popping up throughout Europe, there was no real organized Methodist church. The Methodists still operated under the Church of England, and Wesley worked within this structure by encouraging people to attend their local parishes and receive Holy Communion. However, the Wesley followers found they were more comfortable praying within their own society. So they did. They confessed their sins to each other as a group; they obeyed the leadership of their various communities; and they prayed and sang as a means of devotion.

ESSENTIAL

Charles Wesley wrote more than 7,000 hymns in his lifetime—which is perhaps his greatest legacy, in addition to being one of the founders of Methodism. His most popular hymns, which are still sung in Protestant churches throughout the world, are "Jesus, Lover of My Soul," "Hark the Herald Angels Sing," and "Christ the Lord Is Risen Today."

The Methodist Church

John decided to follow the structure of the Moravian Pietists and form the Methodist societies in small groups that he called "classes," meaning divisions. The classes met once a week, and each member encouraged another in their Christian experience. As the system grew and flourished,

Wesley began to implement church leadership in the form of laymen from the societies and classes. These laymen severed as preachers and assistants, but they were not allowed to administer the sacraments.

The Annual Conference

The Methodist societies grew to such huge proportions that there was no way Wesley could keep in touch with each one of them, so he began the Annual Conference, where church leaders gathered and discussed policy and doctrine. Eventually, the Methodist Church became a church in its own right but still under the domain of the Church of England. Even under great pressure to separate from Anglicanism, Wesley did not budge. That was not his vision for his style of Christian practice. He promised "to live and die a member of the Church of England."

Methodism in America

The Methodists eventually arrived in America. They were sent by John, who hoped for a more successful venture this time around, and soon began caving toward the idea of separation from the Church of England. John sent Francis Asbury to the colonies to oversee the work of establishing Methodist societies and, in Philadelphia in 1773, the first American Methodist conference was held. What the colonists needed to establish the societies was ordained leadership, which the Church of England refused to grant. The colonists had no choice, therefore, but to separate. Wesley saw that this was going to be a problem and took matters into his own hands by appointing Richard Whatcost and Thomas Vasey as lay preachers for the ministry. He sent Dr. Thomas Coke to serve as superintendent. In 1784, the American Methodist Church became a separate and distinct denomination.

Wesley died in 1791. He left behind 79,000 Methodists in England and 40,000 in the Americas. There are more than 20 million Methodists in the world today. Ⓔ

Chapter 21

E **Revolution and Reform**

The world went through tremendous change over the eighteenth and nineteenth centuries. With dreams of individual happiness—sparked by the Age of Reason and a renewed religious fervor as witnessed by the Great Awakening—America was headed for a lasting freedom apart from Great Britain and the Church of England. The stage was set for a "New World" order.

Religion and Revolution

The Great Awakening had a lasting effect on the American Christian perspective. It not only impacted the religious mood of the nation, but it also had psychological consequences that changed the way one Christian would treat another in the future. Ultimately, what came of the Great Awakening was something that had been sorely lacking in the history of Christianity: tolerance.

It was acceptable, for example, for a Baptist to attend a revivalist camp meeting (an outdoor evangelical service) with other Protestant Christians. If the message was about devotion to Christ, then it was a message for all. This opened a door to more diverse communities and acceptance of differences. This was the first step toward a future of democracy and autonomy.

It was inevitable that America would want to break from the dictatorial monarchy overseas and head into a future of further religious freedom. The revivalist movements swept across the country in waves with one "awakening" more powerful than the next.

Appointment of Bishops

England was still appointing bishops of the Church of England to oversee the colonies. It was the only way the monarchs could keep tabs on what was going on across the Atlantic. For the Americans practicing within the Church of England, that was fine; they were happy to have their bishops appointed by England. But the Congregationalists and the Presbyterians did not run their church government according to Church of England structure—they didn't have bishops and, if you recall, the issue of church government was one of the reasons they broke away from Anglicanism to begin with. They wanted autonomy—no interference from outsiders, including the "mother country."

Taxation Without Representation

The infamous Stamp Act of 1765 enacted by the English monarchy was more than most colonists were willing to take. No one consulted them on this tax, and there was no government representation between the colonies and the monarchy—no one to stand up and speak out for their interests in the English House of Parliament.

The tax was imposed on certain goods from the colonies, and the colonists were expected to just live with it. But this was a new generation. The colonies were now well over a century old and feelings of pride and desire for independence had started to grow. Loyalties to Great Britain had changed drastically. People were no longer looking to the monarchy in the same way they might have when they were just fledgling, and often floundering, communities. Certainly, there were some Americans still loyal to Britain, but they were also interested in their own personal well-being, as well as the well-being of their newly found homeland.

FACT

The Loyalists were the settlers who remained true to the English monarchy, while the Patriots wanted independence from the crown. So, the American Revolution was not fought by one united nation against the oppressive mother country, the colonies had their own troubles at home in the division of loyalty, which caused inter-American warfare as well.

Puritan Ideals with a Twist

The Puritan dream of a pure Christian existence in a new land, independent of Anglican control, never left the psyche of future settlers. It was ingrained in the mindset of the colonists and lasted into future generations. With more and more people arriving in the colonies and religious conversions taking place from coast to coast, the Puritan ideal seemed like a real possibility. There was a certain optimism that perhaps this was the land of Christ's vision—a world of love and devotion to God.

Here is a list of how the most popular American Protestant religions felt toward the Revolution:

- **Puritans:** They saw England as their persecutor so it didn't matter to them if they broke away from either the country or the church—they supported the Revolution.

- **Church of England:** Church of England members wanted to stay loyal to England because it meant more power and prestige for themselves—they were against the Revolution.
- **Methodists:** It would seem that the Methodists and their evangelical style would be supportive of the Revolution, but John Wesley spoke out against it.
- **Lutherans:** The Lutherans were divided, with some becoming Loyalists (pro-England) while others became Patriots (pro-independence).
- **Quakers, Moravians, and Mennonites:** These groups did not believe in violent means to an end and to this day they uphold their tradition of pacifism.

Revolutionary Religious Changes

While there were certainly religious and idealistic motives behind the American Revolution, the Revolution also affected lasting changes on American Protestantism. Most of the churches found themselves in shambles with scattered congregations, some disunity, and even disillusionment. Atheism did not exist before the Revolution, but afterward, it found its way into the American psyche—not so much because of the Revolution, but because of the idealism surrounding individuality and freedom. There was a newfound strength in the individual that burst the boundaries of devotion to Christ. But there weren't many that strayed from the fold. Most Americans wanted to rebuild their churches, as well as their faith, and so they did.

ESSENTIAL

The Great Awakening was the American version of the Reformation, only it was unique to a world that was starting from scratch. Protestantism in America became different from that of Europe because it was a unifying force, and not one of dissension, that drove the nation into the future.

The Founding Fathers and Religion

Ironically, George Washington (1732–1799), the first president of the United States of America, was a devout member of the Church of England, so his part in the Revolution had to have had some emotional impact on him. While he chose to fight for Americans against the British, he was not necessarily in favor of a departure from the Church of England. However, he was able to separate his spirituality from his political convictions. The other Founding Fathers, John Adams and Benjamin Franklin for example, were outspoken on the issue now known as the separation of church and state, despite their Protestant and agnostic (religiously ambivalent) beliefs.

Episcopalianism

Many Loyalist members of the Church of England fled America and headed for Canada. While Canada saw an increase in Anglican Church membership, Massachusetts—where most of the American Anglicans were living—saw a tremendous decline. Before the Revolution, some American members of the Church of England believed in the "high" church tradition, which was more in keeping with the Catholic services, while others held to a "low" church tradition, which had more of a flare toward Protestantism.

After the war, they wanted to show their loyalty to the Church of England but on new American ground. So the scattered church members decided to unite under a new theme. They established a more Americanized church by appointing American bishops and archbishops within an American church hierarchy rather than an English one. The English bishops, however, had taken an oath to the monarchy that they would not consecrate any American bishops, so the Americans had to find another route.

After several meetings and the help of some Scottish bishops, in 1784, American clergyman and missionary, Samuel Seabury, was consecrated as the first bishop of the "Episcopal Church"—the American version of the Church of England.

"We give you thanks, O Lord our God, for your goodness in bestowing upon this Church the gift of the episcopate, which we celebrate in this remembrance of the consecration of Samuel Seabury; and we pray that, joined together in unity with our bishops, and nourished by your holy Sacraments, we may proclaim the Gospel of redemption with apostolic zeal; through Jesus Christ our Lord, who lives and reigns with you and the Holy Spirit, one God, now and for ever. Amen."

—Episcopal prayer, *The Collect*

Methodism

Even though John Wesley had opposed the Revolution, he did not want to see Methodism die in America, so he was going to have to find a way to help the Methodists regroup. They still did not have any ordained clergy, and before the war they were participating in Church of England services. John Wesley found a way to ordain Dr. Thomas Coke as superintendent of the Methodist Church and began to produce material that could be used in American Methodist services. Wesley was seen as the founder of the church, so the congregations accepted what he presented to them. Evangelistic practices helped the Methodist numbers grow and by 1790, it was 57,000 members strong in America.

Other Postwar Protestant Changes

The Lutherans in America were still predominantly German speaking and in this new postwar world, they knew they would have to conform to the society around them and learn English. Additionally, they began to cut ties with their sponsor churches in Europe. This was truly an era of independence and self-reliance, and everyone was trying to make their world fit the new one.

The Presbyterians in America had to find a way to organize their own church structure apart from the Scottish home churches. They would have to find a way to organize localized leadership while maintaining the larger church structure of government. The American

Revolution opened the door for all reformed churches to restructure in this new "free" society.

While atheism was virtually nonexistent before the Revolution, pockets of nonbelievers began to sprout up, especially among the educated upper classes. This is something that Europe did not have to contend with, even in its toughest times. Almost everyone had believed in God—it was just a question of how they chose to demonstrate and practice their beliefs.

Deism

After the Revolution and spawned by the Age of Reason (or Enlightenment), "Deism" also found its way into the American psyche, but mostly amongst the wealthy scholars of the upper class, such as Thomas Jefferson and John Adams. Deism was a philosophy that was the antithesis of evangelicalism. It emphasized morality but rejected the divinity of Christ. It upheld that with observance of the design of the universe, one can reasonably draw the conclusion that there is a God. This was more of an intellectual approach to religion versus an emotional or spiritual one particularly popular in revivalist America. Rationalism was the belief in the use of reason as a moral guide to understanding basic truths.

African Americans and Protestantism

The Great Awakening was actually a series of awakenings that rippled through the colonies from the 1730s to the 1770s. Historians refer to it as the first of its kind guiding a nation to spiritual enlightenment. It would not be the only awakening, however. Historians will often break American history in terms of future awakenings. Through American history, various factions of society were affected by different spiritual beliefs. African Americans, for example, were touched by the Second Great Awakening, which is believed to have spanned from 1790 into the

1840s. Inspired by evangelism, the slaves moved from prayer in the fields and slave quarters to African-American church congregations. They drew their inspiration from both Christian belief and African cultural trends. Because of their state in life, the church became a critical survival tool and the number of African-American church-goers continued to grow.

FACT

The first slave church was a Baptist Church that opened in 1773 in South Carolina. When the number of slave congregations across the South continued to grow, they formed the National Baptist Convention. The African-American Christian population grew well into the twentieth century, and from these churches sprang the conviction, confidence, and inspiration to start the Civil Rights Movement in the 1960s.

The Second Great Awakening

The Second Great Awakening was highly significant because it came in the wake of the Revolution. With the rise of atheism, deism, and rationalism, there was more need than ever to turn to evangelical preaching. In the early 1800s, only 10 percent of Americans belonged to an organized religion. The American Revolution had not only scattered church membership, but the Age of Reason had caused people to question religious principles.

Some of the Protestant Church organizations reunited to find a way to spread Christianity to the west of the eastern seaboard. The Congregationalists and the Presbyterians, in particular, banded together on an evangelical mission. This backfired on Congregationalism, in general, as many of the new converts joined the Presbyterian Church instead. But the evangelical movement did spread across the country— first to the midwestern states and then further on to the west.

The Second Great Awakening included many women and African Americans. One of the most famous revivalist women was Ann Randolph Page, a white Episcopalian from Virginia, who is often credited with the beginnings of feminism and the rise of the abolitionism. It was not unusual for a woman to have a leadership role in a revivalist movement and for the evangelicals to speak out against slavery.

Civil War and Reunification

The issue of slavery, economic, and philosophical differences divided the North from the South in America, prompting the American Civil War (1861–1865). When the war came to an end, white Christian churches again faced a crisis of disunity. They had to regroup and restructure, and this time the Protestant division between North and South was even stronger than it was before. There was a great deal of mistrust within one's own Protestant group, depending on which side of the war you fought. But they did reunite.

Slavery

What does this have to do with African Americans and slavery? Well, historians and theologians have debated the topic of slavery throughout the years. Did the settlers merely justify slavery because of their strong work ethic, or did they really believe that an African American was subordinate to them? Well, the answer really is . . . both. Calvinism asserts that there are the "elect" and the "damned." American Protestantism was rooted in Calvinist beliefs and it was a reflex for them to think in terms of who will be saved and who will not. One of the signs of making someone part of the elect was success. If you were successful, you would be saved; if not, well, in all likelihood, you would be damned.

Additionally, Christians turned to the scriptures to find evidence that slavery was an acceptable and necessary part of life. However, it can be argued that there are just as many Bible entries against slavery. On the other hand, it was necessary for the white Americans to insist on slavery in order to get their work done. Obviously, the more money you had, the more slaves you could buy, but also, the more land you had, the more work needed to be done and so the more slaves would be needed. Although the slaves cost money, their labor was free. So, justifying enslavement was convenient more than religious.

ESSENTIAL

Not all Protestant churches approved of slavery. The Quakers, Mennonites, and some of the northern Protestant organizations did not approve and spoke out against it. Many non-Christians also voiced their disapproval and became Abolitionists on a mission to put an end to the barbarism. Since under the Dred Scott Decision in 1857, slaves were considered personal property, an Abolitionist was actually considered a criminal.

African-American Churches

Many plantation owners took it upon themselves to provide spiritual guidance to their slaves—especially the servants who lived in the main houses. One Baptist deacon went so far as to build a church for the benefit of his slaves. With the Abolitionist movement on the upswing, slave owners wanted to keep tabs on their slaves' religious practices and the services they attended. The message they wanted to convey to the slaves through Christianity was that they should obey their masters. Some white churches allowed African Americans in their services, but they were forced to sit in a separate section, usually a balcony overlooking the activities below.

By 1860, the Methodist Church in America had 7,500 members and the Baptist Church had more than 1,000 members. The Presbyterian and Episcopal churches admitted African-American members as full members. But overall, African Americans preferred their own churches and their own services, because not only did they feel more at home, but they had their own African-American preachers. In their own churches, they could practice their own brand of spirituality, which included devotion to Christ accented by their own African cultural heritage. The white services were all about obedience and very little about salvation.

The Importance of Song

Music has played a huge part in many Protestant services with the exception of the Puritans, perhaps. Traditional church music consisted of hymns and anthems sung in a European style—sometimes by congregations alone and other times by a combination of congregation and church choir groups. In the African-American churches, congregations began to merge their belief in Christ with the desire for freedom and salvation in the afterlife, so their music took on a theme of pain and sadness, which came to be known as the "Negro Spiritual."

In the 1920s, gospel music took center stage. It was a mingling of the Protestant hymn, the Negro Spiritual, and African musical culture. Gospel music in itself provided a sort of evangelical revivalism experience that African Americans celebrated every Sunday. White (or southern) gospel music took on more a flare of country and western music, which originated from European folk music styles.

FACT

In many southern regions of the United States, African-American Baptists perform outdoor baptism in true biblical style. A river or lake setting was a common spot for southern baptism—the natural setting was seen as symbolic and spiritual in its purity.

Christianity and Social Reform

In the late nineteenth century, England enacted the Poor Law. This meant that the government would take responsibility for those in financial need, providing them with shelter and food. While this seems like a good thing—it was actually a major deception. The poor who were given this shelter and food were required to perform tasks normally dedicated to prisoners.

England was a society of classes, and class defined the person. The rich were born to wealth, title, and position while the poor had nothing and no hope of anything but a decent job. Jobs were scarce in Victorian England (1837–1901), so the shelters seemed like the best option, but it was really a no-win situation.

The Booths

Enter William and Catherine Booth. William Booth was born to a poor family in Nottingham, England, in 1829. He went to work as an apprentice in a pawn shot to help support his mother and sisters. It was while he was working that he began to understand the plight of the poor. As a teenager, he became a Christian and it became his personal mission to convert others. He moved to London, where he joined the Methodist Church and later became a minister. In 1855, he married Catherine Mumford and began preaching his message across the country.

Catherine, equally devoted to God, was a constant source of support to William. At the time, it was unheard of for a woman to preach, but Catherine devoted her life to the church and found herself preaching at children's services. During these years, she became convinced that a woman should have the right to preach, and so she did—traveling to people's homes and attempting to convert the nonbelievers. Catherine found herself devoting a great deal of her time to helping alcoholics give up their addiction and turn to God.

Catherine and William had eight children, two of whom later became generals of the Salvation Army. William was referred to as the "General," while Catherine was called "The Army Mother." All the members of the Salvation Army are referred to as soldiers in the Army of God. William is also credited with the establishment of the missing persons bureau.

The Birth of the Salvation Army

In 1865, William left his Methodist ministry and devoted his time to preaching on the streets and to small, local gatherings. That same year, he was invited to preach at an outdoor service in Whitechapel, England. He agreed and the event moved him so much that he decided to start "The Christian Mission." The beginning was not easy, however. He held meetings in an abandoned warehouse, where the members were harassed and attacked by locals. William often left the meetings beaten, bloody, and exhausted. At that time, there were hundreds of missions in England, but William felt the message of "The Christian Mission" was different. He later changed the name of the organization to "The Salvation Army."

In 1891, William Booth wrote *In the Darkest England and the Way Out.* It was a controversial book because it basically taught the working class population how to break the boundaries of class and make lives for themselves. William then set out to raise money to set up a labor bureau, which would help people find jobs. He also wanted to purchase a farm where people could be trained in several different kinds of work. However, training workers when there is no work could cause a huge glitch in his plan. Booth, however, foresaw that problem so he trained the workers to find jobs in the colonies where laborers were needed.

This is where the Salvation Army really took hold. By 1912, the Salvation Army existed in fifty-eight countries. Booth's book sold 200,000 copies in the first year and later became the blueprint for the formation of the welfare system set up in England in 1948. William Booth died in 1912. He was eighty-three years old.

The YMCA

The YMCA (Young Men's Christian Association) was founded in 1844 in London by George Williams, a farmer's son, and a group of his London friends. When he was twenty years old, George Williams left the farm on which he was raised, and traveled to London to be a sales assistant in a draper's shop. Like William Booth, Williams was a Christian exposed to the unhealthy environment of the poor. There were too many people and too few jobs. The young men who moved to the city looking for work were living in cramped and uncomfortable living quarters, sometimes over their company's shop.

Williams saw this as a no-win situation and was aware of the gross injustice of the situation. He and a group of friends decided to organize the first YMCA to provide a shelter for young working men of London. There were only two requirements—Bible study and prayer. They called the shelter the Young Men's Christian Association and by 1851, there were more than twenty-four such shelters in Great Britain, with 27,000 members. That same year, the Y (as it is colloquially called today) reached North America with the first opening in Montreal, Canada, and the second in Boston, Massachusetts.

Williams and his friends were Christians determined not only to help their peers but to spread the word of God. They were evangelicals in their own right, struggling to make a life for themselves in the big city. The YMCA was a unique organization in that it broke the boundaries of class and religion. It was a place of shelter, survival, and prayer. The idea eventually grew to include many factions of society, including women (YWCA), children, all races, classes, religions, and nationalities.

A freed slave named Anthony Bowen opened the first YMCA for African Americans in 1853 in Washington, D.C. At this time there were 397 Y's in seven different countries.

In 1894, George Williams became Sir George Williams when he was knighted by Queen Victoria. When he died, this farmer's son was buried with noblemen and statesmen under the floor of St. Paul's Cathedral—a testament to his life and work in uniting all people. A stained glass window in Westminster Abbey bears the Red Triangle symbol for the YMCA. It is dedicated to Sir George Williams and all YMCA organizations. Ⓔ

Chapter 22

(E) **Christianity
in the Modern Age**

Christianity has undergone great challenges in its 2,000-year-old history from heresy, war, and corruption to reform and tolerance. But in the modern era, the church found itself in a compromising position. In order to keep members, both Catholics and Protestants had to reconsider what had never been achieved in the past: an effective form of unity. After all, a Christian is a Christian.

Women in the Church

While women are not allowed to be ordained as priests in the Roman Catholic Church, many Protestant churches are more inclusive in their practices. The Catholic Church has battled the issue of female ordination for decades. As women have taken more powerful roles in society, they would like the option to hold more powerful roles in the Catholic Church as well. But it doesn't seem like the Vatican will budge on the matter any time soon.

Women As Priests?

There are a couple of reasons why Catholics do not want women to be ordained as priests. One of the earliest reasons can be traced back to the apostles and conversion of the "heathens." In pagan times, women were worshipped as goddesses and priestesses. Catholicism, however, did not welcome any form of paganism.

The other reason has to do with the Catholic Church doctrine itself—as a matter of faith. While some critics argue that the Catholic Church merely wants to mire itself in ancient patriarchal tradition, the church claims that Jesus was a man and, therefore, their church leaders should also be men.

FACT

While most Protestant churches do ordain women, there are still some more conservative factions that do not. For example, Southern Baptist Convention (the largest baptism organization in the United States) will not ordain women, while the American Baptist Convention will.

Religion and Communism

Karl Marx was one of the founders of Communism, which changed the face of Europe and caused a major rift between its eastern and western portions. In 1848, Karl Marx and Friedrich Engels published the *Communist Manifesto*, a pamphlet outlining their philosophy. It was not a religious philosophy, but a political one that emphasized a societal structure different than the one they felt existed in Europe.

The basis of communist ideology was that society was built on a class system of the rich and poor (or the employers and workers). Communists claimed the capitalists suppressed the workers by keeping them in a "no-win" situation, not unlike the feudal system that you read about before. History, Marx said, was based on a series of clashes between the classes, and religion was nothing more than an "opium" to suppress the masses and keep them in their place.

Marx's vision was a worldwide class revolution to crush the class system and put everyone on equal footing with equal chances. He wanted to see everyone as the worker and eliminate the upper class. The goal would be to crush existing classes, traditions, and definitely, religions.

Here are just a few of the principles of communism and religion as described by Marx and Engels:

- Life is material and there is no God.
- The current state of law, moral values, and religion is a "bourgeois" (or upper class) concept designed to keep the wealthy rich while the poor stay poor.
- Religion is used for nothing more than spiritual subjugation, while the government is used for economic exploitation.

Dreams of Utopia

The *Communist Manifesto* was the tool used by the Russians during the Revolution of 1919, at which time the Soviet Union was formed. It then conquered several Eastern European countries, bringing them under the communist umbrella as well. While communism was a theory of idealism—of a Utopian society—it proved a failure, as witnessed by the poverty and corruption that ensued.

Why did Communism fail?
Communism suppressed the workers, rather than lifting them from a life of poverty. That's not to say that communism itself is a failure as an ideal, but when put into practice, it seems to defy the laws of human nature.

Charles Darwin

In 1859, Charles Darwin (1809–1882), a British naturalist, wrote *On the Origin of Species by Means of Natural Selection, or the Preservation of Favoured Races in the Struggle for Life* (understandably referred to as *The Origin of Species*), which caused an upheaval for Christianity. His theory of evolution, most likely inspired by the Age of Reason, defied religious concepts of creationism. Darwin believed that human beings came from nature and developed into what they are today through time and a series of natural processes. Some Christian churches put a great deal of emphasis on trying to stop his theory from spreading—but it was an unsuccessful attempt in the end.

Fundamentalism and Radicalism

Between 1910 and 1915, a series of twelve books were published defining fundamental Christian truths. Three million copies of the books were distributed to students of theology throughout the United States. The books contained the work of sixty-four authors, and the series was called *The Fundamentals*.

The books were a way of combating some of the liberal movements taking place throughout the country's various Christian denominations. The Baptists, Presbyterians, Methodists, and Disciples of Christ all contributed to the books and, therefore, to the beginnings of fundamentalism that swept across the United States.

FACT

The Fundamentalist Fellowship was the first group to take the word "fundamental" and apply it to its own religious philosophy. The fellowship believed that the liberal Christians were forfeiting the fundamentals of the scriptures, including the sinful nature of man, the death of Christ as a means of salvation for the individual and society, and the ability for a human being to be saved aside from God's grace.

The fundamentalist movement caused a rift between conservative and liberal Christians, dividing the denominations mostly between conservative and liberal regions of the country. But the rift did not have a lasting negative effect. Ultimately, especially in the late twentieth and early twenty-first centuries, the spirit of Christianity in the United States was one of unification.

Evangelical Renewal

Evangelicalism always seems to be a method that works in the United States. When the evangelicals don't hit the road and preach to the thousands, church denominations tend to settle in their various locals throughout the country and a certain amount of complacency takes hold, sometimes causing numbers of church-goers to decrease. But when the country goes through a period of evangelical awakenings, the numbers soar. Perhaps that has to do with the size of the country.

Getting the word out as a means of unifying Christians (or converting non-Christians) was not easy, simply because of the gigantic land mass, the division of conservative and liberal mentalities, and the ever-increasing population over the centuries. One way or another, the evangelical preachers have always had an impact on American society and religion.

Modern Evangelicalism

There was no greater invention for evangelicalism than the invention of the television. If the goal of the evangelical preacher was to reach the masses, what better way to go than by means of a piece of modern technological equipment, whose very purpose is to reach a large a audience? Had Karl Marx been alive to see this invention, he might have accused it of being the opium of the masses, because of the hold it has taken over modern culture across most of the world.

The Advent of Televangelism

Log on to the Internet and you can stream evangelists into your computer. Turn on the television and you can find Christian networks, such as the

Trinity Broadcasting Network (TBN) and the Christian Broadcasting Network (CBN). Even local television stations broadcast programs such as the *Old Time Gospel Hour* and the evangelist Billy Graham's various programs. Televangelists have been around since television began; however, the advent of cable and satellite television has seen a multitude of a new era of televangelists.

According to the Trinity Foundation (not affiliated with TBN), there are more than 500 televangelists and about 350 religious television stations that are members of the National Religious Broadcaster Association.

While this is true to the American tradition—spreading the word through the evangelicals—with the advent of mass communication, the Christian message can be heard not only all over America, but throughout the world as well. But there is a problem.

Corruption on the Air

Many of the mainline churches, such as the Presbyterians, United Methodists, and Lutherans, take issue with the theology being preached by the televangelists, which many call a "prosperity" theology: "If you give to my ministry you will be rewarded financially by God"—a theme that is echoed many times by these televangelists. Isn't this what Luther objected to in the first place? Isn't this just a system of modern-day indulgences? And where does the money go, exactly?

Abuse of Power

Jim Bakker, an infamous televangelist, was imprisoned for the fraudulent use of millions of dollars donated by his faithful followers—innocent of the knowledge that the preacher they admired was pocketing their hard-earned cash rather than turning it back into his ministry. Bakker told his audience that the money sent to him was going to be used to spread God's word. Despite the fact that the Bible says that adultery is a sin, and this is the message he spread to his followers, Bakker was also involved in an affair with his secretary, Jessica Hahn.

Oral Roberts, another televangelist, abused his followers with his request for $8 million, which he wanted in the form of donations. Roberts locked himself in a tower and proclaimed that if he didn't get the money for his ministry by a specific date, God would "call him home."

There are of course exceptions to this—not all the televangelists are corrupt. Preachers like Billy Graham are greatly respected.

The Reverend Billy Graham is one of today's most popular evangelist preachers in the world. In 1949, when the world was recuperating from World War II, Graham started a popular "tent crusade," in which he took the message of Christ all over the country in evangelical services that raised the Christian spirits of weary Americans. When television became more mainstream, he took to the air waves and reached even more people.

Mixing the Message

Other televangelists have driven wedges through the multicultures of this country. Taking advantage of the September 11, 2001 attacks in the United States, two well-known televangelists, Pat Robertson and Jerry Fallwell, on the *700 Club* (another TV outlet for the televangelists) claimed that certain groups of people were partially responsible for this attack. This was a blatant abuse of faith and freedom of speech, in that a tragic situation was used to push a completely unrelated conservative religious message condemning pro-choice supporters, feminists, and homosexuals. The two did come under fire from their critics, however.

There are other television channels that offer Christian services without any hype at all. Eternal Word Television News (EWTN), a Catholic Channel that airs full Catholic Masses is one such example. Other channels offer Protestant services on Sunday mornings. This is an excellent use of mass communication as a means to reach the homebound or the elderly.

But are all televangelists money-hungry, ultraconservative, sexist bigots? No, of course not. There are people of faith who believe they are doing God's work by preaching through the medium of television. The way for a Christian to identify the corrupt versus the legitimate is to see if they are more interested in selling you blessed holy water or personally signed Bibles (or just ask you straight out for money in the beginning, middle, and end of the program) than they are about preaching faith. As with anything, buyer beware!

Catholics Today

Catholics today are at a crossroads and have faced a great deal of scrutiny in recent years for their conservative stance. The pope still holds spiritual power over Catholics, and his words do have an effect on not only Christianity, but on world affairs as well. Heads of state often visit the pope in the Vatican—a means of recognizing his importance in the world. The current pope never gives approval for war because he believes in diplomacy as a means of solving world problems—not the use of violence.

Pope John Paul II, a native of Poland, has made it his mission to spread the Catholic message throughout the world. Is he a modern-day evangelist or an apostolic messenger? One way or another, he is doing what he vowed to do when he was elected to the papacy in 1978. He is also the most traveled pope in the history of the Catholic Church, having completed ninety-five international trips and 142 trips within Italy.

Current Issues

Catholics today are at a turning point, not unlike the days of the early Reformation. Many devout Catholics who value the traditions and teachings of the Roman Catholic Church are working toward more laity (nonclerical) involvement in the church. Many feel that the clergy have held too much power and authority without any outside checks and balances.

The recent revelation that priests have sexually abused children in their spiritual care is an example of misuse of church power, not to mention a crime. The Catholic Church made little effort to investigate the allegations over the years, which resulted in more and more crimes against children. With the assistance of the church, the abusive priests managed to move from parish to parish when allegations were made against them.

The outcry from the public of these atrocities has finally led the laity to demand more input in the teaching and liturgy of the church. There are pleas for the church to stop covering up rogue priests and allow the laity power to make decisions.

Vatican II

Vatican II was a modern-day Catholic council held in 1962, opened during the papacy of John XXIII and closed by Pope Paul VI. Vatican I was held between 1869–1870, and if you consider everything that occurred in the world between then and now (two world wars, Nazism, nuclear warfare, the rise of the Soviet Union, the Cold War, and so much more . . .), it is understandable that a second Vatican Council was necessary. Catholic leaders felt that society was declining due to so much worldwide atrocity: the breakdown of the family with the increase in divorce, the growth of atheism, and the decreasing number of Christian churchgoers. It was time for an effort at some serious reforms.

FACT

Vatican II was an attempt to create unity within the Christian churches and to request more Catholic involvement in servicing Christians worldwide. Vatican II concluded with several decrees, including the Ecumenical Decree of 1964.

Here are some of the unification principles accepted during the 1962 Catholic council:

1. All those baptized have a right to be called Christian. They are all members of the "Body of Christ."
2. All Christians are encouraged to join ecumenical activity as a means of unification in the name of Christ.
3. While Catholics should not ignore their fellow Christians, their first duty is to put their own house in order.
4. Catholic leadership and theologians should study the history, culture, and practices of the "separated" churches in order to open their hearts to dialogue and future progress.

5. Prayers of unity should be recited jointly by Catholics and Protestants alike. Catholics should be guided in this by Catholic Church clergy.
6. Despite the ecumenical efforts, a Catholic must remain true to his or her faith, as set forth by the Catholic Church.

Protestants Today

The Protestant Church today is at a crossroads as well. With the mainline churches declining and the independents growing, a reassessment of the overall church structure is taking place. However, all is not lost in this conservative movement.

The Message of Inclusion

Many churches—such as Lutheran, Presbyterian, Methodist, and Episcopal churches—are becoming inclusive of all people, despite issues of gender and sexual preferences. Of course, within these churches there is much debate, discourse, and division over homosexuality, particularly in the ordination of pastors. Although many of these churches accept homosexuals into their congregations, they still ban their ordination. Also, while many Protestant churches ordain women, it is, by and large, a male-dominated culture. Women are still fighting their way into church leadership roles, but they do take part in church activity, education, and government. However, there is still a long way to go in order to reach levels of equality in terms of church leadership.

Lessons of a Lifetime

As Christians continue to reform from within by questioning their own behaviors and practices, it is clear that a system of checks and balances is a good way to stay on the straight and narrow. It is also clear that, although great steps have been taken to unite those of Christian faith, there is still a lot of work to be done.

The inclusive church may need to take some lessons from the conservative evangelicals on church growth, but need not compromise the true Christian value of equality among all people. It will be interesting to see where Christianity goes from here. Ⓔ

Appendices

Appendix A

Martin Luther's 95 Theses

Appendix B

Popes of the Roman Catholic Church

Appendix C

Resources

Martin Luther's 95 Theses

Disputation on the Power and Efficacy of Indulgences Commonly Known as The 95 Theses—by Dr. Martin Luther

Out of love and concern for the truth, and with the object of eliciting it, the following heads will be the subject of a public discussion at Wittenberg under the presidency of the reverend father, Martin Luther, Augustinian, Master of Arts and Sacred Theology, and duly appointed Lecturer on these subjects in that place. He requests that whoever cannot be present personally to debate the matter orally will do so in absence in writing.

1. When our Lord and Master, Jesus Christ, said "Repent," He called for the entire life of believers to be one of repentance.

2. The word cannot be properly understood as referring to the sacrament of penance, i.e. confession and satisfaction, as administered by the clergy.

3. Yet its meaning is not restricted to repentance in one's heart; for such repentance is null unless it produces outward signs in various mortifications of the flesh.

4. As long as hatred of self abides (i.e., true inward repentance), the penalty of sin abides, viz., until we enter the kingdom of heaven.

5. The pope has neither the will nor the power to remit any penalties beyond those imposed either at his own discretion or by canon law.

6. The pope himself cannot remit guilt, but only declare and confirm that it has been remitted by God; or, at most, he can remit it in cases reserved to his discretion. Except for these cases, the guilt remains untouched.

7. God never remits guilt to anyone without, at the same time, making him humbly submissive to the priest, His representative.

8. The penitential canons apply only to men who are still alive, and, according to the canons themselves, none applies to the dead.

9. Accordingly, the Holy Spirit, acting in the person of the pope, manifests grace to us, by the fact that the papal regulations always cease to apply at death, or in any hard case.

10. It is a wrongful act, due to ignorance, when priests retain the canonical penalties on the dead in purgatory.

11. When canonical penalties were changed and made to apply to purgatory, surely it would seem that tares were sown while the bishops were asleep.

12. In former days, the canonical penalties were imposed, not after, but before absolution was pronounced; and were intended to be tests of true contrition.

13. Death puts an end to all the claims of the Church; even the dying are already dead to the canon laws, and are no longer bound by them.

14. Defective piety or love in a dying person is necessarily accompanied by great fear, which is greatest where the piety or love is least.

15. This fear or horror is sufficient in itself, whatever else might be said, to constitute the pain of purgatory, since it approaches very closely to the horror of despair.

16. There seems to be the same difference between hell, purgatory, and heaven as between despair, uncertainty, and assurance.

17. Of a truth, the pains of souls in purgatory ought to be abated, and charity ought to be proportionately increased.

18. Moreover, it does not seem proved, on any grounds of reason or Scripture, that these souls are outside the state of merit, or unable to grow in grace.

19. Nor does it seem proved to be always the case that they are certain and assured of salvation, even if we are very certain ourselves.

20. Therefore the pope, in speaking of the plenary remission of all penalties, does not mean "all" in the strict sense, but only those imposed by himself.

21. Hence those who preach indulgences are in error when they say that a man is absolved and saved from every penalty by the pope's indulgences.

22. Indeed, he cannot remit to souls in purgatory any penalty which canon law declares should be suffered in the present life.

23. If plenary remission could be granted to anyone at all, it would be only in the cases of the most perfect, i.e., to very few.

24. It must therefore be the case that the major part of the people are deceived by that indiscriminate and high-sounding promise of relief from penalty.

25. The same power as the pope exercises in general over purgatory is exercised in particular by every single bishop in his bishopric and priest in his parish.

26. The pope does excellently when he grants remission to the souls in purgatory on account of intercessions made on their behalf, and not by the power of the keys (which he cannot exercise for them).

27. There is no divine authority for preaching that when the soul flies out of the purgatory immediately the money clinks into the bottom of the chest.

28. It is certainly possible that when the money clinks in the bottom of the chest avarice and greed increase; but when the church offers intercession, all depends in the will of God.

29. Who knows whether all souls in purgatory wish to be redeemed in view of what is said of St. Severinus and St. Pascal? (Note: Paschal I, pope 817–824. The legend is that he and Severinus were willing to endure the pains of purgatory for the benefit of the faithful).

30. No one is sure of the reality of his own contrition, much less of receiving plenary forgiveness.

31. One who bona fide buys indulgence is a rare as a bona fide penitent man, i.e. very rare indeed.

32. All those who believe themselves certain of their own salvation by means of letters of indulgence, will be eternally damned, together with their teachers.

33. We should be most carefully on our guard against those who say that the papal indulgences are an inestimable divine gift, and that a man is reconciled to God by them.

34. For the grace conveyed by these indulgences relates simply to the penalties of the sacramental "satisfactions" decreed merely by man.

35. It is not in accordance with Christian doctrines to preach and teach that those who buy off souls, or purchase confessional licenses, have no need to repent of their own sins.

36. Any Christian whatsoever, who is truly repentant, enjoys plenary remission from penalty and guilt, and this is given him without letters of indulgence.

37. Any true Christian whatsoever, living or dead, participates in all the benefits of Christ and the Church; and this participation is granted to him by God without letters of indulgence.

38. Yet the pope's remission and dispensation are in no way to be despised, for, as already said, they proclaim the divine remission.

39. It is very difficult, even for the most learned theologians, to extol to the people the great bounty contained in the indulgences, while, at the same time, praising contrition as a virtue.

40. A truly contrite sinner seeks out, and loves to pay, the penalties of his sins; whereas the very multitude of indulgences dulls men's consciences, and tends to make them hate the penalties.

41. Papal indulgences should only be preached with caution, lest people gain a wrong understanding, and think that they are preferable to other good works: those of love.

42. Christians should be taught that the pope does not at all intend that the purchase of indulgences should be understood as at all comparable with the works of mercy.

43. Christians should be taught that one who gives to the poor, or lends to the needy, does a better action than if he purchases indulgences.

44. Because, by works of love, love grows and a man becomes a better man; whereas, by indulgences, he does not become a better man, but only escapes certain penalties.

45. Christians should be taught that he who sees a needy person, but passes him by although he gives money for indulgences, gains no benefit from the pope's pardon, but only incurs the wrath of God.

46. Christians should be taught that, unless they have more than they need, they are bound to retain what is only necessary for the upkeep of their home, and should in no way squander it on indulgences.

47. Christians should be taught that they purchase indulgences voluntarily, and are not under obligation to do so.

48. Christians should be taught that, in granting indulgences, the pope has more need, and more desire, for devout prayer on his own behalf than for ready money.

49. Christians should be taught that the pope's indulgences are useful only if one does not rely on them, but most harmful if one loses the fear of God through them.

50. Christians should be taught that, if the pope knew the exactions of the indulgence-preachers, he would rather the church of St. Peter were reduced to ashes than be built with the skin, flesh, and bones of the sheep.

51. Christians should be taught that the pope would be willing, as he ought if necessity should arise, to sell the church of St. Peter, and give, too, his own money to many of those from whom the pardon-merchants conjure money.

52. It is vain to rely on salvation by letters of indulgence, even if the commissary, or indeed the pope himself, were to pledge his own soul for their validity.

53. Those are enemies of Christ and the pope who forbid the word of God to be preached at all in some churches, in order that indulgences may be preached in others.

54. The word of God suffers injury if, in the same sermon, an equal or longer time is devoted to indulgences than to that word.

55. The pope cannot help taking the view that if indulgences (very small matters) are celebrated by one bell, one pageant, or one ceremony, the gospel (a very great matter) should be preached to the accompaniment of a hundred bells, a hundred processions, a hundred ceremonies.

56. The treasures of the church, out of which the pope dispenses indulgences, are not sufficiently spoken of or known among the people of Christ.

57. That these treasures are not temporal is clear from the fact that many of the merchants do not grant them freely, but only collect them.

58. Nor are they the merits of Christ and the saints, because, even apart from the pope, these merits are always working grace in the inner man, and working the cross, death, and hell in the outer man.

59. St. Laurence said that the poor were the treasures of the church, but he used the term in accordance with the custom of his own time.

60. We do not speak rashly in saying that the treasures of the church are the keys of the church, and are bestowed by the merits of Christ.

61. For it is clear that the power of the pope suffices, by itself, for the remission of penalties and reserved cases.

62. The true treasure of the church is the holy gospel of the glory and the grace of God.

63. It is right to regard this treasure as most odious, for it makes the first to be the last.

64. On the other hand, the treasure of indulgences is most acceptable, for it makes the last to be the first.

65. Therefore, the treasures of the gospel are nets which, in former times, they used to fish for men of wealth.

66. The treasures of the indulgences are the nets to-day which they use to fish for men of wealth.

67. The indulgences, which the merchants extol as the greatest of favors, are seen to be, in fact, a favorite means for money-getting.

68. Nevertheless, they are not to be compared with the grace of God and the compassion shown in the Cross.

69. Bishops and curates, in duty bound, must receive the commissaries of the papal indulgences with all reverence.

70. But they are under a much greater obligation to watch closely and attend carefully lest these men preach their own fancies instead of what the pope commissioned.

71. Let him be anathema and accursed who denies the apostolic character of the indulgences.

72. On the other hand, let him be blessed who is on his guard against the wantonness and license of the pardon-merchant's words.

73. In the same way, the pope rightly excommunicates those who make any plans to the detriment of the trade in indulgences.

74. It is much more in keeping with his views to excommunicate those who use the pretext of indulgences to plot anything to the detriment of holy love and truth.

75. It is foolish to think that papal indulgences have so much power that they can absolve a man even if he has done the impossible and violated the mother of God.

76. We assert the contrary, and say that the pope's pardons are not able to remove the least venial of sins as far as their guilt is concerned.

77. When it is said that not even St. Peter, if he were now pope, could grant a greater grace, it is blasphemy against St. Peter and the pope.

78. We assert the contrary, and say that he, and any pope whatever, possesses greater graces, that is the gospel, spiritual powers, gifts of healing, etc., as is declared in I Corinthians 12:28.

79. It is blasphemy to say that the insignia of the cross with the papal arms are of equal value to the cross on which Christ died.

80. The bishops, curates, and theologians, who permit assertions of that kind to be made to the people without let or hindrance, will have to answer for it.

81. This unbridled preaching of indulgences makes it difficult for learned men to guard the respect due to the pope against false accusations, or at least from the keen criticisms of the laity.

82. They ask, e.g.: Why does not the pope liberate everyone from purgatory for the sake of love (a most holy thing) and because of the supreme necessity of their souls? This would be morally the best of all reasons. Meanwhile he redeems innumerable souls for money, a most perishable thing, with which to build St. Peter's church, a very minor purpose.

83. Again: Why should funeral and anniversary masses for the dead continue to be said? And why does not the pope repay, or permit to be repaid, the benefactions instituted for these purposes, since it is wrong to pray for those souls who are now redeemed?

84. Again: Surely this is a new sort of compassion, on the part of God and the pope, when an impious man, an enemy of God, is allowed to pay money to redeem a devout soul, a friend of God; while yet that devout and beloved soul is not allowed to be redeemed without payment, for love's sake, and just because of its need of redemption.

85. Again: Why are the penitential canon laws, which in fact, if not in practice, have long been obsolete and dead in themselves, why are they, to-day, still used in imposing fines in money, through the granting of indulgences, as if all the penitential canons were fully operative?

86. Again: since the pope's income to-day is larger than that of the wealthiest of wealthy men, why does he not build this one church of St. Peter with his own money, rather than with the money of indigent believers?

87. Again: What does the pope remit or dispense to people who, by their perfect repentance, have a right to plenary remission or dispensation?

88. Again: Surely a greater good could be done to the church if the pope were to bestow these remissions and dispensations, not once, as now, but a hundred times a day, for the benefit of any believer whatever.

89. What the pope seeks by indulgences is not money, but rather the salvation of souls; why then does he suspend the letters and indulgences formerly conceded, and still as efficacious as ever?

90. These questions are serious matters of conscience to the laity. To suppress them by force alone, and not to refute them by giving reasons, is to expose the church and the pope to the ridicule of their enemies, and to make Christian people unhappy.

91. If therefore, indulgences were preached in accordance with the spirit and mind of the pope, all these difficulties would be easily overcome, and indeed, cease to exist.

92. Away, then, with those prophets who say to Christ's people, "Peace, peace," where in there is no peace.

93. Hail, hail to all those prophets who say to Christ's people, "The cross, the cross," where there is no cross.

94. Christians should be exhorted to be zealous to follow Christ, their Head, through penalties, deaths, and hells.

95. And let them thus be more confident of entering heaven through many tribulations rather than through a false assurance of peace.

Popes of the Roman Catholic Church

1. St. Peter (32–67)
2. St. Linus (67–76)
3. St. Anacletus (76–88)
4. St. Clement I (88–97)
5. St. Evaristus (97–105)
6. St. Alexander I (105–115)
7. St. Sixtus I (115–125)
8. St. Telesphorus (125–136)
9. St. Hyginus (136–140)
10. St. Pius I (140–155)
11. St. Anicetus (155–166)
12. St. Soter (166–175)
13. St. Eleutherius (175–189)
14. St. Victor I (189–199)
15. St. Zephyrinus (199–217)
16. St. Calixtus I (217–222)
17. St. Urban I (222–230)
18. St. Pontain (230–235)
19. St. Anterus (235–236)
20. St. Fabian (236–250)
21. St. Cornelius (251–253)
22. St. Lucius I (253–254)
23. St. Stephen I (254–257)
24. St. Sixtus II (257–258)
25. St. Dionysius (259–268)
26. St. Felix I (269–274)
27. St. Eutychian (275–283)
28. St. Caius (283–296)
29. St. Marcellinus (296–304)
30. St. Marcellus I (308–309)
31. St. Eusebius (309 or 310)
32. St. Miltiades (311–314)
33. St. Sylvester I (314–335)
34. St. Marcus (336)
35. St. Julius I (337–352)
36. Liberius (352–366)
37. St. Damasus I (366–384)
38. St. Siricius (384–399)
39. St. Anastasius I (399–401)
40. St. Innocent I (401–417)
41. St. Zosimus (417–418)
42. St. Boniface I (418–422)
43. St. Celestine I (422–432)
44. St. Sixtus III (432–440)
45. St. Leo I (the Great) (440–461)
46. St. Hilary (461–468)
47. St. Simplicius (468–483)
48. St. Felix II (483–492)
49. St. Gelasius I (492–496)
50. Anastasius II (496–498)
51. St. Symmachus (498–514)
52. St. Hormisdas (514–523)
53. St. John I (523–526)
54. St. Felix III (526–530)
55. Boniface II (530–532)
56. John II (533–535)
57. St. Agapetus I (535–536)
58. St. Silverius (536–537)
59. Vigilius (537–555)
60. Pelagius I (556–561)
61. John III (561–574)
62. Benedict I (575–579)
63. Pelagius II (579–590)
64. St. Gregory I (the Great) (590–604)
65. Sabinian (604–606)
66. Boniface III (607)
67. St. Boniface IV (608–615)
68. St. Deusdedit (Adeodatus I) (615–618)
69. Boniface V (619–625)
70. Honorius I (625–638)
71. Severinus (640)
72. John IV (640–642)
73. Theodore I (642–649)
74. St. Martin I (649–655)
75. St. Eugene I (655–657)
76. St. Vitalian (657–672)
77. Adeodatus (II) (672–676)
78. Donus (676–678)
79. St. Agatho (678–681)
80. St. Leo II (682–683)
81. St. Benedict II (684–685)
82. John V (685–686)
83. Conon (686–687)
84. St. Sergius I (687–701)
85. John VI (701–705)
86. John VII (705–707)
87. Sisinnius (708)
88. Constantine (708–715)
89. St. Gregory II (715–731)
90. St. Gregory III (731–741)
91. St. Zacharias (741–752)
92. Stephen II (or III) (752–757)
93. St. Paul I (757–767)
94. Stephen IV (768–772)
95. Adrian I (772–795)

96. St. Leo III (795–816)
97. Stephen V (816–817)
98. St. Paschal I (817–824)
99. Eugene II (824–827)
100. Valentine (827)
101. Gregory IV (827–844)
102. Sergius II (844–847)
103. St. Leo IV (847–855)
104. Benedict III (855–858)
105. St. Nicholas I (the Great) (858–867)
106. Adrian II (867–872)
107. John VIII (872–882)
108. Marinus I (882–884)
109. St. Adrian III (884–885)
110. Stephen VI (885–891)
111. Formosus (891–896)
112. Boniface VI (896)
113. Stephen VII (896–897)
114. Romanus (897)
115. Theodore II (897)
116. John IX (898–900)
117. Benedict IV (900–903)
118. Leo V (903)
119. Sergius III (904–911)
120. Anastasius III (911–913)
121. Lando (913–914)
122. John X (914–928)
123. Leo VI (928)
124. Stephen VII (or VII) (928–931)
125. John XI (931–935)
126. Leo VII (936–939)
127. Stephen VIII (or IX) (939–942)

128. Marinus II (942–946)
129. Agapetus II (946–955)
130. John XII (955–963)
131. Leo VIII (963–964)
132. Benedict V (964)
133. John XIII (965–972)
134. Benedict VI (973–974)
135. Benedict VII (974–983)
136. John XIV (983–984)
137. John XV (985–996)
138. Gregory V (996–999)
139. Sylvester II (999–1003)
140. John XVII (1003)
141. John XVIII (1004–1009)
142. Sergius IV (1009–1012)
143. Benedict VIII (1012–1024)
144. John XIX (1024–1032)
145. Benedict IX (1032–1044)
146. Sylvester III (1045)
147. Benedict IX (1045)
148. Clement II (1046–1047)
149. Benedict IX (1047–1048)
150. Damasus II (1048)
151. St. Leo IX (1049–1054)
152. Victor II (1055–1057)
153. Stephen X (1057–1058)
154. Nicholas II (1058–1061)
155. Alexander II (1061–1073)
156. St. Gregory VII (1073–1085)
157. Victor III (1086–1087)
158. Urban II (1088–1099)
159. Paschal II (1099–1118)
160. Gelasius II (1118–1119)
161. Callistus II (1119–1124)
162. Honorius II (1124–1130)

163. Innocent II (1130–1143)
164. Celestine II (1143–1144)
165. Lucius II (1144–1145)
166. Blessed Eugene III (1145–1153)
167. Anastasius IV (1153–1154)
168. Adrian IV (1154–1159)
169. Alexander III (1159–1181)
170. Lucius III (1181–1185)
171. Urban III (1185–1187)
172. Gregory VIII (1187)
173. Clement III (1187–1191)
174. Celestine III (1191–1198)
175. Innocent III (1198–1216)
176. Honorius III (1216–1227)
177. Gregory IX (1227–1241)
178. Celestine IV (1241)
179. Innocent IV (1243–1254)
180. Alexander IV (1254–1261)
181. Urban IV (1261–1264)
182. Clement IV (1265–1268)
183. Blessed Gregory X (1271–1276)
184. Blessed Innocent V (1276)
185. Adrian V (1276)
186. John XXI (1276–1277)
187. Nicholas III (1277–1280)
188. Martin IV (1281–1285)
189. Honorius IV (1285–1287)
190. Nicholas IV (1288–1292)
191. St. Celestine V (1294)
192. Boniface VIII (1294–1303)
193. Blessed Benedict XI (1303–1304)
194. Clement V (1305–1314)

195. John XXII (1316–1334)
196. Benedict XII (1334–1342)
197. Clement VI (1342–1352)
198. Innocent VI (1352–1362)
199. Blessed Urban V
    (1362–1370)
200. Gregory XI (1370–1378)
201. Urban VI (1378–1389)
202. Boniface IX (1389–1404)
203. Innocent VII (1406–1406)
204. Gregory XII (1406–1415)
205. Martin V (1417–1431)
205. Eugene IV (1431–1447)
206. Nicholas V (1447–1455)
207. Calixtus III (1455–1458)
208. Pius II (1458–1464)
209. Paul II (1464–1471)
210. Sixtus IV (1471–1484)
211. Innocent VIII (1484–1492)
212. Alexander VI (1492–1503)
213. Pius III (1503)
214. Julius II (1503–1513)
215. Leo X (1513–1521)
216. Adrian VI (1522–1523)
217. Clement VII (1523–1534)
218. Paul III (1534–1549)
219. Julius III (1550–1555)
220. Marcellus II (1555)
221. Paul IV (1555–1559)

222. Pius IV (1559–1565)
223. St. Pius V (1566–1572)
224. Gregory XIII (1572–1585)
225. Sixtus V (1585–1590)
226. Urban VII (1590)
227. Gregory XIV (1590–1591)
228. Innocent IX (1591)
229. Clement VIII (1592–1605)
230. Leo XI (1605)
231. Paul V (1605–1621)
232. Gregory XV (1621–1623)
233. Urban VIII (1623–1644)
234. Innocent X (1644–1655)
235. Alexander VII (1655–1667)
236. Clement IX (1667–1669)
237. Clement X (1670–1676)
238. Blessed Innocent XI
    (1676–1689)
239. Alexander VIII (1689–1691)
240. Innocent XII (1691–1700)
241. Clement XI (1700–1721)
242. Innocent XIII (1721–1724)
243. Benedict XIII (1724–1730)
244. Clement XII (1730–1740)
245. Benedict XIV (1740–1758)
246. Clement XIII (1758–1769)
247. Clement XIV (1769–1774)
248. Pius VI (1775–1799)
249. Pius VII (1800–1823)

250. Leo XII (1823–1829)
251. Pius VIII (1829–1830)
252. Gregory XVI (1831–1846)
253. Pius IX (1846–1878)
254. Leo XIII (1878–1903)
255. St. Pius X (1903–1914)
256. Benedict XV (1914–1922)
257. Pius XI (1922–1939)
258. Pius XII (1939–1958)
259. John XXIII (1958–1963)
260. Paul VI (1963–1978)
261. John Paul I (1978)
262. John Paul II (1978–Present)

Appendix C

Resources

Books

Church History in Plain Language, 2nd Edition, by Bruce Shelley (Nashville, TN: Thomas Nelson Publishing, 1982).

Chronological Charts of Church History, by Robert C. Walton (Grand Rapids, MI: Zondervan, 1986).

Will the Real Heretics Please Stand Up, by David Bercot (Tyler, TX: Scroll Publishing, 1999).

Christian History Made Easy, by Timothy Paul Jones (Torrance, CA: Rose Publishing, 1999).

The Everything® Catholicism Book, by Helen Keeler and Susan Grimbly (Avon, MA: Adams Media, 2003).

Church History, The Essential Guide, by Justo Gonzalez (Nashville, TN: Abingdon Press, 1996).

Web Sites

Catholicism:

www.britishhistory.about.com
www.catholic-forum.com
www.whatsaiththescripture.com

Reformation:

www.brittanica.com
www.eldrbarry.net
www.forerunner.com
www.williamtyndale.com

Christianity Now:

www.christianity.com
www.christianity.about.com
www.christianitytoday.com
www.everystudent.com
www.gospel.com.net

Women:

http://historymedren.about.com
www.womeninworldhistory.com
www.womenshistory.about.com

Jesus:

www.lifeofchrist.com
www.jesusjournal.com

Church History and Theology:

http://biblegospelcom.net
www.biblehistory.net
www.biblicalstudies.com
www.deism.com
www.factmonster.com
www.humanismbyjoe.com
www.monergism.com
www.skepdic.com

THE EVERYTHING SERIES!

BUSINESS

Everything® **Business Planning Book**
Everything® **Coaching and Mentoring Book**
Everything® **Fundraising Book**
Everything® **Home-Based Business Book**
Everything® **Leadership Book**
Everything® **Managing People Book**
Everything® **Network Marketing Book**
Everything® **Online Business Book**
Everything® **Project Management Book**
Everything® **Selling Book**
Everything® **Start Your Own Business Book**
Everything® **Time Management Book**

COMPUTERS

Everything® **Build Your Own Home Page Book**
Everything® **Computer Book**
Everything® **Internet Book**
Everything® **Microsoft® Word 2000 Book**

COOKBOOKS

Everything® **Barbecue Cookbook**
Everything® **Bartender's Book, $9.95**
Everything® **Chinese Cookbook**
Everything® **Chocolate Cookbook**
Everything® **Cookbook**
Everything® **Dessert Cookbook**
Everything® **Diabetes Cookbook**
Everything® **Indian Cookbook**
Everything® **Low-Carb Cookbook**
Everything® **Low-Fat High-Flavor Cookbook**

Everything® **Low-Salt Cookbook**
Everything® **Mediterranean Cookbook**
Everything® **Mexican Cookbook**
Everything® **One-Pot Cookbook**
Everything® **Pasta Book**
Everything® **Quick Meals Cookbook**
Everything® **Slow Cooker Cookbook**
Everything® **Soup Cookbook**
Everything® **Thai Cookbook**
Everything® **Vegetarian Cookbook**
Everything® **Wine Book**

HEALTH

Everything® **Alzheimer's Book**
Everything® **Anti-Aging Book**
Everything® **Diabetes Book**
Everything® **Dieting Book**
Everything® **Herbal Remedies Book**
Everything® **Hypnosis Book**
Everything® **Massage Book**
Everything® **Menopause Book**
Everything® **Nutrition Book**
Everything® **Reflexology Book**
Everything® **Reiki Book**
Everything® **Stress Management Book**
Everything® **Vitamins, Minerals, and Nutritional Supplements Book**

HISTORY

Everything® **American Government Book**
Everything® **American History Book**
Everything® **Civil War Book**
Everything® **Irish History & Heritage Book**

Everything® **Mafia Book**
Everything® **Middle East Book**
Everything® **World War II Book**

HOBBIES & GAMES

Everything® **Bridge Book**
Everything® **Candlemaking Book**
Everything® **Casino Gambling Book**
Everything® **Chess Basics Book**
Everything® **Collectibles Book**
Everything® **Crossword and Puzzle Book**
Everything® **Digital Photography Book**
Everything® **Easy Crosswords Book**
Everything® **Family Tree Book**
Everything® **Games Book**
Everything® **Knitting Book**
Everything® **Magic Book**
Everything® **Motorcycle Book**
Everything® **Online Genealogy Book**
Everything® **Photography Book**
Everything® **Pool & Billiards Book**
Everything® **Quilting Book**
Everything® **Scrapbooking Book**
Everything® **Sewing Book**
Everything® **Soapmaking Book**

HOME IMPROVEMENT

Everything® **Feng Shui Book**
Everything® **Feng Shui Decluttering Book, $9.95 ($15.95 CAN)**
Everything® **Fix-It Book**
Everything® **Gardening Book**
Everything® **Homebuilding Book**

All Everything® books are priced at $12.95 or $14.95, unless otherwise stated. Prices subject to change without notice.
Canadian prices range from $11.95–$31.95, and are subject to change without notice.

Everything® **Home Decorating Book**
Everything® **Landscaping Book**
Everything® **Lawn Care Book**
Everything® **Organize Your Home Book**

EVERYTHING®
KIDS' BOOKS

All titles are $6.95

Everything® **Kids' Baseball Book, 3rd Ed.** ($10.95 CAN)
Everything® **Kids' Bible Trivia Book** ($10.95 CAN)
Everything® **Kids' Bugs Book** ($10.95 CAN)
Everything® **Kids' Christmas Puzzle & Activity Book** ($10.95 CAN)
Everything® **Kids' Cookbook** ($10.95 CAN)
Everything® **Kids' Halloween Puzzle & Activity Book** ($10.95 CAN)
Everything® **Kids' Joke Book** ($10.95 CAN)
Everything® **Kids' Math Puzzles Book** ($10.95 CAN)
Everything® **Kids' Mazes Book** ($10.95 CAN)
Everything® **Kids' Money Book** ($11.95 CAN)
Everything® **Kids' Monsters Book** ($10.95 CAN)
Everything® **Kids' Nature Book** ($11.95 CAN)
Everything® **Kids' Puzzle Book** ($10.95 CAN)
Everything® **Kids' Riddles & Brain Teasers Book** ($10.95 CAN)
Everything® **Kids' Science Experiments Book** ($10.95 CAN)
Everything® **Kids' Soccer Book** ($10.95 CAN)
Everything® **Kids' Travel Activity Book** ($10.95 CAN)

KIDS' STORY BOOKS

Everything® **Bedtime Story Book**
Everything® **Bible Stories Book**
Everything® **Fairy Tales Book**
Everything® **Mother Goose Book**

LANGUAGE

Everything® **Inglés Book**
Everything® **Learning French Book**
Everything® **Learning German Book**
Everything® **Learning Italian Book**
Everything® **Learning Latin Book**
Everything® **Learning Spanish Book**
Everything® **Sign Language Book**
Everything® **Spanish Phrase Book,** $9.95 ($15.95 CAN)

MUSIC

Everything® **Drums Book (with CD),** $19.95 ($31.95 CAN)
Everything® **Guitar Book**
Everything® **Playing Piano and Keyboards Book**
Everything® **Rock & Blues Guitar Book (with CD),** $19.95 ($31.95 CAN)
Everything® **Songwriting Book**

NEW AGE

Everything® **Astrology Book**
Everything® **Divining the Future Book**
Everything® **Dreams Book**
Everything® **Ghost Book**
Everything® **Love Signs Book,** $9.95 ($15.95 CAN)
Everything® **Meditation Book**
Everything® **Numerology Book**
Everything® **Palmistry Book**
Everything® **Psychic Book**
Everything® **Spells & Charms Book**
Everything® **Tarot Book**
Everything® **Wicca and Witchcraft Book**

PARENTING

Everything® **Baby Names Book**
Everything® **Baby Shower Book**
Everything® **Baby's First Food Book**
Everything® **Baby's First Year Book**
Everything® **Breastfeeding Book**

Everything® **Father-to-Be Book**
Everything® **Get Ready for Baby Book**
Everything® **Getting Pregnant Book**
Everything® **Homeschooling Book**
Everything® **Parent's Guide to Children with Autism**
Everything® **Parent's Guide to Positive Discipline**
Everything® **Parent's Guide to Raising a Successful Child**
Everything® **Parenting a Teenager Book**
Everything® **Potty Training Book,** $9.95 ($15.95 CAN)
Everything® **Pregnancy Book, 2nd Ed.**
Everything® **Pregnancy Fitness Book**
Everything® **Pregnancy Organizer,** $15.00 ($22.95 CAN)
Everything® **Toddler Book**
Everything® **Tween Book**

PERSONAL FINANCE

Everything® **Budgeting Book**
Everything® **Get Out of Debt Book**
Everything® **Get Rich Book**
Everything® **Homebuying Book, 2nd Ed.**
Everything® **Homeselling Book**
Everything® **Investing Book**
Everything® **Money Book**
Everything® **Mutual Funds Book**
Everything® **Online Investing Book**
Everything® **Personal Finance Book**
Everything® **Personal Finance in Your 20s & 30s Book**
Everything® **Wills & Estate Planning Book**

PETS

Everything® **Cat Book**
Everything® **Dog Book**
Everything® **Dog Training and Tricks Book**
Everything® **Golden Retriever Book**
Everything® **Horse Book**
Everything® **Labrador Retriever Book**
Everything® **Puppy Book**
Everything® **Tropical Fish Book**

All Everything® books are priced at $12.95 or $14.95, unless otherwise stated. Prices subject to change without notice.
Canadian prices range from $11.95–$31.95, and are subject to change without notice.

REFERENCE

Everything® **Astronomy Book**
Everything® **Car Care Book**
Everything® **Christmas Book, $15.00**
    ($21.95 CAN)
Everything® **Classical Mythology Book**
Everything® **Einstein Book**
Everything® **Etiquette Book**
Everything® **Great Thinkers Book**
Everything® **Philosophy Book**
Everything® **Psychology Book**
Everything® **Shakespeare Book**
Everything® **Tall Tales, Legends, &**
    Other Outrageous
    Lies Book
Everything® **Toasts Book**
Everything® **Trivia Book**
Everything® **Weather Book**

RELIGION

Everything® **Angels Book**
Everything® **Bible Book**
Everything® **Buddhism Book**
Everything® **Catholicism Book**
Everything® **Christianity Book**
Everything® **Jewish History &**
    Heritage Book
Everything® **Judaism Book**
Everything® **Prayer Book**
Everything® **Saints Book**
Everything® **Understanding Islam**
    Book
Everything® **World's Religions Book**
Everything® **Zen Book**

SCHOOL & CAREERS

Everything® **After College Book**
Everything® **Alternative Careers Book**
Everything® **College Survival Book**
Everything® **Cover Letter Book**
Everything® **Get-a-Job Book**
Everything® **Hot Careers Book**

Everything® **Job Interview Book**
Everything® **New Teacher Book**
Everything® **Online Job Search Book**
Everything® **Resume Book, 2nd Ed.**
Everything® **Study Book**

SELF-HELP/ RELATIONSHIPS

Everything® **Dating Book**
Everything® **Divorce Book**
Everything® **Great Marriage Book**
Everything® **Great Sex Book**
Everything® **Kama Sutra Book**
Everything® **Romance Book**
Everything® **Self-Esteem Book**
Everything® **Success Book**

SPORTS & FITNESS

Everything® **Body Shaping Book**
Everything® **Fishing Book**
Everything® **Fly-Fishing Book**
Everything® **Golf Book**
Everything® **Golf Instruction Book**
Everything® **Knots Book**
Everything® **Pilates Book**
Everything® **Running Book**
Everything® **Sailing Book, 2nd Ed.**
Everything® **T'ai Chi and QiGong Book**
Everything® **Total Fitness Book**
Everything® **Weight Training Book**
Everything® **Yoga Book**

TRAVEL

Everything® **Family Guide to Hawaii**
Everything® **Guide to Las Vegas**
Everything® **Guide to New England**
Everything® **Guide to New York City**
Everything® **Guide to Washington D.C.**
Everything® **Travel Guide to The**
    Disneyland Resort®,
    California Adventure®,
    Universal Studios®, and
    the Anaheim Area
Everything® **Travel Guide to the Walt**
    Disney World Resort®,
    Universal Studios®, and
    Greater Orlando, 3rd Ed.

WEDDINGS

Everything® **Bachelorette Party Book,**
    $9.95 ($15.95 CAN)
Everything® **Bridesmaid Book, $9.95**
    ($15.95 CAN)
Everything® **Creative Wedding Ideas**
    Book
Everything® **Elopement Book, $9.95**
    ($15.95 CAN)
Everything® **Groom Book**
Everything® **Jewish Wedding Book**
Everything® **Wedding Book, 2nd Ed.**
Everything® **Wedding Checklist,**
    $7.95 ($11.95 CAN)
Everything® **Wedding Etiquette Book,**
    $7.95 ($11.95 CAN)
Everything® **Wedding Organizer,**
    $15.00 ($22.95 CAN)
Everything® **Wedding Shower Book,**
    $7.95 ($12.95 CAN)
Everything® **Wedding Vows Book,**
    $7.95 ($11.95 CAN)
Everything® **Weddings on a Budget**
    Book, $9.95 ($15.95 CAN)

WRITING

Everything® **Creative Writing Book**
Everything® **Get Published Book**
Everything® **Grammar and Style Book**
Everything® **Grant Writing Book**
Everything® **Guide to Writing**
    Children's Books
Everything® **Screenwriting Book**
Everything® **Writing Well Book**

Available wherever books are sold!
To order, call 800-872-5627, or visit us at everything.com